Cogley: Original Edition

THOMAS S. COGLEY

HISTORY
of the
Seventh Indiana
Cavalry Volunteers

by
THOMAS S. COGLEY
Late First Lieutenant Company "F."

A Complete Reprint of the Original by:

Morningside
1991

ISBN: 0-89029-543-3

This book was completely reset on the Intertype
in Morningside's own printing plant in eleven
and eight point Caledonia and Printed on
Glatfelter Acid-Free Paper and Hand Bound
in "C" Grade Cloth.

Morningside House, Inc.
260 Oak Street, Dayton, Ohio 45410

HISTORY

OF THE

Seventh Indiana Cavalry Volunteers,

AND

THE EXPEDITIONS, CAMPAIGNS, RAIDS, MARCHES,
AND BATTLES OF THE ARMIES WITH
WHICH IT WAS CONNECTED,

WITH

BIOGRAPHICAL SKETCHES

OF

BREVET MAJOR GENERAL JOHN P. C. SHANKS,

AND OF

BREVET BRIG. GEN. THOMAS M. BROWNE,

AND OTHER OFFICERS OF THE REGIMENT;

WITH AN ACCOUNT OF THE BURNING OF THE
STEAMER SULTANA ON THE
MISSISSIPPI RIVER,

AND OF THE CAPTURE, TRIAL, CONVICTION AND EXECUTION OF

DICK DAVIS, THE GUERRILLA.

———

BY
THOMAS S. COGLEY,
LATE FIRST LIEUTENANT COMPANY "F."

———

1876:
HERALD COMPANY, STEAM PRINTERS,
LAPORTE, INDIANA

DEDICATED

TO

THE MEMORY OF THE MEN

OF

THE SEVENTH INDIANA CAVALRY,

BY

THE AUTHOR

CONTENTS.

PART I.

PART II.

HISTORY OF THE SEVENTH INDIANA CAVALRY.

CHAPTER I.

ORGANIZATION OF THE REGIMENT.

COMPANY ROSTERS.

CHAPTER II.

Seventh Indiana leaves Indianapolis for Columbus, K'y—Reports to Col. Waring at Union City and assigned to the 1st Brigade of the 6th Division of the 16th Army Corps—Expedition to Dresden, Tenn.—Rebels escape in the night—Return to Union City—Expedition to Jackson, Tenn., and escape of Forrest—Return to Union City, terrible New Year, men and horses frozen—Cavalry

1

Chapter III.

MERIDIAN CAMPAIGN.

Chapter IV.

GUNTOWN EXPEDITION.

CHAPTER V.

EXPEDITION TO PORT GIBSON.

CHAPTER VI.

CHAPTER VII.

MISSOURI CAMPAIGN.

CHAPTER VIII.

GRIERSON'S RAID THROUGH MISSISSIPPI

CHAPTER XIV.

DICK DAVIS, THE GUERRILLA.

PART III.

SKETCHES OF

INTRODUCTION.

As a teenager living across the street from General Shanks Elementary School in Portland, Indiana (Jay County) in the 1950's, I was curious about the individual for whom the school was named. A neighbor informed me that an elderly lady living down the street knew about Gen. John P. C. Shanks. I knocked on her door one afternoon to ask if she would tell me the story. The lady who answered the door was advanced in years and somewhat timid, but when I asked about "the General," she escorted me into her home and, for the next two hours, I listened to fascinating, emotional stories which had been told to her as a youngster by the "boys" and "heroes" who left the area and fought a war in faraway regions of the South. This was one of many incidents of my youth which led me to tread the battlefields, research the facts and strategies, and encourage the preservation of that tragic American era we call the Civil War. Little did I know in the spring of 1988, in conversation with Bob Younger when the decision was made to republish the 1876 regimental history of the *Seventh Indiana Cavalry Volunteers* by Thomas S. Cogley, the "boys" and "heroes" contained in these pages were the same individuals I had heard about from my neighbor nearly forty years ago.

CHARLES F. BRAGG
Winchester, Indiana
September 1991

The Seventh Indiana Cavalry was recruited and mustered into service in the late summer and fall of 1863. Bull Run, Antietam, and Gettysburg had occurred in the East. Shiloh, Stones River, Vicksburg, and Chickamauga were history in the West. Ahead lay the battles of The Wilderness, Spotsylvania, Cold Harbor, and Petersburg, along with Atlanta and Savannah.

7

The Seventh Indiana Cavalry was destined to face Lt. Gen. Nathan Bedford Forrest, a leader who has been ranked by military historians as the greatest cavalry commander of the Civil War. This was to be a most difficult endeavor for the Hoosiers.

The Seventh Indiana Cavalry was the 119th regiment in the line of Indiana regiments. Typical of cavalry regiments, twelve companies comprised the organization, rather than ten, as in infantry regiments. The young men and boys who filled the ranks came from vast areas of Indiana extending to all borders of the state, from the Lake Michigan counties, to the Ohio River, and from Ohio to their Illinois neighbors. The geographical center of the state running from north to south produced large numbers of volunteers, who, together under Brig. Gen. Samuel D. Sturgis, were all too soon to feel the sting of "That Devil Forrest." The Indiana Historical Society, in December of 1961, listed the companies by county of origin of this regiment (APPENDIX A).

Frederick H. Dyer's narrative of the Seventh Indiana Cavalry is reprinted in APPENDIX C. Cogley mentioned several veterans of the Seventh Indiana Cavalry as exchanged prisoners who perished on the steamboat *Sultana* on April 27, 1865. Rev. Chester D. Berry listed more in 1863 (APPENDIX D). *The Official Records* contains many references to the Seventh Indiana Cavalry (APPENDIX E). Many sources were consulted to gain background data and information. These are listed under REFERENCES REVIEWED.

PREFACE.

To preserve the record of the sufferings, fatigues, raids, expeditions, skirmishes and battles, of as gallant a military organization, as ever drew saber in a holy cause, is the purpose of writing this book. The general historian deals only with general facts. Armies, corps, divisions, brigades and regiments, are swallowed up in the names of their commanders. Were it possible for him to gather the information necessary to give the personal experiences of the officers only, of armies, the great space necessary for such a work, will forever preclude the possibility of the general historian engaging in such an undertaking. There never was, never can be, and never will be, a complete history of any war written, although the greater portion of the history of all countries relates to war. The great volume of blood is not complete, until it has the personal experience of each individual soldier. But such a record can be approximated, so far as integral portions of armies are concerned, by works of this character. Although this is a history of the 7th Indiana Cavalry, yet it is by no means complete, because it does not contain the individual military history of each member of the regiment. Even if it were possible to obtain information necessary for such a work, to publish it, would require several volumes of the size of this, the expense of which, with its necessarily limited sale, would forbid such an undertaking.

Although this only purports to be the history of a single military organization, yet it is more. It is as complete a history of the operations of the armies with which the regiment was connected, as will be found in works of greater pretentions. All of it, except such portions as relate solely to the organization of the regiment, will be of interest to the general reader.

Sketches of only a part of the officers of the regiment are given. But it must not be understood that those whose names do not appear in that part of the book, did nothing worthy of record. The reason of the omission simply is, the failure to get in communication with them, has rendered it impossible to obtain the facts necessary to write of them properly.

Of most that is written, the author had personal knowledge. Being a prisoner of war at the time of the expedition to Missouri, in the Fall of 1864, I have had to rely on the statements of others, and on official documents for what is written of that brilliant campaign.

Reasonable accuracy has been attained, by reference to the official reports, the correspondence, and the journal of Gen. Thomas M. Browne, which he kindly placed at my disposal.

Valuable information has been obtained from a history of company "I," written and published in the *Northern Indianian,* by Major James H. Carpenter, after his return from the army. Also valuable information has been furnished by Major Joseph W. Skelton and Capt. John R. Parmelee.

Without further explanation or introduction, this book is submitted to the public—

By the Author.

Michigan City, Ind., November 1, 1876.

PART I.

Biographical Sketches of General Thomas M. Browne and Gen. John P. C. Shanks.

BREVET BRIGADIER GENERAL THOMAS M. BROWNE.

The institution of African slavery was fastened on the people of this country at an early period of their colonial history. It existed at the time our famous Declaration of Independence was promulgated. At the time the Constitution of the United States was adopted, it was a recognized competitor with freedom in the race of life.

Our statesmen and lawyers succeeded in establishing the doctrine that inasmuch as slavery existed at the time the Declaration and Constitution were adopted, the slaves were not included in, but were excluded from their provisions. That they were not thought of as human beings, but were considered by the framers of the Constitution, only as property. This doctrine was at a later day gravely affirmed by the Supreme Court of the United States.

Our nation presented the strange spectacle of one race of people enjoying the most enlarged liberty, while another race were subjected to a more abject slavery than was tolerated under the most absolute autocratic government and that, too, under the same Constitution.

The Constitution was referred to, as the warrant for the existence of both freedom and slavery.

It could not be otherwise, than that the institution of slavery, that had nothing to recommend it to a candid and refined mind, should arouse philanthropists to a warfare against it.

Protests against the institution were made by the convention assembled at Philadelphia, for the adoption of the Constitution, but were unheeded. Organized opposition to slavery, ante-dates both the Declaration of Independence, and the Constitution of the United States.

11

The opponents of Slavery, armed, not with weapons from Vulcan's armory, but with justice, right, and religion, waged their moral warfare against our great national sin.

The slavery propagandist, conscious of the intrinsic wrong of their favorite institution, that it was at war with every principle of natural justice, and in defiance of the inalienable rights announced in the Declaration of Independence, grew intolerant of those who had clearer ideas of liberty. Fearful that the doctrines promulgated by the Abolitionists would be favorably received by the masses of the people, they adopted a system of persecution and ostracism against their opponents.

Slavery entered the pulpit and divided the churches. It entered society, and arrayed neighbor against neighbor. It strode haughtily into the national Congress, where its advocates insulted civilization, and outraged decency, by hurling defiance at those who dared to question their right to buy and sell their fellows like beasts of burden, and making it the especial object of the protection of the Government. Year after year the contest waxed hotter and hotter. The persecution of tthe Abolitionists, by the Pro-slavery men, was intolerable. It seems incredible that such a state of affairs could exist in a free country. To add insult to injury, the Pro-slavery element secured the enactment of the infamous fugitive slave law, which compelled people of the North to become slave hunters for the people of the South.

The accumulating insults and outrages of the champions of slavery, and their demand for its expansion roused the people of the North to the dangers threatening the Union, and they formed the resolution to restrict slavery to the territory it already occupied. For that purpose, the Republican party was organized in 1856. As a twin sister of slavery was the dogma of secession, the right of a State to withdraw from the Union. The threat to dissolve the Union was like a sword, suspended over the heads of the Republicans. Notwithstanding, the champions of freedom did not yield their ground, and the "irrepressible conflict" went on.

Of those who fought on the side of liberty and union in that conflict, and in the rebellion inaugurated by the fairly defeated Pro-slavery men, was Thomas W. Browne, the subject of this sketch. He was born on the 19th day of April, 1830, at New Paris, in Preble county, in the State of Ohio.

John A. Browne, his father, was a native of the State of Pennsylvania, and his mother of Kentucky. The latter died at New Paris, Ohio, in the year 1843.

This calamity broke up the family circle, and John A. Browne took his son Thomas M. to Spartanburg, Randolph county, Indiana, where he apprenticed him to Ralph M. Pomeroy, a merchant of that place. Thomas M. Browne inherited his mother's great mental faculties, and business capacity. His father, after apprenticing him to Mr. Pomeroy, went to Grant county, Kentucky, where he died in 1865. But his eyes were not closed in death, until his ears had caught the sweet accents of praise spoken of his noble son. He lived to see the vast assemblies swayed by that peculiar eloquence, that has placed his son in the front rank of the great men of Indiana. The breezes from the far off battle-fields, wafted to him the gratifying intelligence of the noble manner in which his son, sustained, with his sword, the honor of our national flag.

In his youth, Thomas M. Browne, was a close observer, and acquired a remarkable knowledge of human character. By close application he speedily acquired knowledge, and correct business habits. His honesty and truthfulness, were the chief beauties, not only of his youth, but are also of his mature manhood.

His means of acquiring knowledge, so far as institutions of learning are concerned, were confined to the common schools of Spartanburg, and one term in the Randolph county Seminary. But so indefatigable has been his pursuit of learning, that no one can clothe his thoughts in a more beautiful garb of language, or embellish them with nobler flights of fancy.

In the Lyceum at Spantanburg, he became the acknowledged leader. A ready and fluent speaker and a splendid reader, he distanced all of his competitors.

A friend of his, having a law suit before a justice of the peace, at Spartanburg, and having against him one of the best lawyers of Winchester, and being himself without counsel, and knowing of young Browne's fluency as a speaker, importuned him to appear and defend his case. Browne did so, and with such shrewdness and address, that he won the case. It may be that that incident decided him to study law.

At any rate in the Spring of 1848, he left the store of Mr. Pomeroy, went to Winchester, entered the law office, as a student, of the Hon. William A. Pelle, and applied himself earnestly to the study of law. In 1849, after a reading of only a year, he successfully passed an examination in open court, and was admitted to practice in all the inferior courts of the State, and in 1851, he was admitted to the bar of the Supreme Court of Indiana.

In August, 1850, just one year after his admission to the bar, and before he was twenty-one years of age, he was elected prosecuting attorney of Randolph county, which office he held two years. In 1855, after the adoption of our present State Constitution, which made the office co-extensive with the judicial circuits, he was elected prosecutor of the thirteenth judicial circuit. He was re-elected to the same position in 1857, and again in 1859. He discharged the duties of his office with ability, and his labors were attended with more than usual success.

At New Paris, Ohio, on the 18th of March, 1849, he married Miss Mary J. Austin, who has been his faithful companion in adversity and prosperity, and who has watched with the just pride of a wife, the honorable advancements of her husband.

The election of Abraham Lincoln, to the Presidency of the United States, was seized upon by the traitors of the country as a pretext for dissolving the Federal Union. War, with all its attendant evils, was precipitated on the Government, for which it was wholly unprepared.

Thomas M. Browne was among the host of patriots, who by their eloquence and patriotism, did wonders for the preservation of the Union, by inducing the people to rally around the National Government, and sustain it in its hour of sore trial.

At Morristown on the 27th day of August, 1861, he delivered a great speech on the crisis of the country, replete with patriotism and eloquence. We could not give the reader a better idea of Gen. Browne as an orator and patriot, and of the causes that led to the war, and of the complications of those time, than by giving the speech in full, which we now do:

MORRISTOWN SPEECH.

MY FELLOW CITIZENS: At a time like this, it is more pleasant to review the past, than the present, of our history. A brief reference to what we have been may yet excite emotions of patriotism in the hearts of the people, for as the past passes before us, we find that almost every field has its tale of blood, and every shore its

14

record of suffering, and not a mountain lifts its head unsung or unworthy of heroic strains!

Less than two centuries and a half ago, the May Flower planted on the shores of the Atlantic the germ of a mighty Republic. Driven from their altars and their homes, persecuted and hunted down by a relentless despotism, the indomitable Puritan stepped upon Plymouth Rock, imbued with a love of liberty, and a hatred to tyranny which were destined to achieve stupendous results. The pilgrim found a new world, boundless in its extent, spread out before him. Its resources were to be developed—the hardships and dangers of pioneer life were to be met and surmounted. Fearlessly did he enter upon his task—right valiantly did he struggle until surmounting obstacles the most formidable ever conquered by human genius or human prowess, he was enabled to bequeath to posterity a legacy more valuable than the world had ever known before. If we did not inherit from the Puritan of the May Flower and Plymouth Rock, our Republican institutions, we did that which was equally valuable, we inherited that spirit of liberty which inspired the revolutionary fathers to strike for freedom—and that unconquerable bravery which endured an almost hopeless contest through years of toil, despondency and peril.

But two centuries have passed and the result of the Pilgrim's work is before you. Look at it and say, has it not been done well? See you nowhere the hand of an Almighty Providence in it? Then the sound of the woodman's ax seldom disturbed the stillness of our boundless forests. Nature, in its variegated wildness, in its forests and prairies, in its river and rivulet, in its mountain and valley, wrote its own history. Wrapped in this grand seclusion a great continent had lain for fifteen centuries. How now? A nation stretches itself out from the Atlantic over the Alleghenies, the valley of the Mississippi, scales the Rocky Mountains, and stops only when it reaches the surge-washed shores of the Pacific. Northward it reaches the lakes—Southward to the orange and palmetto groves of the States of the Gulf. Thirty millions of people populate its fertile valleys and its mountain acclivities. In all that constitutes national greatness it is rich; rich in revenue, in strong arms and patriotic hearts. Millions of acres groan under their heavy harvests, and the music of the loom and forge is heard in almost every village. The map of the nation presents a network of canals and railroads, those great arteries of commerce.

15

Its form of government is the model of Republics. The world over, whenever Liberty has gained even a temporary triumph over despotism, a government is formed or attempted upon the plan of ours. The destruction of this government would be a terrible blow, and one that might be eternal in its effects, at civil and religious liberty throughout the world. Prove this to be a failure, and to what people, let me ask you, will the down-trodden and tyranny-smitten subjects of existing despotisms, look for hope and encouragement? Destroy our Constitution, and you establish the divine right of kings—you give the lie to man's capacity for self-government.

But I have spoken of our country as it was, before treason crept into its councils, before its Catilines had conspired against its life, and before it had been ascertained by traitors that this thing of beauty and vigor, had hidden within it some infernal machine, prepared by the makers of the Constitution themselves, by which the government could be utterly annihilated by the act of a single State. Secession is claimed as a constitutional right, although the destruction of that Constitution is the result. Secession is the assassination of the government—it is to suppose that the Constitution has armed a State against itself, and conspired against its own existence. To concede the right of secession is to admit our most solemn statues but mere figures of speech, and that our Constitution is but as the empty declamation of the school-boy. Can it be that all the blood of the Revolution was poured out so freely to secure us a government bound in bonds more feeble than ropes of sand? Secession, disguise it as you may, cover it over with whatever plausible pretext you may, is but treason—treason blacker than Burrs', and as damnable as that which has given Benedict Arnold an immortality of infamy. It is treason because it is a conspiracy against the liberty of the people, and would not only destroy a nation so good, so beneficent, but seeks to inaugurate anarchy and ruin in its stead. I do not propose to argue the question; the mere statement of the proposition is sufficient, but if more were required, if the constitution needs an interpreter more certain than the hearts of a patriotic people, I would again bring to mind the patriotic sages of the past. The cold, lifeless forms of the patriot sires who repose at Mount Vernon, at Monticello, at the Hermitage, at Marshfield, and at Ashland, rise animate before you and utter words of ear-

16

nest and terrible condemnation against this infernal heresy of secession.

Our national existence is threatened. Already we hear the tramp of armed men. American citizens have met American citizens in conflict, and patriot and rebel blood have commingled upon the same battle field. The government has resolved upon the policy to be pursued, and is devoting its best energies in arranging its forces for the struggle. From the plow-share the nation is forging swords, and pruning hooks are being transformed into spears. Fear and hope alternate in every heart. Strong men tremble as they contemplate events. The public mind is deeply moved. What has produced this mighty convulsion? Some cause exists and we may ascertain it without treading upon forbidden ground. Let us examine the question as patriots, and see if we can see the true source of this treasonable conspiracy against Federal authority. Why then, this attempt to destroy the Union of the States, and to overturn the best and freest government the world has ever seen? Is the solution of this question to be found in the result of the late presidential election? That Mr. Lincoln was elected in strict conformity with the Constitution, no one doubts. There is certainly nothing either unusual or dangerous in the legal and peaceful triumph of the popular will. The right of the people to determine by the arbitrament of the ballot, by whom they shall be governed, is and must ever be the corner-stone of a Republican government. It is part of our national pride that under our system of government, sovereign power resides with the people. Those who would attempt to thwart their will when legally expressed, by revolt and revolution, inaugurate a bold and fearful experiment. In popular elections some party must triumph—others suffer defeat. To govern in conformity with the Constitution and laws of the country is the RIGHT of the one, while submission by the minority to the will of the majority is a cardinal one, and no compromise is demanded, and none will be demanded to change it. Tested by this acknowledged rule, the loyal citizen owes the same allegiance to the government administered by Lincoln, that he did in the days of Washington, Jefferson and Jackson. But we are told that the recent triumph of the people was a sectional one, sectional in the geographical position of the party, and sectional in view of the principle upon which its supremacy was secured. The charge is made and it is denied. I will not pass judgment in

17

the case, lest I should judge as a partisan. Who shall judge the people? Who so pure a patriot that he could hold the balances of justice evenly in such a case? To whose arbitrament will politicians submit this question of sectionalism? I will not assume that the party in power or the one out of power, is sectional. It is a question which legitimately belongs at all times TO THE PEOPLE. For the present they have settled it, and if any feel aggrieved by the result, let the question be again submitted to the same supreme tribunal, and trust that the people's patriotism and intelligence will cheerfully correct any error that may have been committed. The right was intended, and if wrong has been done— if their action has tended to the weakening of the bonds that unite these States in a common government, and a common destiny, I have sufficient confidence in their prudence and loyalty to believe that they will at once retrace any inconsiderate step they may have taken, or repair any wrong they may have done. The Constitution recognizes no sections; it does not require a candidate for the Presidency to receive a part or all of his vote from a particular locality; it does not demand that he shall receive the vote of a single slave State, or of a single free State, but provides that whenever he receives a majority of the electoral votes he shall be the legally chosen Chief Magistrate of the Confederacy. But the recent election did not transfer the power to control the government to the Republican party. While in one department—the Executive—it was omnipotent, in two others—the Judicial and Legislative—it was absolutely powerless. That it is now in power in all these departments is because of the rebellion. The treason of certain Representatives and Senators in Congress, and of certain Judges, and the pretended withdrawal of certain States from the Federal Government, has given it powers that it could not have possessed if every officer had been true to his duty and his oath. I speak of this simply to prove that this pretext of sectionalism is as base as it its groundless. No considerable party exists in the Northern States that meditates an assault upon State rights, or upon Southern institutions. While slavery is condemned and abhorred by many, its existence in certain States is recognized as a constitutional right with which they have neither the power or desire to interfere. A majority of the people in the non-slaveholding States are opposed to its expansion, to its being extended to territories now free, to bringing slave labor into competition with free labor of the white man, but they seek to secure their object by no other means than those provided by the Constitution. They conceive it no more sectional in them to resist slavery extension, than it is for others to insist upon it. They cannot see why anti-slavery is more sectional than pro-slavery. But there is a sectionalism which has had much to do in bringing the present troubles upon the country. When you see a State array itself against the Federal power and resist Federal authority; when you see one section of the Union demand unconstitutional concessions and compromises to insure the continuance of its loyalty; when local interests are held to be higher and more sacred than the Constitution and laws of the government, then you have an exhibition of a sectionalism which is the cause of the present national commotion.

There are those who profess to believe that our present calamities are the results of the agitation of the slavery question in the North. Burk said, years ago, in the oldest existing monarchy in the world, "that where there was evil there ought to be agitation —that it was better to be awakened from our slumber by the fire bell, than to perish in the flames." The free people of the North thought that they might speak for the honor and integrity of the Republic without endangering its existence. No wrong to the Constitution was intended. Statesman and Philosopher, Poet and Divine, the world over had condemned the system of human slavery. The civilized world protested against it. None have left stronger or more burning words of reproach to the institution than slave-holders themselves. Turn back but a few years in the country's history and you find Patrick Henry saying: "that it is a debt we owe to the purity of our religion to show that it is at variance with the law which warrants slavery . . . We ought to lament and deplore the necessity of holding our fellow men in bondage." Thomas Jefferson could speak of slavery, and tremble when he reflected that God was "*just* and that his justice would not sleep forever," and Washington—the nation's idol—could express the ardent hope that some means would be devised for its abolition. Henry Clay could denounce it as the "everlasting curse," and Randolph, in his place in the Senate, could hurl his bitter sarcasms at the "man from the North who attempted to defend it upon principle."

The North taking their political lessons from masters like these, learned to believe slavery wrong in morals, and at the same time

19

bad political economy; and while they were willing to tolerate its existence where it was, thought that every principle of duty in justice called upon them to resist its further extension. Upon that platform the political victory of 1860 was achieved. No intermeddling with slavery in the States was contemplated. This embraces the full extent of our offending. In all this I can see no wrong—certainly none but that can be corrected at the ballot box. Let all this be as it may. At all events civil war with its unspeakable calamities, is a poor corrective. No one but a traitor or a madman would think of resorting to so fearful an expedient upon a pretext so paltry and contemptible. If war must come—if anarchy must take the place of order, it is to be hoped that the Robespierres, Marats and Dantons of this conspiracy will find some better excuse than this for their carnival of blood.

But why did we not compromise existing differences and save the Union without the sacrifice of life and treasure? Very many reasons exist why this course was not adopted. If loyalty barters with treason today, when and where will it end? The compromise of today is but a pretext for another to-morrow and every inch treason exacts, adds to its strength and detracts from that of the government. The Constitution is itself a compromise, and the administration of the government according to its letter and spirit is all that any State has a right to expect or demand. The Constitution provides ample protection for the institution and interests of every section of the country. If one provision in it is altered today to suit the caprice of some fastidious State, for the same reason another must be to-morrow, and thus in a few years the greatest work of the fathers will have departed from our government forever.

It is true that popular governments like ours must be administered upon principles of mutual concession and forbearance. If there be conflicting sectional interests, let each section exhibit an honest disposition to adjust the trouble. A spirit that demands everything—exacts everything, and is willing to concede nothing in return, has no element of compromise in it.

In the opinion of our political gamblers, no wrongs are ever committed against human liberty; they demand no concessions to be made to foster the interests of free white labor, but the eternal cry has been "slavery and Cotton demand this thing and we must give it and save the Union." In this way the Union has been saved

20

already too often. Every pretended compromise has weakened the government and tended to precipitate the present condition of things.

But there has been no existing necessity for a compromise. No changes in the law, Constitution, or condition of the nation, or of any part of it, made concession necessary, or even proper. To have made compromise a condition of loyalty was unjust, and the government would not have been true to itself, had it submitted to the condition. A compromise under such circumstances, might have secured a temporary peace, but it would have done a great wrong to the people. In Athens once, its greatest statesman and general, proposed to do a thing of great advantage to the Athenians. The matter was referred to Aristides, a man eminent for his sense of justice, who reported "that the enterprise which Themistocles proposed was indeed the most advantageous in the world, but at the same time it was the most unjust." The Athenians refused the most advantageous thing in the world, because it was tainted with injustice. The American people have done well in imitating this Athenian virtue. A great nation can always afford to repudiate a wrong that would dishonor it. The proposition to compromise was as unnecessary as it was unjust. No seceding State asked it and no one met it in the spirit of kindness. While we were halting and parleying, holding mass meetings and conventions, and discussing propositions of adjustments, they were arming and drilling, forging swords and casting cannon. They used the delay given by the nation, to plunder its arsenals and navy yards, and rob its mints. They presented the one alternative to the government; either to recognize the independence of the Confederate States, or to prepare for war. The government dared not accept the one, and the other became a necessity.

But secession had its origin long before 1860. On the 15th day of May 1828, the Congress of the United States passed a law levying duties on the importation of foreign goods. The act levied higher duties than any previous revenue law of the government. It was passed by a full congress in strict accordance with the Constitution, and avowedly for the protection of American industry. The Gulf States at once commenced devising means by which to resist Federal authority, and to prevent the execution of the law. They insisted then, as now, that the revenue act was both sectional and unconstitutional. It was sectional because it benefited Northern manufacturers, while in the South there were none to protect. It was sectional for the further reason, that one hundred and five votes against it were from the slave States.

The philosophy of sectionalism is indeed a singular one; a combined pro-slavery interest may thrust any measure upon the country or defeat any object, but let the North do that thing—let free labor attempt to thwart the cherished projects of the Cotton power by a united vote, and how soon the howl of sectionalism resounds from one end of the land to the other. Again, it was insisted that this tariff was unconstitutional because it imposed unequal taxation. If it was true, the North might have claimed that slavery was unjust and anti-Republican, because it gave unequal representation. However, seizing these pretexts, South Carolina immediately commenced proclaiming her resistance to the laws of the government. Hasty and heretical then as now, in less than thirty days after the passage of the tariff act, a public meeting was held at Walterburough in that State, at which an address to the people was adopted, containing the following passage:

"What course is left to pursue. If we have the common pride of men, or the determination of freemen, we must resist the imposition of this tariff. To be stationary is impossible, we must either retrograde in dishonor and in shame, and receive the contempt and scorn of our brethren superadded to our own wrongs and their system of oppression strengthened by our toleration; or we must 'by opposing end them.' In advising an attitude of open resistance to laws of the Union, we deem it due to the occasion, and that we may not be misunderstood, distinctly, but briefly to state, without argument, our constitutional faith. For it is not enough that imposts laid for the protection of domestic manufacturers are oppressive, and transfer in their operation millions of our property to Northern capitalists. If we have given our bond, let them take our blood. Those who resist these imposts must deem them *unconstitutional*, and the principle is abandoned by the payment of one cent as much as ten millions."

Open resistance to the laws of the Union are here explicitly proclaimed one-third of a century ago. A state assumes to declare in the face of Congress, and in the face of a Supreme Court, that a particular law is unconstitutional, and boldly and openly defied the nation to execute it. All over South Carolina, meetings were held and similar sentiments expressed. The soil which grew Tories so abundantly in the Revolution, was prolific of traitors. Georgia openly co-operated with South Carolina, while Mississippi and the other Cotton States contented themselves by more, or less boldly expressing their sympathy with treason.

In December 1828, the Senate of South Carolina passed a resolution condemning the tariff as unconstitutional, asserting that its enforcement ought to be resisted and concludes by inviting other States to co-operate with her in devising means of resistance. Thus thirty-three years ago the State which leads in this rebellion, was actively engaged in conspiring against the government. Nothing but her weakness prevented her attempting to leave the Union then. But the first paroxyms of frenzy passed off, and she gradually relapsed into her former condition.

In 1832, Congress thought best to revise the tariff and modify the duties imposed by it, so as to make it less distasteful to the Cotton States. It was thought to conciliate South Carolina, but true to her nature, she grew suddenly furious and would have been out of the Union without the ceremony of a final good bye, had not the strong arm of the government been interposed. The tariff could not be made to suit our rebellious sister State; in 1828 it was too high—in 1832 she would not consent to have it made lower. The spirit of disunion again became rite within her borders: Demagogues advocated it on the stump, and ministers from the pulpit called the blessing of God to consecrate the treason; Statesmen gave it countenance, and Calhoun publicly announced "Nullification to be a peaceful solution of existing difficulties." In 1832, the Legislature called a convention of delegates to be elected by the people of the State, "to take into consideration the acts of congress of the United States, and to devise means of redress." The convention contemplated by the Legislature assembled on the 19th day of November in the same year. Treason is always in haste. The people must have no time for reflection—no time to allow the passions to cool—for reason to assume her sway, lest returning to their allegiance, they should put their feet upon the necks of the traitors who would have rushed them out of the Union. In this respect the conduct of the conspirators was not unlike that of the rebels of to-day. They meet and resolve States out of the Union—form new governments and put them into operation, without thinking of submitting their work to a vote of the people. But to proceed with the history: The convention of

23

South Carolina had met but a brief day, before it arrayed itself in open and flagrant hostility to the general government by adopting the "ordinance of Nullification." The title is a curious and interesting specimen of traitorous impudence. It reads: "An ordinance providing for *arresting* the *operation* of certain acts of the Congress of the United States, purporting to be laws laying duties and imposts on the importation of foreign commodities." Think for a moment of the monstrous absurdity of the proposition! A State in the Union owing allegiance, bound to aid in its defense, and assist in the execution of its decrees, presumes to pass an ordinance *arresting* the operation of the laws within its limits! The ordinance next proceeds to pronounce the revenue laws of 1828 and 1832, "null and void, neither binding upon the State, its officers or citizens." It declares it unlawful to attempt the collection of duties or the enforcement of these laws within the limits of the State. It made the decisions of its own courts upon the validity of these laws, final and conclusive, by prohibiting appeals or writs of error from such decisions to the Federal courts. It required every one who held an office of honor, trust or profit, civil or military, to take an oath to obey the ordinance only, and the laws of the Legislature passed in pursuance to it.

Its iniquities culminated in its final proposition, which declared that in case the general government should employ *force* to carry into effect its laws, or should endeavor to coerce the State by shutting up its ports, that South Carolina would consider the Union dissolved, and would proceed to organize a separate government. I have been somewhat minute in stating the facts, that you might, in the meantime, in your own minds, run the parallel between that and the present conspiracy. Traitors then hated coercion—declared that "coercion was disunion." They only wanted to be let alone. They did not intend to resist the government, unless the government undertook to enforce the laws. If it assumed to do so monstrous a thing as that, and war came of it, the United States only would be to blame, because they were forewarned that "coercion was disunion." In such an event the traitors would not be responsible for desevering the Union. Northern fanatics only could be blamed for foolishly insisting that the constitutional obligations of each State should be faithfully and rigidly enforced. Strange logic is that of secession!

Notwithstanding South Carolina's belligerent attitude, and her

24

terrible threats, the government did enforce the revenue laws, and she did not go out—did not proceed to "organize a separate government." Georgia and Mississippi saw in the flashing eye, and determined visage of the hero of New Orleans an unanswerable argument to Nullification. They abandoned Palmettodom to its fate. But the action of the convention did not end the treason of the Carolina Catilines. Immediately upon its adjournment the Legislature was convened and laws were passed to carry into effective operation the ordinance of the convention. This legislature hurriedly adjourned its session upon the promulgation of President Jackson's proclamation. The nation had at its head a hero and a patriot equal to emergencies of the great occasion. He called no convention to propose measures of peace and compromise. He held no parley with traitors—agreed upon no terms of armistice by which they were enabled to make their conspiracy more formidable. So lame and impotent a policy found no place in his councils. He had taken an oath to preserve the inviolability of the Constitution, and kept that oath. General Scott was dispatched to Charleston with instructions to put the fortifications there in a condition of defense. He was authorized to reinforce the forts and he did it. South Carolina was coerced and the Union was saved. It has been claimed that all these dangers were averted by the compromise of Mr. Clay. I revere the memory of Henry Clay; from youth I have been taught to believe him the statesman of the age, and I would not pluck a leaf from his laurels, but in justice to the history of my country, I must deny that that compromise restored South Carolina to her allegiance. The proclamation of the 10th of December, and the vigorous coercive policy of Jackson, did it. History will so record it—it has so recorded it already.

The Union was saved by the very means that demagogues now tell us will destroy it. A similar policy employed at the beginning of the present rebellion, by the late administration would have saved much blood and treasure. The reinforcement of Moultrie, Sumpter and Pickney might have saved the nation. The Federal Government should have shown its teeth at the outset. An emphatic "by the eternal" by another Jackson, might then have accomplished what years will now be required to perform. But Jackson is entombed at the Hermitage, and it appears that he was "the last of the Romans."

"There are but few giants in these days!" The government triumphed over treason in 1832, but did not annihilate it. Cotton and traitors are produced by the same soil—treason was indigenous in South Carolina. The Cotton States, dissatisfied with their connection with the government, have ever since then been plotting for its overthrow. Feeling their inability to accomplish their purpose at once, they have sought to attain their object by regular approaches. A series of acts were passed by many of these States, in direct conflict with the Constitution and in violation of the rights of citizens of non-slaveholding States. Statutes were passed making free citizens of Massachusetts and of some of the other New England States, slaves, if they entered their ports. When a distinguished and venerable lawyer of Massachusetts was sent to quietly test the constitutionality of these laws in their own courts and before their own judges, he was seized, mobbed and driven from the State. Southern Institutions soon became too sacred for Northern men to think of or talk about. He who dared utter a word against the "peculiar institution," became the victim of indignities and cruelties insufferable by a brave and a free people. It was thought a reproach to be a Northern man, for a man from the North was necessarily an "Abolitionist." The name of an American citizen was no protection even upon American soil.

The slave power was not only imperious within its own borders, but it became dictatorial abroad. It not only managed its own affairs at home without interference, but demanded that it should be supreme dictator for the general government. It became frenzied with madness whenever the Representatives of a free laboring North attempted in any way, to provide for the protection of labor.

No tariff suited it—none could be made to suit it. Feeling that its power was on the decline, that soon the offices of the government and their emoluments might pass from its clutches, it demanded "expansion." When the North faltered, King Cotton's statesmen thundered out their treason in the halls of the Capitol; and doughfaces tremblingly and submissively granted their most extravagant demands. Texas must be annexed—slavery extended and the Union weakened. That was done and another State joined the conspiracy.

When it was sought to pass the Wilmot proviso, excluding slavery from the territory to be acquired under a treaty with Mexico, it was only necessary to threaten dissolution and the Wilmot Proviso went down forever. California, with a free constitution of the people's choice, asked to be admitted into the Union as a State, but its admission could not be secured until the country was saved by a compromise, containing some features that will ever disgrace the Republic.

This self-same conspiracy against the government demanded the repeal of the Missouri compromise, and deluded many honest and patriotic men into a support of the measure. It was done, but not precisely to its liking. It was soon discovered that Popular Sovereignty, honestly and faithfully enforced, might prove the death knell of slavery expansion, and required the administration of Buchanan to fetter, and manacle freedom until slavery could fasten its roots deep and wide in the soil of Kansas. The government did its bidding, and the conflict was as deplorable as it was terrible.

Although numerically the lesser power in the government, it controlled its offices and patronage. Having less than a third of the population, it has ever had two-thirds of the Federal offices. This should have satisfied it; but the labor States were increasing too rapidly in population and wealth, the scepter was departing— and dissolution was immediately, but in strict accordance with a long matured plan, adopted as the remedy. To fully prepare the Southern mind for the "consummation so devoutly to be wished." Southern politicians thought it necessary to break the last tie that bound them to the government. This was done at Charleston. The Democratic party was destroyed, and its destruction was premeditated. The disruption of the party was secured to insure its defeat, that the defeat might be used to inflame the Southern heart. Lincoln's election was to be seized upon as a pretext for dissolution. Nothing was too sacred to espace the touch of the conspirators. Everything that could not be moulded to their purpose, they have destroyed. Ties, the most binding, have been ruthlessly broken, and oaths, the most sacred, have been violated without remorse. Southern statesmen thought:

"To reign was worth ambition, tho' in Hell.
Better to reign in Hell than to serve in Heaven."

I have said that this stupendous treason has long been contemplated. The proof of the fact is abundant and overwhelming. No

27

observer of events for the past few years can for a moment doubt it. Why has every recent attempt to increase our naval force, or standing army, been so strenuously resisted? Why has so large a number of the arms of the government and munitions of war been transferred, in times of profound peace, from Northern arsenals and navy yards to those States that were first to engage in the rebellion? Why was it, let me ask, that our ships of war were sent thousands of miles from our shores on cruises of almost indefinite duration! Why was our finances crippled without cause, and our treasury robbed? But one answer can be given; it was to weaken the government, and strengthen the hands of the rebels.

Our officers in the army and navy had been tampered with; when treason first showed its head, they precipitately abandoned their posts of duty, and disgraced the flag of their country. Federal officers unblushingly committed the double crime of treason and perjury.

The President to whom was confided the destinies of a free government, freighted with the hopes of millions of free people, retained in its councils men, who were plotting the downfall of the Republic.

Patriots in the Cabinet, unwilling to be longer identified with the destroyers of their country, resigned their positions. The President, while not a conspirator himself, was either utterly incapable of comprehending the treachery of his advisers, or else he was too indifferent to make any attempt to avert the impending danger. Too long he permitted his confidence to be betrayed by those who were engaged in betraying the nation. To speak plainly, the administration of James Buchanan, while professing to execute the laws and constitution, contributed constantly and largely to strengthen the hands of the rebels. It gave them the very sinews of war. It put arms and ammunition into their hands, and abandoned our forts, arsenals, and navy yards to their mercy. It refused to strike when with a blow the rebellion could have been annihilated—it refused to strike and the government may be lost forever.

The people were loth to believe that the South was in earnest; that the destruction of a government so beneficent as ours, was seriously meditated. It had existed so long, grown so great and glorious that they were wont to believe that it was necessarily eternal.

When South Carolina resolved herself out of the Union by the action of her convention, it was regarded as but an ebullition of passion. When batteries were being built and forts invested, and the rebellion became a reality, the public was startled. The people were divided as to the means to be employed to avert the impending danger. While we quarrelled and delayed and recriminated, the work of investment went on. We played effectually into the hands of the traitors. We abandoned Major Anderson and his gallant little band to their fate. We allowed them to be shut up in Sumpter—a wall of batteries to be built around them, without making an effort to succor or relieve them. No attempt was made to re-enforce our own forts, for fear that such an attempt would endanger the Union. How short-sighted and cowardly we were! United States ordnance were pointed threateningly towards United States forts and upon the National flag—our unarmed ships were fired into, and were driven from our ports, and we had not the courage to resent the indignity. The war was thrust upon the government; no alternative was left the administration but to call the people to arms in defense of their institutions, yet there are persons whose patriotism is above suspicion, who are constantly asking what is this war being prosecuted for? Have they heard that the integrity of the government was in imminent peril? Heard they the loud-mouthed cannon as they belched forth ball and shell upon the government forts in Charleston harbor? Do these persons know that our capital is threatened by an army of rebels? Know they all these things, and do they feel an honest doubt as to the purpose of the government? No man need mistake the object of this war. It is to suppress tthe rebellion, maintain the Union, vindicate the Federal authority, and to restore the supremacy of the Constitution and laws of the United States, to the whole people of the Confederacy. It is to put down treason and punish traitors. It is a contest for the unity and the indivisibility of the nation. It is a war to preserve the life of the nation, and preserve inviolate the Constitution made by the fathers. It is waged to save Republican institutions, and a free government for the untold generations that are to come after us. We are engaged in defending the honor and the liberty of the people. For these objects only, has the government taken up arms. Are you an American citizen, and can you say in your heart, that in such a contest you do not sympathize with your country? When such

29

interests are involved, can you refuse to give your warmest and fullest support to the nation? That these are the objects of the administration, in resorting to the terrible arbitrament of battle, no one need doubt or question. In every proclamation, message or order issuing from the department at Washington, the object is stated fully. Every act of the government since this struggle commenced, without a single exception, has been entirely consistent with this policy. It is charged that this is an abolition war. The Johnsons and Holts and Crittendens do not think so. They are identified with the institution of slavery, and they make no such charge upon the administration. But the question is asked, what will be done with the institution of slavery! I answer, it will not be touched if it does not interfere with the government. If slaves are employed against us, they must be treated as contraband of war. This course is dictated by the great law of self-defence. If this war has a tendency to weaken the tenure of slavery, it is the fault of the rebellion—not of the government in re-asserting its supremacy in the seceded States. Neither slave nor master must stand in the way of the Union. This rebellion formidable as it has grown to be, must be suppressed and such means must be employed to secure this result, as the future contingencies of the contest may demand. I have confidence in the integrity and patriotism of the government, and I will not suspect or assail its motives, until by its conduct, I have reason to believe that it is abusing the trust confided to it by a brave and magnanimous people.

Our country however, is infested with a hoard of miserable grumblers, who appear determined to find fault with everything the government may find it necessary to do. If our citizen-soldiery are called to defend our capital when it is menaced by rebels, they say it is unconstitutional! If the *Habeas Corpus* is suspended within a district where the civil authorities are in sympathy with the rebellion, these men cry out "it is unconstitutional." I would not abridge the liberty of speech, it is one of the safeguards of public liberty. To the fullest extent consistent with public good this right of free speech; is guaranteed to the people, and while it is their right to criticize freely, the acts of their public servants, there are times when such criticisms should not rankle with the bitterness of partisan animosities. This is not the government of a party but of all parties—and patriotism and the safety of the

30

people forbid that it should be abandoned to the controle or support of one party. All parties are protected by its broad shield, and all should cheerfully unite in its defense. Our criticisms should be honorable and just, and with the single view of strengthening and upholding the cause of the government against its enemies. Whatever divides and distracts, weakens us and strengthens the enemies of the Union; and believe me, in this contest, we have less to fear from their strength than our weakness. Let discussion be free, but let it at the same time be just. Do not for party purposes, magnify little things. Let our mantle of charity be broad. Be not hasty to condemn. Regard the spirit of the act, and from that judge the act itself. Do not resort to the trickery and cunning of the demagogue to excite the people against the administration, if it evinces an honest desire to defend the constitution, and preserve the liberties of the people. It may not adopt just such measures for the public good as you would suggest, but differences of opinion must be expected. There is a period in the history of almost every people, when for a time, there must exist a higher law than the written constitution, for the "safety of a people is always the supreme law of the land." Swear your public servants not merely upon constitutions and statutes, but swear them by the memories of the past—by the blood of patriots, and all that is sacred and holy in our nation's history *to preserve the Republic*. Let every thought and act be for the preservation of the Union; bend every energy toward the accomplishment of this glorious result, and when peace is established—when the country is safe from the infamous hands of the traitors who would destroy it, we can return again to our party allegiance. Certainly for a time we can forget that we are partisans and elevate country above party platforms. No greater mistake can possibly exist, than that when a political party in the country succeeds in obtaining supremacy, that for the time being, the government becomes simply that of such party. Admit the correctness of this theory, and government is practically destroyed. Because one party or the other has the assendency, neither absolves the citizen from his allegiance to the government, nor it, from its duty to protect the citizen in every legal right. This is the people's government, they made it—gave its rulers power, and can in the way provided by law, deprive them of it. They are the supreme power in the land; the President and cabi-

THOMAS M. BROWNE
32

net are but their agents executing delegated powers. If the government is destroyed it is not the few officials merely who will suffer, but the whole people. Let treason triumph, and it does not simply destroy the Republican party or the Democratic party, but the constitution and the government of the country, and all parties sink together into a common grave to rise no more forever.

Nothing is to be gained by wanton attacks upon the administration. You may cripple its energies, you may paralyze the arm of the patriot—you may encourage and embolden the traitor, you may possibly succeed in pulling down the pillars of our Temple of Liberty, but be assured you must perish also in the ruins. You may protract this struggle—you may increase the number of the wounded and slain upon the field of battle, but you will live to bear the terrible rebuke of the widow's sigh and the orphan's tear, you can earn the reproach which will cling to your garments through all coming time—that you aided in the destruction of your country.

Fellow-citizens, do not understand me as attacking any political party; nothing could be further from my purpose. On the 13th day of April, when the cannon of the rebels opened upon Fort Sumpter, when the thundering of that fearful cannonading swept over the land, the last party tie was broken. Party names and party distinctions were buried, and Republican, Democrat and American rallied alike under the bright folds of our country's flag. None have shown a more noble devotion to the cause of the Union, than that great party which was defeated in the late exciting Presidential contest. It has furnished its full proportion of brave and noble men to fight the battles of the constitution. Its Statesmen have, in the main, firmly and earnestly stood by the administration and strengthened its hands for the conflict. Democratic fathers and mothers have freely given up their sons to the country—have sent them to the field of battle to maintain the honor of the old flag of stars and stripes, if need be, with their life blood. The leader of that party, the great statesman who fought its battles so ably, and so valiantly, both in the Senate and on the stump, although now an inhabitant of the "city of the dead," forgetting all the exciting past, came promptly and cheerfully, with his whole heart and soul, to the support of the country. I had the pleasure of hearing the next to the last public speech he ever made, and shall never forget how eagerly the people

33

gathered around him, and how patiently they stood in the midst of a drenching rain to catch the words, big with patriotism as they fell from his lips. I confess from that time I loved STEPHEN A. DOUGLAS. I felt that he was one of the pillars of the confederacy. But it pleased the Almighty to call him from the councils of the country, and at a time when his loss is truly a national calamity. His dying admonition was full of devotion to the Union. He sent his sons, with lips almost inarticulate, the request that they *"support the laws and constitution of the United States."* Noble sentiment! He will live longer in that dying utterance, than in the marble monuments that may be erected to his memory.

What will be the result of this war? Can the government suppress this insurrection? He whose eye alone can pierce the future of our history, can answer this question. If we are a united people—if we stand shoulder to shoulder, we have nothing to fear. Those who are depressed at our losses will soon be cheered up. Brave men are rushing to the rescue by the thousand, and to doubt our triumph, is to reproach the just providence of God.

It is however said that Cotton is King, that England and France must have it in defiance of the blockade; that one of our important measures of defense may involve us in a war with one or both of those formidable nations. It is true, that the Gulf States furnish seventy-one per cent. of the cotton heretofore used, and it is equally true that the closing of their ports will seriously embarrass the manufacture of cotton fabrics. But this embarrassment must be temporary in the nature of things. Europe has already turned its attention toward India for this important staple, and will soon be under no necessity of opening the American ports to secure a supply of that article. Indeed, millions of acres, adapted by both soil and climate to the production of cotton, may soon be converted into cotton fields. Europe is by no means dependent upon the Confederate States. Anticipating troubles like the present, she had already begun the organization of companies for the cultivation of cotton in the Indies. The present rebellion will give vigor and activity to this enterprise, and within a few years King Cotton will find a competitor, in the markets of the world more formidable, than any that has ever met him before. The genius of the age will soon supply the article in abundance. But cotton is not king. The world could do without it. From the almost endless quantities of wool, flax, jute, and hemp now produced, fabrics

34

of almost every conceivable kind, can be made both durable and cheap. Necessity will stimulate inventive genius, until soon a substitute will supply its place. It will lose more—infinitely more than it will make by this rebellion. There is more involved in this contest than the mere loss of cotton bales. England and France cannot afford to involve themselves in the present contest, even if every loom, supplied with material by the Gulf States, had to stand idle. To break our blockade, would be to declare war against us; and to prosecute that war would cost them more, by odds, than to support at the government expense, every person thrown out of employment for want of cotton. It would be exceedingly bad economy for these governments to pursue a belligerent policy toward us.

Then the sympathies of the masses of the people are with the North, and if their government espouse the cause of the rebels, they may have trouble with their own refractory subjects.

Europe has other interests to foster, this side of the Atlantic, than that of her trade in cotton. The North exports and imports largely—She feeds five millions of French and British subjects. War would cut off this trade between them and us. Northern ports would be closed to their imports. The products of our abundant harvests would no longer seek a market in French or British ports. Cotton might be procured; but it would be at a loss of bread. The United States, broken and distracted as they are, have still some power left that Europe might feel. Insurrections and rebellions ought not to be in good repute in a monarchy that has already felt the heavy stroke of the guillotine beheading its kings and queens, and saturating its soil with the best blood of its nobility. France should remember 1793 and 1848.

England ought to know the precarious tenure of its union. Its Robert Emmets and Horne Tookes are not all dead yet. Some of its possessions have shown symptoms of disloyalty. Canada may become infected with the secession *mania*, and England should remember that the United States bound it on the South.

Let the result be what it may, whether we are reunited or continue a dissevered people; whether our nation be one of thirty-four States, or of twenty-three States, we must still continue a power of importance among the nations of the world. Every year will increase our wealth and our population, and in a quarter of a century we will have attained an addition to our numbers that

35

will more than supply the loss incurred by the secession of the rebel States. The people of the old world know this, and they know, too, that they cannot afford to incur our displeasure upon trifling pretexts.

Come what will, we must now fight this battle to the end; until we can conclude it upon terms of honorable, perpetual and enduring peace.

Let this war eventuate as it may—whether the nation be destroyed or its supremacy vindicated, the man who has been known in the loyal States to sympathize with this crime against the Union, and Constitution, will receive the merited execration of his countrymen through all coming time.

Those who advocate secession—peaceable secession as a remedy for existing evils, know very little of the temper of the country. It is no time to cry peace; we must buckle on the armor of the warrior, and fight—fight until traitors lay down their arms and sue for peace.

No patriot should despond. Our government has not fully performed its mission. The Almighty will preserve it and guide it safely through the storms that threaten it. The great future has much in store for us yet. For one, I will not believe that this experiment of a Republican government is so soon to prove a failure. The temple of our liberty was reared by our fathers upon foundations too solid to be tottering to their fall in the brief period of three-quarters of a century.

With the great Webster I can devoutly pray, that "when my eyes shall be turned, to behold for the last time, the sun in Heaven, may I not see him shining on the broken and dissevered fragments of a once glorious Union; on States dissevered, discordant, belligerent; on a land rent with civil feuds, or drenched it may be, in fraternal blood. Let their last feeble and lingering glance, rather behold the gorgeous ensign of the Republic, now known and honored throughout the earth, still full high advanced, its arms and trophies streaming in their original lustre, not a stripe erased or polluted, nor a single star obscured—bearing for its motto no such miserable interrogatory as, *What is all this worth?* nor those other words of delusion and folly, *Liberty first and Union afterwards*; but everywhere, spread all over in characters of living light, blazing on all its ample folds, as they float over the sea and over the land, in every wind under the whole

heavens, that other sentiment, dear to every true American heart
—Liberty and Union, now and forever, one and inseparable!"

This noble effort was listened to by a large concourse of patriotic people. It punctured the bubble of secession, and laid bare
the long contemplated treason of the rebels. It is not surprising
that such masterly efforts should batter down party distinctions,
and unite the people on an elevated platform of patriotism.

Early in the year 1862, General Browne entered the United
States service as an Aid-de-camp, on the staff of General Thomas
J. Wood, and served with that General 'till after the battle of
Shilo, and during a part of the time of the seige of Corinth. While
before Corinth, he was stricken down by disease, and for months
his life trembled in the balance. He was taken to his home and
finally recovered his usual health.

At the October election, in 1862, he was elected to represent
Randolph county in the Senate of the Legislature of Indiana.

The ensuing session of that body convened at Indianapolis, on
the 8th day of January, 1863. The Senate was called to order by
Thomas M. Browne, its principal Secretary of the previous session.

On the same day he presented his credentials as Senator-Elect
from Randolph county, and was sworn into office. Although one
of the youngest Senators, yet he became the acknowledged leader
of the Republicans in the Senate. A ready and eloquent debater,
thoroughly versed in the political history of the country, and an
able lawyer, he was eminently qualified for that responsible
position.

The Democrats had a majority in the Legislature of 1863, and
they assumed an undisguised attitude of hostility to the administration of President Lincoln, and of Governor Morton. They
were opposed to the suppression of the rebellion by force of arms,
and wanted to maintain slavery, the Union, and the Constitution
as they were. They denounced the Emancipation Proclamation
of President Lincoln as executive usurpation. They were extremely
hostile to the action of the President in suppressing, in certain
disloyal districts, the writ of *Habeas Corpus.*

The Legislature convened on the anniversary of the battle of
New Orleans. About the first thing Senator Browne did was to

remind the Democratic members of their inconsistency. After organizing in the morning, the Senate adjourned until two o'clock in the afternoon. The roll-call in the afternoon, disclosed the fact, that there was not a quorum present. Senator Browne arose and said, he hoped the further call of the roll would be suspended and the absent members excused, because it being the anniversary of the battle of New Orleans, the absent Republicans were celebrating the occasion, because it was the anniversary of the day on which General Jackson whipped the British; and the absent Democratic members were celebrating it, because it was the anniversary of the suspension, by General Jackson at New Orleans, of the writ of *Habeas Corpus.* The point will be understood when it is remembered, that with Democrats, Jackson was authority not to be questioned, and at that time, the Democrats were complaining loudly of President Lincoln, for suspending the writ, a proceeding all wrong when done by Lincoln, but all right when done by Jackson.

For the purpose of compelling the Democratic members to place themselves on record, either for or against a vigorous prosecution of the war for the suppression of the rebellion, on the 10th of January, he introduced this resolution:

"1. *Resolved,* That we are in favor of a vigorous prosecution of the present war, within the limits of the Constitution, and in accordance with the recognized usages of civilized warfare, for the suppression of the rebellion, and the restoration of the union of all the States; and that all necessary appropriations should be made by this General Assembly to assist the State in answering all requisitions of the general Government in the payment of any proper expenses that have accrued, that have not heretofore been provided for; and are opposed to obstructing, in any manner whatever, the general Government in the exercise of any of its powers."

This resolution was referred to a select committee of nine, consisting of six Democrats and three Republicans. After taking the matter under advisement, the Democratic portion of the committee, submitted a majority report, in which they say, "As it regards the subject matter of the first resolution we know of no disposition or intention on the part of any member of this body, or of the dominant political party in the State, to interfere with the exercise of the rightful powers of the general Government,

38

for the purpose of putting down the rebellion and preserving the national Government under the Constitution. Yet we do not desire to *conceal the fact that we are opposed to much of the policy and conduct of the Administration in its so-called efforts to accomplish those desirable objects*; and especially are we opposed to the Emancipation Proclamation, of September the 22d, 1862, and the entire *Negro policy of the radicals*, who now, unfortunately, have control of the Government, believing that such policy is calculated to destroy, and not preserve the Union and constitutional liberty. And in proof of these opinions, we refer, with pain, to the deplorable condition of our national affairs, which *we believe, is the legitimate result of the cause stated.* 'The Constitution as it is,' and the 'Union as it was,' with 'the Negro where he is,' is *our motto*; and at the proper time we will probably elaborate our views upon these important subjects, so as to give a full and fair expression of the voice of Indiana upon all the questions connected with the momentous crisis of the country—an expression in accordance with the *sentiments of the loyal people* of Indiana, as foreshadowed by the ballot box at the recent election."

In the opinion of those patriotic Democratic Senators, the deplorable condition of the country was not the result of treason, but of the "*Negro* policy of the radicals who had control of the Government." And they intended to give a full and fair expression of the *voice of Indiana* upon all the questions connected with the crisis of the country.

The soldiers of Indiana, with their *guns*, upon nearly every battle-field of the rebellion, spoke the *voice* of Indiana, on all those questions, and after laying King Cotton, Slavery, Secession, States rights, chivalry and treason, in the same bloody grave, they proudly returned to their noble State, with *their* "motto" emblazoned on their *battle-rent flags*—

"Freedom to all, even to the despised slave!"

And the people of the United States not satisfied with the Constitution as it was, changed it. They "put *God* in the Constitution by recognizing the rights of his creature, man."

The minority submitted a report, offering an additional resolution as an amendment, and recommending the adoption of

Senator Browne's resolutions. A Democratic Senator moved to lay the minority report on the table, which motion prevailed by a strict party vote. The ayes and noes were demanded and ordered, and thus the Democratic Senators placed themselves on record against the resolution, to which no patriot could have had the slightest objection.

Senator Browne offered resolutions recommending the abolition of the Common Pleas Court, and the transfer of all cases pending in those courts, to the Circuit courts, and conferring the jurisdiction the former court had on the latter. Such a law was enacted by the Legislature of 1873. He was an earnest advocate of the Grand Jury system.

After the close of the Legislature, General Browne recruited company "B" of the Seventh Indiana Cavalry, and was commissioned captain of the company. He was soon after promoted Lieutenant Colonel of the regiment.

He shared with it, the dangers, fatigues, and privations of all its most trying and dangerous expeditions and battles. In the battle of Okolona, fought February 22d, 1864, by his courage and coolness, he did more than any other man to maintain intact the organization of the regiment, a thing most difficult to do, with the wild confusion and riot reigning supreme around it.

At the battle of Brice's Cross Roads, June 10th, 1864, his courage and skillful management of his regiment, won the enthusiastic admiration, not only of General Benjamin H. Grierson, but of every man in the army. *He was the hero* of that bloody but ill-fated field. With but a handful of men, he held the key of the Federal position, against the repeated and desperate attempts of Forrest to carry it. When the rebels were flanking him with one column, and attacking him in front with a line but a few feet from his position, he withdrew his regiment under a galling fire, and formed it in another a few rods to the right and rear, and compelled his adversaries to keep at a respectful distance. When the battle was raging fiercest, and the lines were but a few feet apart, his horse, a present to him from company "B," was shot under him, himself wounded in the ankle, and his orderly killed at his side. He did not for an instant lose his presence of mind, but issued his commands in a stentorian voice that was heard above the din of conflict.

Early in October, 1864, on account of his known ability as a lawyer, he was selected as President of a Military Commission to convene at Memphis, for the trial of such cases as might be brought before it. He took his seat as such, on the 10th day of October, 1864.

The most important case tried before the Commission, was that of "Dick Davis" the guerrilla. That man, on account of his bloody cruelty, had been the terror of the country within a *radii* of fifty miles of Memphis. He was captured by Captain Skelton on the 2d of October, and put on trial for being a guerrilla. On the 11th of October, his trial commenced. He was ably defended by counsel, who did their utmost to secure the acquittal of their notorious client. But all their arts were turned to confusion, by the watchful, able and sagacious President of the court. The trial ended on the 15th of December, 1864, and resulted in the conviction of the prisoner. The findings of guilty and sentence of death by the court, were approved by General Dana. On the 23d of December, 1864, within the walls of Fort Pickering, at Memphis, Dick Davis suffered death by hanging. An interesting account of the trial and execution, written by General Browne himself, will be found in chapter 14.

He remained on duty as President of the military court till some time in January 1865, when he returned to and assumed command of the regiment. From that time until the final muster out of the regiment, he was in reality its commander.

When the regiment was consolidated at Hempstead, Texas, he became its Colonel.

"For gallant and meritorious conduct," he was commissioned by the President of the United States, Brevet Brigadier General of Volunteers, to date from March 13th, 1865.

During the winter of 1865-6, he was commandant of the military post of Sherman, in the northern part of Texas. By his firmness and kindness, he won the respect and confidence of the people, and when he departed, he left behind him many warm personal friends.

After he was mustered out of the service, he returned to his home at Winchester, Indiana, and entered earnestly on the practice of his profession. But he was not permitted to remain long in private life. In 1866, he was appointed by the President, United States District Attorney for the District of Indiana. He discharged

41

the duties of that office for a number of years with distinguished success.

In 1870, he formed a copartnership with Jonathan W. Gordon and Judge Robert N. Lamb, for the practice of law at Indianapolis. The firm name being Gordon, Browne & Lamb. He remained in business with those gentlemen until June 1876, when he returned to his old home at Winchester.

Although a poor man at the close of the war, yet by his close attention to his profession since, he has succeeded in accumulating a moderate fortune.

Although a thorough statesman, yet he is more widely known as a great lawyer. Thoroughly grounded in the principles of jurisprudence, and master of a peculiar forensic eloquence, there are few lawyers who wield a greater influence in the courts than himself. He is particularly strong before juries. Fully six feet in height, as straight as an arrow, compactly and firmly built, from the crown of his head to the soles of his feet, he is a gentleman of commanding presence. His blue eyes now twinkling with mischievous fun, now flashing with indignation, as he employs judiciously, the weapons of the orator, irony, sarcasm, wit, humor and ridicule, he moulds his "twelvers" to his will. No man has a better enunciation. The words come from his lips like coin fresh from the mint. Although elaborate, yet he never uses a superfluous word. Even in ordinary conversation his language is chaste and precise, yet it comes with such ease and grace, that it never fails to interest and charm the listener.

In 1872, he was nominated at Indianapolis, by the Republican State Convention, as the Republican candidate for Governor. Of this important event in his career, Jonathan W. Gordon, the great lawyer and advocate of Indianapolis, says:

"It was while pursuing the even tenor of his way as a citizen and officer of the government, that some friend mentioned his name in connection with the office of Governor of Indiana, a distinction at which, the writer has reason to know, he never had aimed, and of which it may be doubted whether he had ever so much as thought. Once publicly mentioned for the place it soon became apparent that he would be selected. The young men of his party everywhere were for him, and, without effort on his part, he was chosen by the Republican State Convention of Indiana, on the second ballot, as its standard-bearer in the ensuing political contest over two of the ablest and most deservedly popular men in the State—Godlove S. Orth and Gen. Ben. Harrison. It was a proud day for the lonely orphan who had been left among strangers without means or friends at the age of thirteen, when that great convention—the greatest in many respects that ever assembled in the State—called him to the front and placed in his hands the battle-scarred flag of union, of law, and of liberty, and made him its bearer, and the guardian in the coming strife of all its glorious memories, its undying hopes, 'its honor's stainless folds.' As he came forward, that vast assembly was swept by the spirit of the deepest enthusiasm, and greeted him with cheers and shouts that sprung spontaneously from the hearts and lips of thousands made one by the same inspiration."

He had for his competitor in that political campaign, the present Governor of Indiana, Thomas A. Hendricks. General Browne made an able and thorough canvass of the State. In every county he eloquently advocated the "undying principles" of his party, but the fortunes of the day were against him.

Socially he is genial and polite. As a friend he is steadfast. As an adversary he is honorable, relying solely on truth and reason. At Winchester every one becomes enthusiastic at the mention of the name "General Tom Browne" as he is familiarly called.

At the October election, 1876, Gen. Browne was elected on the Republican ticket, as representative for the Fifth Congressional District, in Congress, over Judge Holman, Democrat, by a majority of fifteen hundred. Gen. Browne had a large Democratic majority to overcome. The fact of his election with the chances against him, shows the estimation in which he is held by the people of his district.

BREVET MAJOR GENERAL JOHN P. C. SHANKS.

The paternal ancestors of John P. C. Shanks came to this country from Ireland, in an early period of our colonial history. His grandfather, Joseph Shanks, fought under the banners of Washington, through the revolutionary war, and took part in the battle of Yorktown, the last of the engagements fought for national independence. His father, Michael Shanks served as a soldier through the war of 1812, and an elder brother through the Mexi-

43

MAJOR JAMES H. CARPENTER

44

can war. Thus it will be seen that the subject of this sketch is a descendant from a military family.

John P. C. Shanks was born on the 17th of June, 1826, at Martinsburg, Virginia. In 1839, his father, on account of his hostility to the institution of slavery, left Virginia and settled in Jay county, Indiana, which at that time was a wilderness. Michael Shanks and his family endured the hardships and privations of pioneer life. It required all their time with their strong arms to hew out a home in the forests of Jay county. John P. C. Shanks enjoyed but few advantages of schools either in Virginia or at his new home in Indiana. The time from his fifteenth to his seventeenth year, being disabled for labor by rheumatism, he industriously employed in the acquisition of learning under the instruction of his father, who was a good scholar. He continued his studies on regaining his health, during the hours not devoted to labor for his father, or in necessary slumber. By the fire-light at home, and the camp-fires in the woods, on the highway while driving his team, and while holding the plow in the field, he studied his book, an earnest devotee at the shrine of learning. Possibly the history of no American who has risen to eminence, will show the acquisition of knowledge under more adverse circumstances. Our Revolution wrought changes other than those of government. It battered down a titled nobility, and erected one based on intellect and worth of character. It placed within the reach of the lonely plow-boy the highest positions of honor, trust and profit. The American youth, conscious of this, have striven through difficulties that seem insurmountable, and have finally reached the acme of their ambition. The people thoroughly imbued with the principles developed by the Revolution, have always delighted to advance their self-made men. They can more surely rely upon them. They are of the people, know their hardships, toils and necessities by experience, and when elevated to positions of honor, are faithful to their trusts. The people of Jay county, and of the congressional district, to which it is attached, have not been forgetful of John P. C. Shanks. He resolved to make a lawyer of himself, but had not the means to pursue the study of law. To acquire them he worked at the carpenter's trade in the State of Michigan. In 1847, he began the study of law in Jay county. To pay for his board while pursuing his studies, he worked a portion of the time, while not unmindful of his filial duties, he devoted every third week to labor for his father on the farm.

During the year 1850, he was acting Auditor of Jay county. In that year he was admitted to practice law, and in the following autumn was, by the unanimous vote of both political parties, elected prosecuting attorney of the Circuit court. That was a flattering recognition of his ability as a young lawyer and of his worth as a citizen.

In early life, he was, in politics a Whig and as such was, in 1853, elected to the Legislature of Indiana. Two years later he was a candidate for re-election, but was defeated as the temperance candidate, and because he was known to be in favor of legal prohibition.

In 1860, he was elected, on the Republican ticket, a representative from Indiana to the Thirty-Seventh Congress. The black cloud of rebellion had broken on the country, and hostilities inaugurated by the rebels by the bombardment of Fort Sumpter. Congress was convened in special session by the proclamation of the President, for the purpose of providing the means for the prosecution of the war. On July 4th, 1861, Gen. Shanks took his seat in Congress. While it was in session the rebels were concentrating their forces in the neighborhood of Manassas Junction. The first battle of Bull Run was fought on the 21st of July, 1861. Gen. Shanks, unable to sit idly by when a great conflict was to occur, voluntarily took part in the battle, and by great exertions, succeeded in rallying a large number of the fugitives from that bloody field. For his valuable services in that battle, he was tendered by President Lincoln the commission of Brigadier General, which he declined on the ground that none should be promoted until they had proved themselves competent to command. After the adjournment of congress, he accepted an appointment on the staff of Gen. John C. Fremont, as volunteer *aid-de-camp*, and served with him in Missouri. When Fremont was superseded, Gen. Shanks remained with his successor, Gen. Hunter, until the reassembling of Congress. He offered a resolution in Congress declaring that the constitutional powei to return fugitive slaves to their masters, rests solely with the civil department of the government, and that the order of the Secretary of War to General Wool to return a slave to Mr. Jessop of Maryland, was an assumption over the civil law and the rights of the slave. Congress sustained him in his position. On the 4th of March, 1862, he made an able speech in Congress, vindicating the course pursued by General Fremont in Missouri, and sustaining his proclamation giving freedom to the slaves of rebels. It will be remembered that that proclamation, through the intrigues of the unscrupulous demagogue, Frank P. Blair, was made one of the causes for the removal of Fremont. That General is amply vindicated by subsequent history. It proves that Fremont in the field, and Shanks, in Congress had clearer conceptions of the war and its final termination, than some of the leading politicians of those days. Freedom was given not only to the slaves of rebels, but to every bondman, and bondwoman and child in the United States.

After the close of that session of Congress, Gen. Shanks again served on the staff of Fremont, in his campaign in West Virginia.

By order of Governor Morton, dated June 24th, 1863, he recruited the Seventh Indiana Cavalry. When that regiment was raised, he was commissioned its Colonel. He gave all his time and energy to arming, equipping, drilling, and fitting the regiment for active service. He commanded it in all its operations till after its return to Memphis from the unfortunate expedition to West Point, Mississippi, in February 1864. At Ivy Farm, February 22d, 1864, he received from the lips of General W. Sooy Smith himself, the order to charge, and had the honor of striking the last blow, that saved the greater portion, if not the entire army from capture. After his return from that expedition, his health was broken down, and for a time, he was compelled to retire from active service. In February 1864, he was commissioned a Brevet Brigadier General, for gallant and meritorious services. As soon as his health permitted he was assigned to the command of a brigade of cavalry. That separated him from the regiment during the most of the remainder of its service. He commanded a brigade of cavalry under Brevet Brigadier General Osborn, on the expedition to Bastrop, Louisiana, in the Spring of 1865.

On the recommendation of E. M. Stanton, Secretary of War, he was breveted Major General of volunteers.

On the 18th of September, 1865, at Hempstead, Texas, he was mustered out of the service, on the consolidation of the regiment, and immediately started for his home.

In 1866, he was elected, as the Republican candidate, to the Fortieth Congress. He introduced a resolution for the appointment of a committee to inquire into the treatment of Union prisoners. After a long and patient investigation, the committee, of which General Shanks was chairman, submitted an elaborate report. Subsequently in an address to the Grand Army of the Republic, in speaking of the treatment of union prisoners, he said:

"I hope that the high moral, political, and military position of our people will enable our government to procure the adoption in the laws of nations of a provision that the captives in war shall not be personally retained as prisoners; but shall, under a flag of truce, be returned to their own lines or vessels, and paroled until properly exchanged, so that the books of the commissioners of exchange of the respective belligerents shall determine the relative advantages in captives, and thus the horrors and sacrifices of prison life be prevented." All Christian people will earnestly pray that such will become one of the rules of civilized warfare. He supported in a speech the bill of Mr. Logan, to furnish to disabled soldiers, free of expense to themselves, artificial limbs, claiming that it was the duty of the government to put them in as good a condition so far as possible, as they were before being injured. He was re-elected to Congress term after term until 1874, when he was defeated by Judge Holman.

He is an able lawyer, and an eloquent speaker, and has a ripe experience in our governmental affairs.

PART II.

History of the Seventh Indiana Cavalry.

CHAPTER I.

ORGANIZATION OF THE REGIMENT.

The Seventh Indiana Cavalry, or One hundred and nineteenth Regiment of Volunteers, was organized pursuant to the following order:

GENERAL ORDERS.

STATE OF INDIANA, ADJUTANT GENERAL'S OFFICE
INDIANAPOLIS, JUNE 24, 1863.

SEVENTH INDIANA CAVALRY.

By virtue of authority from the Secretary of War, another regiment of cavalry will be raised in this State immediately, to serve for three years or during the war. The regiment will be recruited in accordance with the rules and instructions in General Orders No. 75, of the War Department series of 1863.

The privilege will be accorded to each Congressional District, to furnish one company for the regiment, if organized and reported within thirty days. If companies are not likely to be raised in any of the Districts within that time, companies from any part of the State will be accepted.

The regiment will consist of twelve companies, and be officered as follows:

One Colonel, one Lieutenant Colonel, three Majors, one Surgeon, two Assistant Surgeons, one Adjutant, one Quartermaster, one Commissary (extra Lieutenant), one Chaplain, one Veterinary

Surgeon, one Sergeant Major, one Quartermaster Sergeant, one Commissary Sergeant, two Hospital Stewards, one Saddler Sergeant, and one Chief Trumpeter.

Each company will be organized with one Captain, one First Lieutenant, one Second Lieutenant, one First Sergeant, one Quartermaster Sergeant, one Company Sergeant, five Sergeants, eight Corporals, two Teamsters, two Farriers, one Blacksmith, one Saddler, one Wagoner, and seventy-eight Privates. Aggregate, 103.

Any company of fifty-two men will be accepted and mustered with a First Lieutenant, and if they fail to fill up within a reasonable time, they will be consolidated with other parts of companies. The right is reserved to combine incomplete companies or parts of companies, after a fair opportunity has been afforded them to fill up.

In combining parts of companies the following distribution of officers is suggested, and parts of companies will be accepted with a view to making such combinations:

For forty-five men, a Captaincy.

For thirty-five men, a First Lieutenancy.

For twenty-five men, a Second Lieutenancy.

Colonel J. P. C. Shanks has been appointed Commandant of the camp of rendezvous for said regiment, and will be obeyed and respected accordingly.

Applications for authority to recruit companies may be filed at these headquarters or with the commandant.

Camp Morton will be the rendezvous of said Regiment.

Recruiting officers and others raising companies, may contract for the subsistence and lodging of recruits at places away from the camp of rendezvous, for a period not exceeding one week, at not exceeding thirty cents per day, and the accounts therefor properly verified by the recruiting officer, and approved by the Governor, or Adjutant General, will be paid by the U. S. Disbursing officer, provided the recruits so subsisted are received into the United States service.

When companies have been accepted they will be furnished with transportation passes to enable them to reach the rendezvous.

$25 OF BOUNTY IN ADVANCE.

Every volunteer shall receive in advance twenty-five dollars

50

of the one hundred dollars bounty, to be paid him immediately upon the muster of such regiment into service.

O. P. Morton, Governor.

LAZ. NOBLE, Ad'jt Gen. Ind.

From all parts of the State, companies were recruited for this regiment. On their arrival at Indianapolis they rendezvoused at Camp Shanks.

The regimental officers were as follows: Colonel, John P. C. Shanks; Lieutenant Colonel, Thomas M. Browne; Majors, Christian Beck, Samuel E. W. Simonson, and John C. Febles; Adjutant, James A. Price; Quartermaster, John W. Martin; Commissary, First Lieutenant, —— Holliday; Chaplain, James Marquis; Surgeon, William Freeman; Assistant Surgeon, Joshua Chitwood, promoted to Surgeon, May 11th, 1864, *vice* William Freeman dismissed; Veterinary Surgeon, Lysander S. Ingram; Hospital Steward, Daniel B. Roether.

The regiment was composed of the following companies:

COMPANY A.

COMMISSIONED OFFICERS.

Captain—John C. Febles of Valparaiso, Indiana, promoted to Major, October 27th 1863. John R. Parmelee, of Valparaiso, promoted from First Lieutenant, *vice* Febles, promoted to Major.

First Lieutenant—Henry S. Stoddard, of Valparaiso, commissioned First Lieutenant, but did not muster as such. Resigned as Second Lieutenant, Nov. 25th, 1863.

John Douch, of Valparaiso, commissioned Second Lieutenant, but being immediately promoted to First Lieutenant *vice* Stoddard resigned, he did not muster as Second Lieutenant, but mustered as First Lieutenant, November 25th, 1863.

Second Lieutenant—John C. Hanson, of Valparaiso, and a private of company G, was commissioned Second Lieutenant of this company, and mustered as such November 26th, 1863.

ENLISTED MEN.

First Sergeant—Charles H. Gleason of Valparaiso.

Sergeants—Francis J. Miller, Americus Baum, Edmond L. Robinson, promoted to First Sergeant, on promotion of Charles H.

51

JOHN C. FEBLES, 1st Lieutenant, Major, Co. A, F, S

Gleason to Second Lieutenant; Benjamin M. Brown, Albert H. Jackson.

Corporals, Rufus H. Norton, George K. Ritter, John Marsh, Avery Jones, deserted Oct. 4th, 1863; William Gogan, Henry Fairchild, and Orin S. Clark.

Musicians, Charles M. Gogan, Cornelius O'Neal, Samuel H. Jones.

Saddler, William A. Wise.

Wagoner, Rieden McDorman.

Privates, Stillman F. Andrews, Stephen Adams, Perry Brandon, Orlando Bagley, George Bundy, Clark B. Booth, John Brock, Levi B. Bible, Cleveland A. Bishop, William Curtis, John R. Crawford, William Crawford, John Clark, Henry W. Clark, Cassius Clark, John W. Cook, James Demmick, Samuel P. Dunn, Elias Davis, Clark S. Durkee, James A. English, Joseph Earnest, James Eahart, George W. Easterly, Franklin Furguson, Henry Fisher, Francis Foley, George Frazee, Thomas Fox, Wm. Gardner, Norah H. Gordon, Adolphus Hardesty, James G. Hughs, Berzillian Homer, Nicholas Haskins, George W. Huntington, Geo. W. Jones, David Ketchall, Wesley B. Kelley, Perry Lageston, Moses Livingstone, John W. Matheny, Alonzo McMurphy, Abram McArty, Henry B. Miller, Isaac J. Margeston, William McWindle, Isaac R. McBride, James M. C. Meyers, John R. Mills, Felix J. Murphy, William Mossholder, Thomas Nickson, Winfield Pierce, Lewis Porter, James W. Pollett, Noah F. Rodabaugh, Sumner T. Robinson, Hiram Ramey, Rheimer Roweder, Allen Rains, James T. Ragan, James Spaulding, John H. Skinner, William C. Sparks, James Smith, Thomas H. Smith, Lyman Temple, John W. Trubarger, James M. Williams, Alvin Welch, Clark S. Williams, Sylvester B. Willis, George A. Youngs, William Younglove, John B. Brewer, Charles P. Smith.

Mustered into service August 24th, 1863.

Mustered as recruits, William Ayers, John Davis, James Hodges, William Leaky, Leny Maulsby, John Robinson, John Seibert, Oliver P. Saint.

COMPANY B.

COMMISSIONED OFFICERS.

Captain, Thomas M. Browne, of Winchester, Randolph county, Indiana. Promoted Lieutenant Colonel, October 30th, 1863.

GEORGE BUNDY, Corporal, Private, Co. A

George W. Branham, of Union City, Indiana. Promoted from First Lieutenant *vice* Browne promoted to L't Col.

First Lieutenant, Francis M. Way, of Winchester, mustered October 10th, 1863, *vice* Branham, promoted Captain.

Second Lieutenant, Sylvester L. Lewis of Union City, Randolph county, Indiana, mustered August 28th, 1863.

ENLISTED MEN.

First Sergeant, Charles A. Dresser, promoted Quartermaster of 130th Regiment of Indiana infantry.

Quartermaster Sergeant, William C. Griffis.

Commissary Sergeant, William A. Dynes.

Sergeants, David S. Moist, Elisha B. West, William R. Schindel, Edwin M. Lonsey, Cyrus B. Polly.

Corporals, Jacob Hartman, Robert G. Hunt, John R. Perkins, Samuel Coddington, Joseph L. Coffin. Granbury B. Nickey, Zachariah Pucket, Joseph W. Ruby.

Bugler, Joel McBrown.

Farrier and *Blacksmith*, John B. Lennington and George D. Huffman.

Saddler, Martin Lardner.

Wagoner, James Bright.

Privates, Jeremiah D. Armstrong, John F. Arnold, George W. Allison, Edmond Anderson, Charles L. Brenham, Justice Brumel, Orin Barber, Benjamin L. Beaden, Hunter Berry, Anthony S. Cost, James K. Clear, Alpheus Congers, Edmond D. Cortes, Edward Calkins, Sanford Crist, Daniel Coats, John J. Dillon, Nelson H. Elliott, Eli Frazer, Isaac M. Gray, Edward E. Gray, George W. Gray, Nathan Garrett, Hamilton C. Gullet, Elias Helffine, Alfred Hall, Edward D. Hunt, Andrew Huffman, Vinson Huston, Elijah Hazelton, John C. Henshaw, Mordica W. Harris, Samuel F. Jean, John F. Jones, Francis M. Johnson, Stephen Kennedy, John E. Keys, John Keesy, Hiram Lamb, Urias Lamb, Erastus Ludy, Thomas Little, Alexander Little, William Milles, John Murphy, John F. Matheny, Franklin McDaniel, James W. Matox, Patrick McGettigan, George W. Monks, James Moore, John R. Mauzy, Harrison C. Nicky, Henry S. Peacock, Cass M. Peterson, Orvil R. Peterson, Leander Pugh, Ninnian Robinson, George W. Shreve, David H. Seamons, Clement Strahan, George

55

W. Smith No. 1, George W. Smith No. 2, Sampson Scott, John F. Shirly, William Stine, William Skinner, Benjamin Throp, Alva Tucker, Luther C. Williamson, Elijah T. Wood, Henry Worgum, John D. Williamson, Daniel Woodbury, John M. Woodbury, Christian H. Wright, Francis M. Way, D. McMahan.

This company was mustered into the service August 28th, 1863, at Indianapolis. Afterwards John B. Hughs, Lewis Reeves, Joseph Shaffer, Elisha B. Wood, joined the company as recruits. The members of this company were from Randolph county, Indiana.

COMPANY C.

The members of this company were from Dearborn, Grant, Marion, and Ripley counties. They were mustered into the service September 2d, 1863, at Indianapolis.

COMMISSIONED OFFICERS.

Captain, John W. Senior, of Aurora, Dearborn county.
First Lieutenant, George R. Kennedy.
Second Lieutenant, James W. Spence, died October 2d, 1863. Peter Platt, promoted from First Sergeant *vice* Spence, deceased.

ENLISTED MEN.

First Sergeant, Peter Platt, promoted to Second Lieutenant.
Sergeants, James W. Marshall, Benjamin E. Bleasdell, Philip Piercy, William C. Stark, James Kennedy, Francis M. Hinds, and Robert Whitecer.
Corporals, Nathaniel Miller, Jacob H. Garrigus, Marius Kelly, John Q. Overman, John H. Hustis, Landon F. Whithrow, Chester C. McCabe, and Harvey P. Richardson.
Buglers, Joseph Lansing and Thomas J. Palmers.
Farriers and *Blacksmiths*, Stephen Smith, Charles Wilson.
Saddler, Mason Bradshaw.
Wagoner, Ambrose Jones.
Privates, Alkana Adamson, John M. Bradford, Alexander Bradburn, John P. Batlaro, Silas E. Burr, Henry Borgman, Joshua Bratton, William Bates, Clark Cash, George Charman, George W. Conal, Ruben Cooper, Linman C. Clark, Isaac Cristy, Henry Carter, John S. Ducate, Franklin Daggy, John P. Ewing, George

S. Eubanks, Oliver W. Frazee, Phillip Fisher, George W. Goth, John H. Gathman, Joseph G. Gould, Frederick Gardner, William Grant, Joshua Henderson, Seth S. Heaton, Louis Hall, Myron Harding, Edward Marsh, William Hiatt, Benjamin Hiatt, David Harding, Joseph Hull, Frederick J. Hurst, George W. Isabel, Charles Jones, James Johnson, Franklin Johnson, Otto Kratz, George W. Knapp, Thomas Lytle, Julius Lane, Joseph Laird, Albert Laird, Samuel Land, Jones Mires, Jacob W. H. Mayers, Daniel B. Morgan, James Nemire, Henry Oppy, Jacob Orn, Levi Oliver, William H. Osborn, William Patterson, Samuel Pendergast, George W. Rush, John Rees, Joseph Ruble, Elijah Stevens, Jacob Shaffer, John Shaffer, Joseph Straley, Chester F. Smith, Christian Sohly, Eliphalet Stevens, Samuel Squibb, Ferdinand Santz, John Schumas, John Sparks, Frederick Trane, John Tullock, Frederick Tafhon, Philander Underwood, George W. Woodward, Erastus Wells, John Wilson, Charles Wince.

Recruits, William Colshear, Joshua M. Conn, Benjamin J. Harding, Ezekiel Horsley, David P. Row.

COMPANY D.

Mustered into service September 3d, 1863, at Indianapolis.

COMMISSIONED OFFICERS.

Captain, Henry F. Wright, of Aurora, Indiana.
First Lieutenant, Abram Hill, of Aurora, Indiana.
Second Lieutenant, Jacob C. Skirvin, of Sturgis, Michigan.

ENLISTED MEN.

First Sergeant, John F. Dumont, of Marion county.
Quartermaster Sergeant, Lewis F. Brougher.
Commissary Sergeant, Joseph McCarthey.
Sergeants, Albert E. Trister, George Patrick, John W. Desheil, John A. Talley, George W. Spieknall.
Corporals, John T. Lemon, Robert J. Ewbank, Francis V. Pearson, Andrew D. Brougher, Franklin P. Wagner, William H. Day, Joseph A. Erwin and John W. Lewis.
Farriers and *Blacksmiths*, William Saddler, Dirlam Stilwell.
Musicians, James W. Graydon and Henry Bunger.

HENRY F. WRIGHT, 2d Lieutenant, Captain, Co. D
Died of Disease September 25, 1864

Wagoner, Varnel D. Trulock.

Saddler, Israel Warner.

Privates, William Allerton, Amer Abden, Edward Ayers, James Agin, Francis Anderson, John Bruce, William Ball, Joseph F. Burns, Richard Bigelow, John Barber, Enoch Colon, George L. Canon, George Clark, Perry Cosairt, George W. Carr, James M. Disbro, Joseph Dingman, Jackson Dean, John Denble, Eli Dahuff, John E. Elmer, Joseph Eberle, John Earl, George W. Fegley, George Frederick, Anthony Frederick, Moses Fostnaucht, John Fitch, Cyrus J. Gilbert, Charles E. Green, William F. Green, Anthony Gucket, Richard Guthrie, Thomas S. Hunt, Henry H. Hughs, Henderson Huffman, Andrew H. Hess, Henry (Charles) Heiger, John Hall, Frederick Hoffman, Samuel D. Hoffman, George Hamlin, George Johnson, Nickolas Johnson, Andrew A. Johnson, Josiah Jillison, George C. James, Hiram J. Kail, Adam Lidge, Mathas Martin, Richard Mullis, Michael Mondary, John W. Mullen, Wesley Moore, Arthur McCueon, Samuel Mortorff, George L. Miller, Edward Norton, William Neff, Isaac Neff, Benjamin Russell, Samuel Roberts, Andrew Stevinson, Smith Sampson, John Salgers, George W. Swindler, Owen Stevinson, Robert Scrogins, Marcus Slater, Jonathan Swisher, Robert H. Snowberger, Daniel G. Shaffer, Thomas Starkey, Chester V. Tuttle, Theodore F. Tuttle, Adam C. Wagner, Brazillian Woodworth, John Whipple.

Recruits, James B. Gordon, William Loftus, James Norman, John Truelove, Harvey Williams.

COMPANY E.

Mustered at Indianapolis, September 3d, 1863.

COMMISSIONED OFFICERS.

Captain, David T. Skinner, of Jay county.

First Lieutenant, Joel H. Elliott, of Centerville, Indiana. Promoted to Captain of company M, October 23d, 1863. James E. Sloan, promoted from Second Lieutenant, *vice* Joel H. Elliott, promoted.

Second Lieutenant, Lee Roy Woods, of Centerville, Indiana, promoted from First Sergeant *vice* James E. Sloan, promoted.

JACOB C. SKIRVIN, 2d Lieutenant, 1st Lieutenant, Co. D
Killed in Action on April 3, 1865

First Sergeant, Lee Roy Woods

Quartermaster Sergeant, John W. Lee.

Commissary Sergeant, Harris J. Abbott.

Sergeants, William M. Skinner, John Rowlett, Barton B. Jenkins, Harrison Booth, and James Stansbury.

Corporals, Henry Hawkins, William Underwood, Thomas J. Updike, Daniel Van Camp, George M. D. Frazee, Richard Dilworth, George W. Ford, John K. Teters.

Musicians John W. Legg, and Charles W. Coffin.

Farriers and *Blacksmiths,* William Vanskyhawk, Francis M. Johnson and Thomas Montieth.

Saddler, James Bowen.

Wagoner, Jeremiah W. Hunt.

Privates, John Abadie, Philemon Abadie, John Adair, William Adair, Sanford P. Aimes, Philip Austin, John W. Babb, Edward Baldwin, Anthony Bunussi, Joseph Blackburn, Charles Bromfield, Henry Carter, August T. Cailliel, Charles Claverie, John G. W. Clevenger, Andrew Crews, Daniel B. Crow, Abijah Crow, Humphrey Davis, James Deal, Daniel W. Doner, John Dupuy, David T. Edwards, John H. Elliott, David Farris, Franklin Forrest, Obediah Gardner, Michael Gillegan, William Glendenning, Morgan L. Gray, Samuel J. Gray, Isaac A. Gorman, Edward Green, Isaac Griffith, George Haley, George W. Hambleton, George W. Hilton, Frederick Hive, Richard D. Hoover, Jerome Hiatt, James Inks, James B. Jay (promoted assistant Surgeon), John E. Karch, William C. Kittsmiller, Emanuel Knepper, Joseph Knepper, Ely Lehr, Thomas Lahmmon, John W. Lott, George W. Lutes, Gramaliel McLeod, Lemuel McLeod, George Miller, Francis Moore, Benjamin F. Paxton, John Q. Paxton, Jacob A. Poinier, Alfred Poindexter, Costan Porter, Hickason Ramsbottom, Jonathan Ray, John Roberts, John Schneider, Judson Skinner, James C. Snyder, William H. Smith, Paul Storms, Michael Solar, H. J. Van Benthuysen, Jacob Wallick, Enos Walker, John Ware, John Watts, John Watson, Aaron Whetsel, William Whetsel, Morris P. Wood.

Joined subsequently to the muster of the company, as recruits: James G. Cloud, Thomas Mericle, Charles W. Ward, Joseph Watts.

JOHN W. SHOEMAKER, Acting 2d Lieutenant, Captain, Co. F

COMPANY F.

This company was mustered September 3d, 1863, at Indianapolis. The men composing it were principally from LaPorte county.

COMMISSIONED OFFICERS.

Captain, John W. Shoemaker, of LaPorte county.
First Lieutenant, Joseph W. Skelton of Princeton, Gibson county, Indiana.
First Lieutenant, George W. Dunkerley, of Covington, Indiana.

ENLISTED MEN.

First Sergeant, Thomas S. Cogley, of LaPorte.
Quartermaster Sergeant, James C. Barnes.
Commissary Sergeant, Rhynear S. Mandeville.
Sergeants, Orlando Ballenger, William H. Ellsworth, Talcut Miller, William W. Frasier.
Corporals, Andrew J. Woolf, Edward Kent, George Dudley, Ransel B. Cuttler, Adam H. Shoemaker, Jacob Cranse, William H. Crane, Francis J. M. Titus.
Bugler, Daniel Devrew.
Farrier, John Ritter.
Saddler, William H. Parker.
Wagoner, Fred Demzine.
Privates, Thomas Able, Aaron Alyea, Fred Anthon, Joseph R. Aurand, John Best, Charles Bishop, William Barneby, Lewis Bright, Samuel Clark, Leon Carle, Lafayette Crane, Daniel Crites, William B. Crocker, Jacob Dilman, Thomas Duncan, Dudley C. Dugan, John Edwards, Franklin Erwin, Charles Fennimore, John Fugate, William A. Flynn, Oliver Frame, John Florharty, William A. Fink, Bennett Forrester, Joseph Gaw, Henry Gabler, William Gilespie, George Hammond, Greenbury Hall, William H. Hunter, Amasy Howell, Holbert Iseminger, Hiram Iseminger, Archibald F. Inglis, Harrison Jones, James M. Jackson, Henry Jessup, Herman Kile, Andrew Kerwan, John R .Kelley, John P. Knowlton, John B. Kisner, Alexander Kansas, William A. Kent, John J. Link, John Lemon, Thomas A. Lantsford, Jared B. Mandeville, Jesse M. Meacham, David H. McNeece, Lorain J. Moore, Peter Meredith, Edward D. Morden, John McCarty, James McCune, James

63

GEORGE W. DUNKERLEY, 1st Lieutenant, Co. F.

McKinney, Andrew Myres, Bernard Mullingate, Oliver Newcomb, Chester G. Pierce, Horace Pierce, James M. Parker, Dennis J. Peer, Chas. E. Ruple, John L. Redding, Ashbury Ritter, Stephen Rice, Albert Ray, Alexander Schultz, Sanford H. Steward, John Slagel, John Sims, David Sweigart, Edward Tracy, John P. Townsend, Alpheus Thomas, Henry H. Vandusen, Johnson C. Vandusen, Landon Williams, William Whipple, George Wilson, Philander Wheeler.

COMPANY G.

Mustered September 5th, 1863, at Indianapolis. The members of this company were from Vigo, Delaware, Franklin, Marion, Lake and Grant counties.

COMMISSIONED OFFICERS.

Captain, Walter K. Scott, of Indianapolis.
First Lieutenant, William A. Ryan, of Terre Haute.
Second Lieutenant, Oscar Rankin, of Terre Haute.

ENLISTED MEN.

First Sergeant, James H. Lowes.
Sergeants, Andrew J. Thompson, John Hurley, Austin H. Piety, Isaac Sowerwine, James Dundon, Basil M. Warfield, and John W. Hamilton.
Corporals, John Jones, Charles E. Cottrill, James A. Pinson, James T. Vinnedge, John C. Shannon, Samuel H. Wells, Charles Wilson, William S. Corbin.
Buglers, James McKanon and Edward McBride.
Farrier and *Blacksmiths*, Robert McCoy and William H. Oberdurf.
Saddler, Patrick Kelley.
Wagoner, Daniel C. Brenner.
Privates, George W. Acker, Christopher C. Burny, Isaac Budd, George W. Brandon, Alfred Culbertson, Joseph Carter, William N. Cole, George Carmichael, George Crow, Milton Davis, Joseph B. Dickey, Alfred O. Dewitt, Leander Downing, William T. Downing, James P. Frazier, David Freeman, Andrew Falkner, William H. Grow, William Grisham, Hiram Goad, William H. Gray, John C. Hanson (promoted 2d Lieutenant of company A),

Courtesy: Mick Hissick

ANDREW J. THOMPSON, Sergeant, 1st Lieutenant, Co. G, F

66

Benjamin Hamilton, Daniel C. Hunneford, James H. Hunt, Joseph Isabel, Timothy Kelley, Joseph R. Lane, Henry E. Luther, Wesley B. Lambert, Andrew F. Lakin, Abraham Mitcham, Henry H. Muthert, John H. Matherly, John Mentor, Joseph Massacre, Jacob Miller, Daniel C. Nash, Issac Needham, George W. Needham, Abraham Nicely, Adam Nearon, James C. Powers, John Rankin, Andrew G. Richardson, John Rex, Leokalas Ryan, Jacob E. Shirley, Hezekiah Stout, William R. Shoemaker, Silas M. Shoemaker, Sanford Shoemaker, William Sisk, Jasper Smock, John W. Sparks, Henry Stewart, John Smith, Reason Trueblood, Joseph J. Vanmeter, Francis M. Vinnedge, Christian M. Williams, William Welsh, Sanford Whitworth, Enoch M. Windsor, Joseph A. Young.

Joined as recruits: John Clevenger, Henry Cory, Robert M. Dillman, Daniel G. Downing, Samuel Downing, Lewis F. Edgerton, John Gay, Richard Highton, John Heck, George W. Kennedy, William Moore, William M. Moore, John Myres, Bluford Peake, Henry C. Richards, Charles Saughter, John W. Lidwell, Isaac H. Truitt, Jacob Warnock.

COMPANY H.

Mustered at Indianapolis, September 5th, 1863. The members of this company, were principally from Marion, Tippecanoe, and Lagrange counties.

COMMISSIONED OFFICERS.

Captain, John M. Moore, of Plymouth, Indiana.
First Lieutenant, John Q. Reed, of Lagrange.
Second Lieutenant, Edward Calkins, of Winchester, Indiana.

ENLISTED MEN.

First Sergeant, Robert G. Smithers, of Indianapolis.
Sergeants, Henry L. Green, Michael Giles, John F. Morris, John Kelley, Ezekiel Brown, James Green, Rollo Hall.
Corporals, John A. King, Robert C. Redenbo, James P. McKinney, Jacob Aylea, John Q. Watson, William Wrick, Hugh Hefferman, and William H. Kline.
Buglers, John Cleland and Dewitt C. Watson.
Farrier and *Blacksmith*, Samuel Briley, Benjamin Beck.

ROBERT G. SMITHERS, 1st Sergeant, 1st Lieutenant, Co. H, A

Saddler, Christian Winger.

Wagoner, Charles McCann.

Privates, William Armington, George Allen, James Andrew, Thomas Alford, Harrison Anderson, George F. Andrews, Gideon Aylea, James Banogan, Samuel Bryant, Albert Brown, Andrew Bates, William Barnett, Solomon Bolder, Reason Browning, Charles Burgner, Henry Ballabend, Morris Currin, Michael Cavanaugh, Charles Cavanaugh, James Chisam, William Carrell, Edward Carpenter, Barnard Detta, Mathew Dwighman, Frank Englehart, Michael Ferall, Charles Flynn, Edward G. Gilson, John Gleason, Noah Gilbert, John Herrell, Jeffrey Harrington, Willard Johnson, Augustus Johnson, Ephriam Lattae, Dennis Lowrey, Edward Lahoe, Arthur F. Lamson, Francis Mellville, James McCabe, Robert McQuillan, James Maskell, Ambrose McKinney, James McGrain, Patrick Mitchell, Benjamin Mashone, James Maxville, James McNamara, Albert Morris, Abraham Oliver, John Paine, Thomas Robinson, James Rowe, Francis Robinson, John Reinkins, Clark Spidle, Samuel P. Sams, Marcus W. Stoner, Fred Strance, William Smith, Ed Smith, Edward St. John, John Shaw, Max Shoen, John Traiy, Jackson Tabb, Peter Vevasa, Lemuel Waddle, William Yarbrough, Francis Waddle.

Mustered September 26th, 1863, as recruits: Lewis Bodel, David Beckett, John P. Baker, Sylvester Dunn, John J. Gardner, James Kitchen, John F. Myres, Henry Sherman, John Smith, and William Winfield.

COMPANY I.

Date of muster, September 5th, 1863, at Indianapolis. The members of this company were principally from Kosciusko and Marion counties.

COMMISSIONED OFFICERS.

Captain, James H. Carpenter, of Warsaw, Kosciusko county, Indiana.

First Lieutenant, Charles H. Hare, of Shelbyville, Indiana.

Second Lieutenant, Benjamin F. Bales.

ENLISTED MEN.

First Sergeant, Elijah S. Blackford.

Sergeants, William W. Kelley, John M. Longfellow, Robert

BENJAMIN F. BALES, 2d Lieutenant, Captain, Co. I

S. Richart (promoted captain 12th Indiana cavalry, October 31st, 1863), Thomas J. Howard, Horace W. King, Cornelius E. Cartwright, and George D. Sayler.

Corporals, Nelson H. Hunt, Lewis Gerrean, Alexander Walker, George S. Jones, John B. Cole, Henry C. Clifford, Justice M. Denton, John W. Barger.

Buglers, John R. Harrel, Michael C. Grey.

Farrier and *Blacksmith*, Joseph C. McClary and Cyrus Bennett.

Saddler, Allen J. Watson.

Wagoner, William E. Hampton.

Privates, Adoniram Allen, Robert B. Armstrong, John H. Arnold, John L. Arnold, George W. Barger, William Babcock, William Barrack, John Cook, James Chery, Enoch Crowl, Adoniram Carr, Jacob Crevaston, Erasmus M. Chaplin, Delancy A. Dockham, Martin L. Frank, Joseph Felton, Asbury C. Garrard, Abraham Gasper, Azariah Griffin, Slavan Graham, John M. Hendrickson, Tunis Hendrickson, Lawrence Howser, Joseph Helms, Henry Hight, Sylvester C. Hogle, John B. Holmes, Burt C. Hilligoss, Solomon Hines, Josiah Jordan, John W. Jarrett, John N. Lynn, Benjamin Maze, Alfred Mitchell, John McMarth, William Morgan, John H. McMillan, Simon H. Moore, James K. Miller, Ephriam Maple, John McCorkle, Robert McConahay, William McGrath, Jesse Merical, John McCune, Richard J. Nolan, William Patterson, Taylor Parish, John W. Phillippe, Noble Ross, Lewis Robinson, Joseph R. Ringgold, Brantley Rayle, James Sullivan, Ambrosia Smith, George Swords, Elisha Swords, Albert St. John, Charles Smith, Abraham Stainetts, Ruben A. Sisk, John Tignor, Samuel Whitten, Jeremy Walker, Alvin Wiley, James H. Wasson, Nicholas Wilkins, David Whistler, Henry C. Willard, Calvin Warwick, Charles A. Younce.

Joined as recruits, Michael Ash, Franklin Anthony, George T. Andrews, James E. Arnold, Henry C. Blackford, Joel Bacon, Vinnedge R. Cox, George W. Davis, John Dixon, Albert Judd, Joseph Lossing, James McCarthy, William F. Morrison, Sylvester Michael, Abijah Sismore, Headly Thomas, James S. Veach, Gideon Wing.

COMPANY K.

Mustered September 11th, 1863, at Indianapolis. The members of this company were principally from Marion county.

SAMUEL M. LAKE, 2d Lieutenant, Captain, Co. K

Captain, William S. Hubbard, of Indianapolis.
First Lieutenant, Siegfried Sahm, of Indianapolis.
Second Lieutenant, Samuel M. Lake, of Indianapolis.

ENLISTED MEN.

First Sergeant, Charles T. Noble, of Terre Haute, Indiana.

Sergeants, John Lasch, Jerome B. Ketcham, Lafayette Burkett, John D. Longfellow, Danford Edwards, Nathan Boulden, and William H. Dangerfield.

Corporals, William H. Eldridge, John B. Mellott, Valentine Backer, Freeman Shepard, Julius Oppero, John H. Matchett, Charles Schott and John Reed.

Privates, Wesley Alexander, William H. Baker, Augustus Barrett, George M. Bascom, William Blowers, Elias Boughton, John W. Baler, John M. Cashman, John J. Collins, Micajah Cox, Robert E. Cherry, Edwin Cary, William A. Chew, John Cogan, John V. Crail, John M. Cook, Almon S. Carpenter, Calvin P. Corbit, James R. Daugherty, Benjamin F. Drake, Francis M. Elkins, David Fisher, Frederick Fribes, John W. Gard, John W. Godbey, James Gray, Samuel Ganitt, William Gillan, Alexander Gillan, Wheeler Gould, Winfield Gunckle, James A. Hopkins, Samuel Hull, Uriah G. Hatley, William Hyatt, Marvin Hix, Calvin Harlin, Henry C. Johnson, Charles Jacob, John Jennings, James Jones, George W. Kitt, George Krinkle, Christian Krahmer, William H. Kennedy, John Kelley, James Lyle, James H. Lewis, John McKenily, Thomas McAvoy, William H. Mann, Louis Monewitz, John McDermott, Jesse Matthews, Isaac McCabe, John McAree, Benjamin S. Myres, Richard E. Matchett, John Montony, James Oakey, Albert Partie, John P. Parr, Mathew Paff, Henry W. Pool, John Poe, James M. Ricketts, William Sampson, William W. Scott, Andrew Schmurr, John Shea, Joseph Schmidt, Charles Smith, William D. Tingle, John Turner, Oren Taylor, David Tomelson, Abraham Watkins, James S. Whiting, Henry C. Wills, Frank Williams, Joseph Wintzen, Leopold Woerner, Ellory P. Willitt, William Woodard, and Milo Wilkinson.

COMPANY L.

Mustered September 14th, 1863, at Indianapolis. The members of this company were all from Wabash county.

Captain, Benjamin F. Daily, of Wabash, Indiana.

First Lieutenant, Alpheus T. Blackman, of Liberty Mills, Wabash county, Indiana.

Second Lieutenant, James A. Fisher, of Wabash, Indiana.

ENLISTED MEN.

Sergeants, Champion Helvey, Albert Kline, William Wampler, Samuel B. Henderson, Savanah Leonard, Rutherford M. Beetley, Edwin Sheets.

Corporals, James L. Ellis, Joseph S. Craig (promoted captain of company G, 130th regiment Indiana infantry), Richard Ring, Oscar J. Cox, Iremis Shortridge, Joseph L. Todd, James M. Reed, William L. Scott.

Buglers, Robert Helvey, and Joseph N. Tyler.

Farrier and *Blacksmith*, Benjamin F. Ryman, Humphrey Stahl.

Saddler, Nathaniel Benjamin.

Wagoner, Milton M. Swihart.

Privates, John Anson, George A. Armstrong, John Q. Adams, David Anderson, Isaac Burk, John B. Blockson, George Baugher, Samuel S. Barkeley, Mannasseh Buzzard, Joseph Clark, Calvin Custer, Gilbert M. Depo, Charles Dorsey, Henry Deshong, George P. T. Douglass, Samuel Deeter, John Ennis, William Egbert, William F. Filson, Calvin Griton, James Highland, Peter Hager, John W. House, Martin S. Hubbard, Lysander S. Ingram, Amos A. Kellis, Ruben R. Krebs, Albert T. Lowrey, William L. Logan, William A. Lockhart, James Leason, Charles Lyons, John Lawson, Daniel Miller, Alexander McCutcheon, Robert Miller, Simon H. Malotte, Peter S. Murphey, Mathew Munjoy, Vance McManigal, Oliver H. P. Meek, John H. Maxville, David McDaniel, James Meniers, Myer Newberge, James Oliver, Joseph Phipps, Sirenius Porter, William S. Prichett, Henry C. Pruitt, Hiram F. Price, Isaac S. Peterson, Daniel Roether (promoted hospital steward), Jeremiah Reed, George W. Stover, James Smith, Franklin Sowers, James S. Tilberry, Joseph Thrush, James W. Thompson, Elias S. Totten, John Tuttle, Louis S. Todd, James Walton, William Wilson, Henry K. Zook.

Joined as recruits, John Core, John Dubois, Milton K. Fleming, William Headley, Elbridge S. Hilligoss, Daniel Kitson, Jeremiah

Murry, John Osborn, Morris E. Place, George W. Read, David Walters and Benjamin White.

COMPANY M.

Mustered September 19th, 1863, at Indianapolis. The members of this company were principally from Madison county.

Captain, Joel H. Elliott, of Centerville, Indiana.
First Lieutenant, John G. Mayer, of Indianapolis.
Second Lieutenant, Benjamin O. Deming, of Lafayette.

ENLISTED MEN.

First Sergeant, Charles P. Hopkins.
Sergeants, John W. Denny, John N. Gilbert, Abraham Wilson, Thomas W. Gibson, James McNaughten, James Woodard, and James H. Jackman.
Corporals, Thomas C. Poyns, George A. Cotton, Daniel Grebe, Willard O. Story, Elias Green, Rollin W. Drake, George Howard, and George Lutz.
Buglers, Ruel C. Freeman, and David Falkner.
Farriers and *Blacksmiths*, Jordon Markle, Edward R. Reynolds.
Saddler, Robert H. Ferry.
Wagoner, James McFadden.
Privates, Moses Altizer, George Antle, Frank Akerman, Frank J. Ball, James Buchannan, Philo E. Brittingham, Henry Brown, George Conover, Charles Conover, George D. Craig, John Clutter, Theodore P. Cotton, Jeptha Downs, Joseph Deversey, John H. Davis, Samuel Dohoney, Harmon Dixon, James A. Dixon, William Day, Charles Fred, John R. Garrott, James B. Glasscock, George Hinds, Thomas Heath, Cyrus Hall, James M. Hand, Theodore F. H. Hinton, Richard Hayes, Samuel W. Hostetter, John H. Jones, Henry A. Johnston, James W. Keith, William Kelly, Joseph Linnenweber, George Linnenweber, Samuel Lanham, John S. Lash, William H. Lee, Asbury Lunger, Joseph Martin, Thomas McVey, Adam McKand, Benjamin Mathews, Charles Middleton, Nathan McDonald, Eli Moyer, Richard Nolen, Philip F. Osborne, Robert R. Patton, Oliver N. Ratts, Calvin R. Royce, John H.

Starks, Zachariah T. Sanders, Charles Smith, Squire A. Story, Truman Selee, William F. Thompson, Henry C. Thomas, Benjamin F. Temple, Wiseman Vest, Joseph Walker, George W. Wood, George Whitham, William Ware, Daniel B. Williams, Huey Washam, Edmond West, James T. Wise, and Christian M. Warring.

The interval from the muster in of the companies of the 4th or 5th of December, 1863, was busily employed in learning the cavalry drill, in which the regiment acquired great proficiency.

Its first appearance on parade, mounted, was ludicrous in the extreme. The Governor had not appointed the Majors of the regiment. As usual, there were several applicants for those positions. Governor Morton resolved to review the regiment, and form, from personal observation, his opinion of the fitness of some of the captains for promotion. Accordingly, he notified Col. Shanks, that he would, on a certain day, review the regiment. The Colonel was naturally ambitious that his men should present as fine an appearance as possible. He therefore issued orders for the regiment to appear mounted, on the field for review.

The horses, having been but recently drawn, had never been exercised in drill. Some of them had never been backed.

The captains, some time before the hour for review, formed their companies on the company parade grounds to see how it would go. The men were as green as the horses. Some of them never having been on a horse's back, did not know how to mount. Those who had wild steeds, had great difficulty in maintaining their positions in the saddle, and some in attempting to mount, suddenly found themselves on the ground. However, after great effort, the horses were sufficiently quieted, so as to stand in reasonable proximity to each other. The hour having arrived for the review, the companies were marched to the regimental parade ground, and the regiment, after long and patient effort, formed in a reasonable straight line.

Governor Morton and his Staff, accompanied by Colonel Shanks, took their positions in front of the regiment.

Colonel Shanks in genuine military style, gave the command, "Draw sabres." The men obeyed the order. The sabres in being drawn made a great rattling and clatter, and waved over the horses heads, the sound and sight of which greatly frightened them. This was more than they could bear. Some of them reared and plunged, depositing their riders on the ground; some wheeled and dashed madly for the company quarters; others darted over the commons, their riders hatless, holding on with both hands to the horses' manes, or the pommels of their saddles, presenting pictures not in keeping with accomplished equestrianism. In a twinkling the entire regiment was dispersed over the surrounding country. The Governor maintained his gravity, but it must have cost him an effort to have done so. So ended the first *grand review* of the regiment.

But drill accomplishes wonders, and the mounted parades of the regiment, before it left Indianapolis, was worth seeing.

REV. JAMES MARQUIS, Chaplain, Co. F, L

CHAPTER II.

The 7th Indiana Cavalry left Indianapolis, on the 6th of December, 1863, by railroad, for Cairo, Illinois. At that place it embarked on steamboats and steamed down the Mississippi to Columbus, Kentucky, where it disembarked, and reported to General A. J. Smith, and by his order, camped for the night near the fortifications of the town. By way of introduction to military life, the rain fell in torrents during the night, extinguished all the camp-fires, and the country being flat, completely deluged it with water. In the morning the men were completely drenched, and presented a disconsolate appearance.

After remaining at Columbus one day, by order of Gen. Smith. the regiment started to report to Col. George E. Waring, Jr., at Union City, Tenn., where it arrived at the end of a march of two days. It was there assigned to the First Brigade of the Sixth Division of the Sixteenth Army Corps. The Brigade was commanded by Col. George E. Waring, Jr., of the 4th Missouri Cavalry, and was composed of the following regiments of cavalry:

Fourth Missouri, Col. George E. Waring, Jr.
Second New Jersey, Col. Joseph Kargé.
Seventh Indiana, Col. John P. C. Shanks.

79

Sixth Tennessee, Col. Hurst.

Nineteenth Pennsylvania, Col. Hess.

Second Iowa, four companies, Maj. Frank Moore, and Captain Copperfair's Battery.

Maj. Beck was sent with a detachment of the 7th Indiana, from Union City, to disperse a body of rebels at Dresden, Tenn. On arriving there the Major discovered that the enemy was too strong for him to attack, and reported the fact to the regiment. Lt. Col. Browne, with one hundred men from the 7th Indiana, went to his assistance, and met the Major slowly retiring. But the force was still too weak to safely risk an attack, and Col. Browne sent such a report to headquarters, when Col. Shanks took the balance of the regiment, overtook the other two detachments, and with the entire regiment marched to Dresden, arriving there at night. Under cover of the darkness, and the heavy rain that fell all night, the rebels stole away. In the morning, finding that the game had flown, Col. Shanks marched the regiment back to Union City.

On the morning of December 23d, 1863, Gen. A. J. Smith with his entire command, began his march on Jackson, Tenn., sixty miles from Union City. His object was to drive out the rebel, General N. B. Forrest, who was engaged in conscripting and gathering forage for the rebel army. On the approach of Gen. Smith, Forrest retreated.

Gen. Smith remained at Jackson, till the 1st of January, 1864. Christmas was a pleasant day, and so warm, the men could sit in their tents with their coats off. On New Years day Gen. Smith was on his return to Union City. In the forenoon the weather was pleasant, but early in the afternoon, it began raining, and rapidly grew intensely cold, the rain was changed to a terrible sleet. The cold increased in intensity, and the men, to keep from freezing, were obliged to walk most of the time. Notwithstanding their precautions, the feet of some of them were so badly frozen that amputation was necessary, from the effects of which some of them died. Among these were Alvah Tucker of Company B, and Joseph Gaw of Company F, of the 7th Indiana. Even some of the horses perished of the cold, and fell dead in the road.

On the return of Gen. A. J. Smith to Union City, Lieut. Col. Browne was sent to Hickman, Kentucky, to take command of a detachment of three hundred and fifty men of the 7th Indiana cavalry, that had been left there.

About the 7th of January, 1864, the cavalry under Gen. Grierson, expecting the detachment under Lt. Col. Browne, started on the march through West Tennessee, to join the cavalry force organizing at Colliersville, under Gen. Sooy Smith, for an expedition into Mississippi, in aid of the movement of Gen. W. T. Sherman from Vicksburg to Meridian.

This march was a hard one, particularly on the horses. In crossing the swamps of the Obine river, they were constantly breaking through the ice, and floundering in the ice, mud and water.

At Boliver Tenn. Col. Waring ordered Capt. John W. Shoemaker to take Company F, of the 7th Indiana, and escort his aid-de-camp, bearing dispatches, to Memphis. At Grand Junction, the escort ran into a large body of rebels, and captured five prisoners. Lt. Skelton with two men by Capt. Shoemaker's order, returned to Boliver for reinforcements. Lt. Skirvin with Company D, of the 7th Indiana, returned with Lt. Skelton. By the time the reinforcement arrived, the rebels had withdrawn in the direction of Lagrange, Tennessee. At that place, Lt. Skelton, having command of the advance guard, charged them, and drove them through the town, and captured nineteen prisoners. He pursued them four miles south of Lagrange, and in the chase captured one or two more prisoners and several horses and mules, abandoned by the rebels in escaping to the woods to avoid capture. There were three or four hundred of the rebels, who must have taken the escort to be the advance guard of Grierson's force, and hence allowed themselves to be driven by inferior numbers. While Lt. Skelton was pursuing the rebels south of Lagrange, Capt. Shoemaker, with the aid, and part of the escort, marched rapidly north to Summerville, and from thence through Raleigh to Memphis, and thus got separated from Lt. Skelton, who followed up, and safely delivered his prisoners at Memphis.

General Grierson, with the division, arrived at Colliersville, twenty-five miles from Memphis, early in February.

Col. Browne, with his detachment, on the 8th of February, embarked on a steamboat, for Memphis, where he arrived on the 9th. On the evening of the 10th, after a march of twenty-five miles, he joined the regiment and brigade at Colliersville.

JOHN M. MOORE, 2d Lieutenant, Captain, Co. H, A

CHAPTER III.

The campaign, as sketched by Gen's Grant and Sherman—Gen. Sooy Smith to cooperate with Gen. Sherman, by destroying Forrest's cavalry—2d and 3d brigades march from Germantown to New Albany—The First from Colliersville to Moscow, thence to New Albany via Holly Springs—Skirmish beyond Holly Springs—Concentration of Smith's army, "pomp and glorious circumstance of war"—Preparations for battle; rebels retire— Redland burned, the whole country in a blaze—Head of column to the left—Skirmish beyond Okolona—2d brigade goes to Aberdeen—Egypt station burned—Fight at West Point, rebels retire across the river, and burn the bridge—Bivouac on the battle field—Smith retreats, heavy fighting in the rear—Stampede of the 3d brigade at Okolona, on the morning of Feb. 22d —Desperate fighting of the 7th Indiana, makes a brilliant sabre charge at Ivy farm, and saves the army from capture—Return to Memphis—Official report of the expedition.

This campaign was one of the many planned by those master Generals of the age, U. S. Grant and W. T. Sherman. Its object was to give greater effect to the grand strategic conception of the war—the possession by the Government, of the Mississippi river from its source to its mouth. The importance of that river to the national arms, was seen in the early stages of the war, and for its capture, the movements and battles of the Union armies in the West, were mainly directed. Once in the possession of the Government, and constantly patroled by gunboats, not only would the rebel armies east and west of the river be separated from each other, but also the pretended Southern Confederacy cut in twain. General Grant, in this brilliant campaign, unsurpassed in the annals of war, placed his army in the rear of Vicksburg, and in a series of rapid brilliant victories, separated the two Confederate armies, one under Johnson, and the other under Pemberton, and compelled the former to retreat into the interior, and the latter to seek safety in the fortifications of Vicksburg. That place he invested on the 18th of May, 1863, and closely beseiged till the 4th of July of the same year, when Pemberton and his entire army unconditionally surrendered. With the capture of that stronghold, and the surrender to Gen. Banks, four days later, of Port Hudson, the great Mississippi became once more the thoroughfare of the nation.

Notwithstanding the large force distributed at the various garrisons, employed in guarding it, yet the navigation of the river was interrupted, and rendered dangerous, by the sudden and frequent attacks on the weak garrisons, by the rebel General N. B. Forrest, a daring and accomplished cavalry officer. So frequent and annoying were his dashes, that Generals Grant and Sherman resolved to put a stop to his depredations, by the complete destruction of his command. The time selected for the accomplishment of this purpose was, when the military operations about Chattanooga and Knoxville were suspended by the severity of the winter of 1864. The destruction of Forrest's cavalry was not the only purpose of the campaign. It was the preliminary step in the operations that resulted in the capture of Atlanta.

That the purposes of the campaign may be fully understood, the following extracts, from the correspondence of the projectors of it, are given.

On December 11th, 1863, in writing to Gen. McPherson, Gen. Grant says, "I will start a cavalry force through Mississippi in about two weeks, to clean out the State entirely of all rebels."

On December 23d, he writes to Gen. Halleck, "I am now collecting as large a cavalry force as can be spared, at Savannah, Tenn., to cross the Tennessee river, and cooperate with the cavalry from Hurlbut's command, in cleaning out entirely the forces now collecting in West Tennessee, under Forrest. It is the design, that the cavalry, after finishing the work they first start upon, shall push south, through East Mississippi, and destroy the Mobile road, as far south as they can. Sherman goes to Memphis and Vicksburg in person, and will have Greneda visited, and such other points on the Mississippi Central railroad as may require it. I want the State of Mississippi so visited that large armies cannot traverse there this winter." [Badeau's history of Grant, Vol. 1, pp. 552, 553.]

January 15th, 1864, he again writes to Halleck, "Sherman has gone down the Mississippi, to collect at Vicksburg, all the force that can be spared for a separate movement from the Mississippi. He will probably have ready, by the 24th of this month, a force of twenty thousand men. . . . I shall direct Sherman therefore, to move out to Meridian, with his spare force, the cavalry going from Corinth; and destroy the roads east and south of there so effectually, that the enemy will not attempt to rebuild them during the rebellion. He will then return unless opportunity of going into Mobile with the force he has appears perfectly plain. Owing to the large number of veterans furloughed, I will not be able to do more at Chattanooga than to threaten an advance, and try to detain the force now in Thomas' front. Sherman will be instructed, whilst left with these large discretionary powers, to take no extra hazard of losing his army, or getting it crippled too much for efficient service in the Spring. . . .

The destruction Sherman will do to the roads around Meridian will be of material importance to us, in preventing the enemy from drawing supplies from Mississippi, and in clearing that section of all large bodies of rebel troops. . . . I do not look upon any points, except Mobile in the south and the Tennessee river in the north, as presenting practicable starting points from which to operate against Atlanta and Montgomery."

Sherman, in Chapter 14, vol. 1, of his memoirs, says: "The winter of 1863-4 opened very cold and severe; and it was manifest after the battle of Chattanooga, November 25th, 1863, and the raising of the seige of Knoxville, December 5th, that military operations in that quarter must, in a measure, cease, or be limited to Burnside's force beyond Knoxville. On the 21st of December, General Grant had removed his headquarters to Nashville, Tennessee, leaving Gen. George H. Thomas at Chattanooga, in command of the Department of the Cumberland, and of the army round about that place; and I was at Bridgeport, with orders to distribute my troops along the railroad from Stephenson to Decatur, Alabama, and from Decatur up towards Nashville.

Gen. G. M. Dodge, who was in command of the detachment of the Sixteenth Corps, numbering about eight thousand men, had not participated with us in the battle of Chattanooga, but had remained at and near Pulaski, Tenn., engaged in repairing that railroad, as auxiliary to the main line which led from Nashville to Stephenson and Chattanooga. Gen. John A. Logan had succeeded to the command of the Fifteenth Corps, by regular appointment of the President of the United States, and had relieved Gen. Frank P. Blair, who had been temporarily in command of that Corps during the Chattanooga and Knoxville movement.

At that time I was in command of the Department of the Tennessee, which embraced substantially the territory on the east bank of the Mississippi river, from Natchez up to the Ohio river, and thence along the Tennessee river as high as Decatur and Bellfonte, Alabama. Gen. McPherson was at Vicksburg and Gen. Hurlbut at Memphis, and from them I had regular reports of affairs in that quarter of my command. The rebels still maintained a considerable force of infantry and cavalry in the State of Mississippi, threatening the river, whose navigation had become to us so delicate and important a matter. Satisfied that I could check this by one or two quick moves inland, and *thereby set free a considerable body of men held as local garrisons*, I went up to Nashville and represented the cast to Gen. Grant, who consented that I might go down the Mississippi river, where the bulk of my command lay, and strike a blow on the east of the river, while Gen. Banks, from New Orleans, should in a like manner strike another to the west; thus preventing any further molestation of the boats navigating the main river, and thereby *widening the gap in the Southern Confederacy. . . .*

About the 10th of January we reached Memphis, where I found Gen. Hurlbut, and explained to him my purpose to collect from his garrisons and those of McPherson, about twenty thousand men, with which in February to march out from Vicksburg as far as Meridian, break up the Mobile and Ohio railroad, and also the one leading from Vicksburg to Selma, Alabama. I instructed him to select two good divisions and be ready with them to go along. At Memphis I found Brigadier Gen. W. Sooy Smith, with a force of about twenty-five hundred cavalry, which he, by Gen. Grant's orders, brought across from Middle Tennessee, to assist in our general purpose, as well as to *punish the rebel General Forrest*, who had been most active in harrassing our garrisons in West Tennessee and Mississippi. . . .

A chief part of the enterprise was to *destroy the rebel cavalry commanded by General Forrest,* who were a constant threat to our railway communications in Middle Tennessee, and I *committed this task to Brigadier General W. Sooy Smith.* Gen. Hurlbut had in his command about seven thousand five hundred cavalry, scattered from Columbus, Kentucky, to Corinth, Mississippi; and we proposed to make up an aggregate cavalry force of about seven thousand 'effective,' out of these and the twenty-five hundred which Gen. Smith had brought with him from Middle Tennessee. With this force Gen. Smith was ordered to move from Memphis straight for Meridian, Mississippi, and to *start by February 1st.* I explained to him personally the nature of Forrest as a man, and of his peculiar force; told him that in his route he was sure to encounter Forrest, who always attacked with a vehemence for which he must be prepared, and that after he had repelled the first attack, *he must in turn assume the most determined offensive, overwhelm him, and utterly destroy his whole force.* I knew that Forrest could not have more than four thousand cavalry, and *my own movement would give employment to every other man of the rebel army, not immediately present with him,* so that he (Gen. Smith) might safely act on the hypothesis I have stated. . . .

On the 1st of February we rendezvoused in Vicksburg, where I found a spy who had been sent out two weeks before, had been to Meridian, and brought back correct information of the state of facts in the interior of Mississippi. Lieut. General (Bishop) Polk was in chief command, with headquarters at Meridian, and had two divisions of infantry, one of which (General Loring's) was posted at Canton, Mississippi; the other (General French's) at Brandon. He had also two divisions of cavalry—Armstrong's, composed of the three brigades of Ross, Stark and Wirt Adams, which were scattered from the neighborhood of Yazoo City to Jackson and below; and Forrest's which was united towards Memphis, with headquarters at Como. General Polk seemed to have no suspicion of our intentions to disturb his serenity." Now the reader has a correct idea of the Meridian campaign as mapped out by General Sherman. It is shown that the cavalry under Sooy Smith, was designed to play an important part, in one of the most skillfully planned campaigns of the war.

General Smith did not start with his command until the time he was to have formed a junction with Sherman at Meridian. His force consisted of three brigades of cavalry, and sixteen pieces of cannon, and numbered fully seven thousand men.

On the 9th of February, Gen. Smith with the 2d and 3d brigades left Germantown, Tennessee on the Memphis and Charleston railroad, and marched to New Albany, Mississippi on the Tallahatchie river, where he waited for the arrival of the first brigade.

On the morning of the 11th of February, the first brigade, to which the 7th Indiana was attached, broke camp at Colliersville and moved east along the Memphis and Charleston railroad, to Moscow, a small town eighteen miles distant.

On the 12th, it left the railroad, and marching south, arrived at midnight at Hudsonville, the ruins of which marked the trail of hostile armies. After a rest of two hours, it proceeded on the line of march, and at dawn arrived at what was, before the hot breath of war swept over it, the beautiful town of Holly Springs. That place presented a strange appearance of desolation. The echoing tread of the horses' hoofs, and the clank of the sabres, produced a weird effect, as the column rode in silence through the streets.

Just beyond the town, the advance guard met some resistance from a company of rebel cavalry, and in the skirmish that ensued, the 2nd Tennessee lost three men killed, but it inflicted equal sanguinary punishment on the rebels, and captured nine prisoners with their horses and equipments. The brigade proceeded without further interruption, to Walker's Mills, eight miles from Holly Springs, and camped. Foraging parties were sent out to get subsistence for the men and horses. While on this duty, a member of the 2d New Jersey regiment was killed at a farm house. The perpetrator of the deed, was, by way of retaliation, shot, and his house burned to the ground.

The brigade remained in camp on the 14th. The monotony of the rain that fell all day, was relieved by an almost constant fire on the picket lines.

Early on the morning of the 15th, the command was in motion, and proceeded to the Tippah river, arriving there about nine o'clock in the morning. The recent heavy rains had rendered it unfordable. The only means of crossing was on an old horse ferry. To have crossed on it, would have consumed too much time. A bridge was, therefore, constructed under the supervision of Col. Shanks, over which the entire command passed in safety.

At six o'clock on the morning of the 16th the march was continued. The Tallahatchie river was crossed at New Albany. Four miles from this place, the brigade went into camp on the plantation of a rebel by the name of Sloan. He had been a member of the secession convention of Mississippi, that had resolved the State out of the Union. When the brigade marched the next morning, he was a poorer man by many thousand dollars, by cotton and fence-rails burned, and meat, meal and corn eaten and taken away.

At three o'clock on the morning of the 17th, the brigade was mounted and on the march. On this day Smith's army was concentrated. The 1st brigade was commanded by Col. George E. Waring, Jr., of the 4th Missouri; the 2d by Col. Hepburn, and the 3d by Col. McCrillis. Seven thousand mounted men make a great show. The day was clear, and the sun shone brightly. The long line as it filed out on its march, with its nodding guidons and waving banners, as it wound along the road, the proud step of the steeds champing their bits, and the gleam of the brightly polished arms, presented a spectacle grand and splendid in the highest degree. In the afternoon the advance had a slight skirmish, with this exception nothing of particular interest occurred through the day. The army passed through Pontotoc towards Houston, and after a march of thirty miles went into camp.

General Smith expecting an attack from the rear, ordered the 7th Indiana to go back three miles on the road it had traveled, and picket and hold the crossing at a swamp. Though the men were so fatigued they could scarcely sit in their saddles, yet the regiment remounted, and went to the point designated, and stood by their arms, patiently awaiting the anticipated attack. Night, however, wore away without any hostile demonstrations being made.

The march was continued on the 18th toward Houston. Throughout the day everything indicated the presence of the enemy in force. An engagement was expected at any moment. Everything was got in readiness for sanguinary work. Ambulances were cleared for the reception of the wounded; the surgeons placed their knives, bandages and lint, where they could be conveniently reached; the officers gave their commands in a sterner tone of voice, while their faces wore a solemn and anxious look. But the men, what of them? A soldier is a strange being. He trusts everything to his officers, and borrows no trouble about passing events. He views the preparations for battle with apparent indifference, cracks his jokes, and belches out his hearty laugh, as if danger was not near.

The enemy, evidently, were not yet ready for battle, for he steadily fell back before the advance of the federal army.

Redland, a small town ten miles from Pontotoc, lay in the path of this day's march, and was given over to the torch. When Smith's army left it, it was a heap of smouldering ruins. In every direction, except the immediate front, as far as the eye could see, smoke and flames shot up from burning mills, cotton-gins, and corn-cribs.

The work of desolation, designed for this army to accomplish, as foreshadowed in General Grant's correspondence with Gen. Halleck, had commenced. When within about thirteen miles of Houston, the head of the column was directed towards Okolona, while a small force proceeded towards Houston, to engage the attention of the rebels behind the Hulka swamp. The army passed at nightfall through Okolona, and went into camp two miles south of it on the edge of a large and fertile prairie. Here the advance guard had a heavy skirmish in which the enemy were discomfited.

Early on the morning of the 19th, the 2d battalion of the 7th Indiana, under the command of Maj. Simonson, was sent back to Okalona, with orders to burn the depot, and warehouses, and to destroy the railroad for several miles to the north of the town and to rejoin the command in the evening. It returned, having faithfully performed its mission.

From Okolona the army moved in two columns. The 2d brigade going to Aberdeen, the 1st and 3d south on the Mobile and Ohio railroad. Lieut. Col. Burg with the 19th Illinois, dashed into Aberdeen so unexpectedly, that several Confederate soldiers fell into his hands.

The 1st and 3d brigades marched along the railroad to Egypt Station, a small village. It is situated in one of the most beautiful and fertile prairies in the world, that produced wonderful crops of corn and cotton. The former were mainly relied on to subsist the Confederate armies in the south-west. At this place vast cribs of corn, belonging to the Confederate government stood by the roadside. The warehouses were filled with meal, tobacco, guns, and baggage for the Confederate army, awaiting shipment. The railroad was destroyed, and the torch applied to the depot, warehouses, and corn-cribs, and entirely consumed by fire. When the army left it, only two dwelling houses remained to mark the spot where "Egypt" had been. From this place the 1st brigade marched towards Aberdeen, but it had not gone far when it was overtaken with an order to countermarch, and go to the assistance of the 3d brigade, which was reported to be engaged with the enemy. The order was promptly obeyed, and after a march of a few miles, came up to the 3d brigade drawn up in line of battle. Without stopping, the 1st brigade filed past and went to the front, when the bugles sounded the "trot" and off the brigade went on the hard, smooth road. After a ride of an hour the brigade halted and formed in a wood, without having met the enemy. Two companies of the 7th Indiana were sent out to burn corn-cribs on the left of the road. It was now night, and as the command rode along, the sky was reddened in every direction, by the flames that shot up from corn-cribs and cotton-gins. At ten o'clock at night the army went into camp at Prairie Station. The brigade that went by way of Aberdeen had reached this place, and Smith's army was again concentrated. It was now ascertained that Forrest was concentrating his army at West Point, a small town on the Mobile and Ohio railroad, thirteen miles distant.

Early on the morning of the 20th, the entire army was on the march toward the enemy, moving slowly and cautiously to avoid falling into ambuscades.

Small bodies of rebels were constantly in sight, hovering on the flanks and in the front. The advance guard was continually firing and charging, to clear the road of the enemy. Near West Point, the advance guard met with considerable resistance, the account of which and the balance of this day's operations, is given in Colonel Browne's own language. He says: "Arriving within a mile of West Point, quite a force, probably a battalion, was drawn up in line to oppose our advance. Quite a spirited skirmish ensued, and the rebels fled, having lost two or three killed, and a captain taken prisoner. We lost a lieutenant killed, and a few men wounded. When this skirmish occurred our brigade was moved forward on a double quick, and our regiment constituting its advance, was soon on the ground and in line of battle. The

91

men were dismounted, fences thrown down, howitzers put in position, and every preparation made for battle. Here we stood in readiness for an hour, and I had an opportunity of studying the conduct of the men. The joke and laugh went round as if no foe was near. Officers and men were calm, not a sign of cowardice could be seen anywhere. About sundown, and while we were still in line, four or five hundred rebels moved around to our right. The 4th Regulars and 7th Indiana were ordered forward, and after them we went, with a whoop and a yell, and as fast as horse-flesh could conveniently go. The rebels having the start and making equally as good time as ourselves, were enabled to keep out of the way. It was now night, and soon a huge column of flame and smoke went looming up in our front. We soon learned that the foe had retreated to the south side of the Bigbee, tributary of the Tombigbee, and set fire to the bridge. We then went into camp to await the coming morrow. On that night our forces were within a short mile of each other. One camp-fire could be seen from that of the other. Two brigades of our command were kept saddled during the night, and the men slept with their arms by their sides. Stronger pickets than usual were thrown out. That blood would flow on the next day all believed. I could see no way of avoiding it. The foe was in our front, and in a favorable position, and if we went forward we would have to give battle, if we turned backward Forrest was too good a General not to see that he could pursue and annoy our rear and flanks."

Early on the morning of the 21st, the bugles called the soldiers from their slumbers to the saddle. The regiments were formed in line awaiting orders. Pursuing further the account given by Col. Browne, he says: "I awaited impatiently the order of march. Just then Gen. Smith rode up in front of our regiment and halted by the roadside surrounded by a knot of Aids and officers. They seemed engaged in eager conversation I did not go near enough to hear what was passing, but I imagined I saw anxiety or apprehension depicted in the General's face. In a short time afterwards, Hepburn's brigade moved past on the road we came, in a brisk and hurried trot. Why this retrograde movement? It excited my curiosity. I enquired of an officer the reason for it, and being answered that the rebels were attempting to flank us upon the left, was satisfied. As soon as that brigade passed, ours formed in its rear, and backward we went. This left McCrillis and Grierson to bring up the rear. I soon became convinced that we were on the march back to Memphis, that it was a retreat—and subsequent events have proven the correctness of my suspicions. Before proceeding a mile the sharp, quick volleys of musketry, and the loud, deep roar of the cannon, told us in language that could not be misunderstood, that our rear was engaged with Forrest. And gallantly did they stand and hold their own ground, and drive back the enemy. Every hour during that long and bright Sabbath, they were skirmishing and battling, always doing their work well. Till 4 o'clock p.m., we (the 7th Indiana) were out of sight of the enemy. About this hour they made a demonstration on Maj. Simonson's battalion, it being the rear guard of our brigade. The Major promptly deployed two companies and held them at bay. Just then the column was halted, and the 7th was ordered back to reinforce Gen. Grierson. Moving back a half mile, we discovered a long line of rebels upon our right, moving leisurely through the prairie on a parallel line with ourselves. A company was deployed under the command of Maj. Beck, and he rode gallantly out into the open field to feel for them. Col. Shanks followed to feel for them. Col. Shanks followed to his support with another company, and I was left with the regiment. We threw down fences and formed in line of battle. Maj. Beck soon came upon their main column. He would have charged them but was unable to do so because of the intervening hedges and ditches. The same obstacles prevented the regiment from engaging them. In the meantime, Grierson's command came up and we moved forward. That the rebels intended to pursue our retreating forces, and harrass us at every suitable moment, was now quite apparent. At near midnight we went into our old camping ground near Okolona, and a more weary and worn command had seldom been seen. We were now hurrying rapidly forward to the day of our trouble."

On the morning of February 22d, the anniversary of Washington's birth, the sun rose gloriously in an unclouded sky. At an early hour the army was in the saddle and on the march. The splendor of the morning, and the sight of the long column moving on the edge of the prairie, gave the men a glow of pleasure, and a feeling of confidence.

Hepburn's brigade had the advance, the 1st the centre guarding the trains, and the 3d, under Col. McCrillis, brought up the rear.

93

Across the prairie, to the east about half a mile, in the edge of the woods, marching on a line parallel with the Union army, was seen the advance of the enemy. Both armies were making for Okolona.

A company of rebels were in the town, when the 1st brigade arrived at the south edge of it, the 2d brigade having passed through. Gen. Grierson ordered Col. Browne to throw forward a company of skirmishers. The Colonel ordered Lieut. Calkins to move company H forward, which he did, and deploying it as skirmishers, was soon delivering a brisk fire into the rebels, and gallantly drove them through the town. The rest of the regiment, with Gen. Grierson and Col. Browne at its head, advanced rapidly into the middle of the town. While passing along the main street, a rebel appeared at the corner of a house, and leaning against it, took deliberate aim at Col. Browne and fired. The ball passed, to use the language of the Colonel, in speaking of it afterwards, "in uncomfortable proximity" to his head. The regiment moved through on the trot, to the north side of the town, and under the personal supervision of General Grierson, formed in line of battle on the crest of a hill facing the prairie. A battery was placed in position, and the 3d brigade was hurrying forward to take position on the field. In front of the federal line, about a quarter of a mile distant, the rebels were formed in the open prairie. Between the two lines was a high railroad embankment, behind which either side could have offered a stubborn resistance, had one or the other ventured on an attack. The two forces stood watching each other for the space of an hour, without a shot being fired on either side.

The soldiers now thought that the long expected battle was to come off. When they saw the superior position they occupied, to that of the rebels, they felt confident of defeating them. Back of the federal line was a dense woods and the town of Okolona, and the rebels to attack, must advance across a level prairie, every man of them in full view of their adversaries, in the face of a murderous fire from behind the railroad embankment. If driven from that, they had the houses of the town, and the woods from which to deliver their fire into the ranks of the rebels, who would have been obliged to advance across an open field. As they sat on their horses awaiting the attack, they beguiled the time, by promising to celebrate Washington's birth, with a glorious victory, and in complimenting Gen. Smith, on his generalship, in drawing Forrest towards Memphis, and in compelling him to attack on a field chosen by his adversary.

The 3d brigade having arrived on the field, the 7th Indiana, which was the rear of the 1st brigade, and being nearest when the enemy was marching into Okolona, was ordered to the position mentioned, because the emergency required it, was ordered to resume its position in its brigade. It slowly withdrew its line, and filed to the rear in column of fours, and started off on the trot to overtake the brigade. The regiment had gone but about half a mile, when the rebels made a furious charge on the 3d brigade. They charged into the town right up to the battery of howitzers, and captured five out of six of them. The scene that followed was terrible beyond description. The 2d Tennessee broke and fled in wild confusion. Soon the entire 3d brigade stampeded, and became an uncontrollable mob. Its regiments lost all semblance of organization. The men threw away their arms, and dashed, hatless, pell-mell to the rear, with terror depicted in their faces, deaf alike to threats or entreaties. Col. McCrillis and Staff, and Gen. Grierson, made superhuman efforts to rally this brigade, but to little purpose.

The 7th Indiana was ordered back to the support of the 3d brigade. Col. Shanks and Majors Beck and Febles, formed the two rear battalions across the road, and Col. Browne and Maj. Simonson the front one. Scarcely was the regiment thus formed, when the fugitives of the 3d brigade went pouring through its ranks. The officers beat them with their swords, and cocked their revolvers in their faces to compel them to halt, but failed. The torrent rushed past the 7th, leaving it to contend with the entire rebel army. This it did until the rest of the 1st brigade, far in advance, could be brought back to its assistance. The two rear battalions under Col. Shanks, were formed on a hill flanked on both sides by ravines. There was room for but one company to fight at a time. This, each company did, till flanked on both sides by the rebels, when it was compelled to retire to escape capture in a body. The one in the rear would then engage the enemy, until flanked in like manner when it would retire. It then came the turn of the battalion under Col. Browne and Maj. Simonson to meet the foe. It was formed across the road with each wing resting on a grove of scrub oaks. Col. Browne dismounted a

95

company, and deployed it forward as skirmishers. It soon opened fire on the advancing enemy. With an exultant yell the rebels charged this skirmish line, but were suddenly brought to a halt by a well-directed volley, that emptied many of their saddles, from the remainder of the battalion. A brisk fire then opened on both sides. The bloody tide surged against the 7th Indiana hour after hour, it yielding its ground only step by step. Many were the anxious glances cast at the sun, whose rising on that day was hailed with a glow of pleasure, but whose setting was now prayed for. As it was about to dip beneath the western horizon, Ivy Farm, eleven miles from Okolona, was reached. Over this distance, from ten o'clock in the morning, the contending armies had fought, contesting the ground foot by foot. The condition of Smith's army, at this time, was critical in the extreme. Forrest was flanking it on both wings. Smith's only hope of avoiding a capture of his entire army, was to give Forrest such a sudden and severe check, that darkness would put an end to the strife, before he could resume the offensive.

The field at Ivy Farm, where the most desperate fighting of that ill-fated day occurred, sloped east an eighth of a mile to a ravine, that lay north and south. It extended south of the road half a mile, where it was skirted with timber.

The 7th Indiana took its position on the crest of the hill, on the south side of the road. The 4th Missouri was formed in close column behind the 7th Indiana. The battery attached to the 4th Missouri, was placed on the left of the column near the road, and was having a duel with a rebel battery on an opposite hill. To the right of the 7th Indiana, a quarter of a mile distant, a regiment was formed in the open field, and was engaging with its carbines, the enemy formed in the edge of the woods. Wreaths of smoke rose from the ranks of the Union regiment and floated gracefully away. The line of smoke at the edge of the woods indicated the position of the enemy.

The rebels in front of the 7th Indiana and 4th Missouri, were formed along the ravine in the edge of the woods. They ceased firing and watched with interest the preparation for the "charge."

Members of the 7th Indiana dismounted and threw down the fence in front, so the cavalry could charge through.

Everything being ready, Gen. Smith, who had personally directed the formation of the troops, rode up to the 7th Indiana, and said, "Colonel Shanks, charge!" The Colonel gave the command, "Draw sabres!" and in an instant every blade flashed in the setting sun-light. "Forward, charge" rang along the line, which was repeated by the bugles sounding the "charge," then off shot the column, like a thunderbolt, down the hill to the ravine, over it, into the ranks of the enemy, through a storm of bullets from their muskets, and shells from their guns. Sabres clashed on muskets, and muskets were fired in the faces of the assailants, or used as clubs over their heads. Owing to the nature of the ground some of the regiment were unable to get close enough to the rebels to use their sabres. Under a galling fire they coolly returned them to their scabbards, drew their revolvers and poured such a deadly fire into the faces of the rebels that it caused confusion in their ranks. The sun having gone down, the blaze from pistol and musket illumined the dusk of evening. Having accomplished the object of the charge, the regiment was withdrawn.

The enemy had been so severely punished, he did not venture in pursuit. A few scouts only went forward to watch the movements of their adversaries, but vanished like specters in the gathering gloom of night. In this last encounter, the rebel Col. Jesse Forrest, a brother of the rebel General N. B. Forrest, was killed.

There were many acts of personal daring performed which will be more fully mentioned in another part of this book. Only one or two instances are given here. Captain James H. Carpenter of company I, with his own hands captured two prisoners and sent them safely to the rear. He killed, with his sabre, a rebel who refused to surrender. He captured a third prisoner, who was in the act of handing him his sabre, when the Captain happening to cast a look to his left, saw not over ten feet from him, the left wing of a rebel regiment that had been stealthily placed in the ravine parallel with and north of the road. To escape capture himself, he was compelled to let his prisoner go, and save himself by flight. In doing so, he had to ride along in front of this rebel regiment, under a fire directed at him, but he escaped unhurt. He and his company saved the battery, that had been abandoned by its support, from capture.

First Lieut. George R. Kennedy of company C, fought with desperation, was wounded and taken prisoner.

Capt. John R. Parmelee of company A, fought valiantly, and

at the time was supposed to have been mortally wounded. His wound however proved not to be fatal. He was taken prisoner, and confined at Macon, Georgia, and Columbia, South Carolina, but succeeded in making his escape from the latter place Nov. 4, 1864, and arrived in safety at the federal lines at Port Royal.

By the pale light of the moon, that rose in a clear sky, the bleeding and exhausted army pursued its retreat. About midnight it halted two hours to rest, and restore order to the ranks of the demoralized regiments. After which it was again on the move, and passed through Pontotoc at daylight.

About this time information was received through a Negro, that the rebels had the day before, burned the bridge at New Albany, on the Tallahatchie, and that a rebel force was moving to intercept Smith's army.

The 2d Illinois and the 2d New Jersey were hurried forward to hold the crossing of the river. They arrived there without interruption, and found the bridge undisturbed. The 2d and 1st brigades arrived and had all crossed except the 7th Indiana. As it was about to cross, Gen. Grierson rode up, and asked for reinforcements for Col. McCrillis, who was reported to be engaged with the enemy. The 7th Indiana was ordered back to his assistance. It soon met the Colonel's brigade, and was formed in a favorable position and awaited the expected attack. The 3d brigade passed by, and after remaining in its position for an hour, an order came for the regiment to fall slowly back to the river. The commanding officer could not complain that the order was not obeyed in its very spirit. Horses that had had no rest, food or drink for forty-eight hours, could not be expected to move otherwise than slowly. It crossed on the bridge, set it on fire, to prevent pursuit, and moved on without stopping, till midnight, and then only for a short time. Near the crossing of the Tippah, the rear guard was attacked by about two hundred Guerrillas, two men were killed, one wounded, and two taken prisoners. The command formed in line of battle and awaited the attack. But none was made. This was the last annoyance from the enemy, except that occasionally a straggler was shot by "bushwhackers." The brigade crossed on the same bridge constructed on going out, and burned it and obstructed the ford, and pushed on towards Holly Springs. Marching one day and night, the Brigade reached its old camp ground at Collierville on the evening of the 25th of

February. From there it marched to Camp Grierson, near Memphis, arriving there on the 27th. Thus ended this ill starred expedition. It was a miserable failure and a disgrace to our national arms.

Some have attempted to make it appear that the expedition accomplished all it was designed to accomplish, and having done so, retired to Memphis. For proof of this they refer to the large amount of property destroyed, and the throng of Negroes that swarmed in from the plantations, and followed the army to and from West Point. But it is poor generalship, that will fail in the accomplishment of the chief object of a campaign, for the sake of securing results of minor importance.

That Gen. Sherman keenly felt Gen. Smith's failure, the following extract from his memoirs will show:

"At the same time, I wanted to destroy General Forrest, who with an irregular force of cavalry, was constantly threatening Memphis and the river above, as well as our routes of supply in Middle Tennessee. In this we failed utterly, because General W. Sooy Smith did not fulfill his orders, which were clear and specific, as contained in my letter of instructions to him of January 27th, at Memphis, and my personal explanations to him at the same time. Instead of starting at the date ordered, February 1st, he did not leave Memphis till the 11th, waiting for a regiment that was ice-bound near Columbus, Kentucky; and then when he did start, he allowed General Forrest to head him off and to defeat him with an *inferior force*, near West Point, below Okolona, on the Mobile and Ohio railroad.

We waited at Meridian till the 20th to hear from General Smith, but hearing nothing whatever, and having utterly destroyed the railroads in and around that junction, I ordered General McPherson to move back slowly toward Canton. With Winslow's cavalry, and Hurlbut's infantry, I turned north to Marion, and thence to a place called "Union," whence I dispatched the cavalry farther north to Philadelphia and Louisville to feel as it were for General Smith, and then turned all the infantry columns toward Canton, Mississippi. On the 26th we all reached Canton, but we had not heard a word of General Smith, nor was it until some time after (at Vicksburg) that I learned the whole truth of General Smith's movement and of his failure. Of course I did not and could not approve of his conduct, and I know that he yet chafes under the censure. I had set so much store on his part of the project that I was disappointed, and so reported officially to General Grant. General Smith never regained my confidence as a soldier, though I still regard him as a most accomplished gentleman and a skillful engineer. Since the close of the war he has appealed to me to relieve him of that censure, but I could not do it, because it would falsify history."

The facts since disclosed, make it apparent that Gen. Smith could have placed himself in communication with Sherman. The same fighting that was done to cover his retreat, would have defeated Forrest, and driven him back into the arms of Sherman.

General Sherman fulfilled to the letter his part of the campaign. He attacked Polk so vehemently, that he had no time to rest till he was driven across the Tombigbee, at Demopolis. He had given out on his line of march that Mobile was his objective point. Not only Polk, but also Johnson in front of Gen. Thomas, believed that that was the point he was aiming for, and the latter sent a detachment to assist the former in defending Mobile. On the 20th, the day on which Gen. Smith was driving Forrest before him to West Point, Gen. Sherman was moving a part of his command northward purposely to cooperate with him. On this day it was known, even to the private soldiers of General Smith's force, that the rebel General Polk had been driven across the Tombigbee. Gen. Smith ought to have known that Gen. Sherman would so maneuver his command as to render him all possible aid.

When Gen. Smith commenced his retreat on the morning of the 21st, Gen. Winslow's cavalry was at Louisville, Mississippi, only forty-five miles distant, and Forrest's army lay between two hostile forces. The retreat was a surprise to every officer in the command.

The cavalry force under Gen. Smith was organized with great care. It was composed of picked men, mounted on fresh horses, and armed with new and improved weapons. It left Memphis feeling itself invincible, but returned a demoralized mob.

It was the cherished object, not only of Gen. Sherman, but also of Gen. Grant, to completely destroy Forrest's army. Gen. Sooy Smith was selected as the man who could and would accomplish this great result. He failed ignominiously.

The casualties of the 7th, in this expedition were as follows:

Killed—John Elmer, of Co. D; Serg't John Rowlett, of Co. E.

Privates, James M. Jackson and Charles E. Ruple of Co. F; Corp'l Jacob E. Shirley, and Private William N. Cole, Co. G; Privates John H. H. McClellan, Abraham Garber, and Albert St. John, and Corp'l John W. Barger, of Co. I; George W. Wood, Co. M.—11.

Wounded—First Lieut. Francis M. Way, Co. B; Second Lieut. Jacob C. Skirvin, Co. D; Privates John L. Babcock, Stillman Andrews, Berzillia Horner, and William Mossholder, Co. A; Private John F. Shirley, Co. B; Privates Levi Oliver and Nathaniel Miller, Co. C; Privates George Frederick, John Fitch, Israel Warner, Jonathan Swisher, Co. D; Privates Dennis J. Peer, George Dudley, and David Sweigert, Co. F; Privates Jacob Miller, Isaac H. Truitt, Isaac Needham, Dan Downing, Henry Stewart, Co. G; Serg'ts Robert G. Smithers and James Chisim, Co. H; Serg'ts Adoniram Carr and Henry C. Clifford, and Privates Erasmus M. Chaplin, Delancy A. Dockham, Corp'l George S. Jones, Co. I; Serg't Lafayette Burket, Co. K; George Antle, Co. M.—30.

Wounded and taken Prisoner—Capt. John R. Parmelee, and First Lieut. John Donch, Co. A; First Lieut. George R. Kennedy, Co. C; Absolem McCarty, Co. A; William R. Shoemaker, Co. G.—5.

Taken Prisoners—First Serg't Cornelius O. Neal, James Earhart, John Johnson, Luna Maulsby, Isaac Margeston, Co. A; George D. Huffman, Co. D; Corp'l Morris Kelley, Henry Oppe, George Rush, Henry Carter, Co. C; Franklin D. Wagner, Co. D; Andrew F. Lakin, Isaac Budd Samuel Downing, Hezekiab Stout, Co. G; James Walton, Co. H; John Tignor, Elisha Swords, Joseph Ringold, Charles A. Younce, Sylvester Michael, Samuel Whitten, Lewis Robinson, Alexander Walker, William F. Morrison, Brantley Rayle, William McGrath, Co. I; Elias Braughten, John McRea, William A. Chew, Co. K; Henry C. Priest, William Filson, Co. L; Joseph Linnenweber, Edmond West, Wiseman Vest, William Ware, Co. M.—36. Total, 82.

The whole number of the regiment engaged in the battle of Okolona was 813. It lost over one tenth of its members. Most of the wounded were left on the field, and unavoidably fell into the hands of the enemy. Lieut. Donch, of company A, was shot through the body. He was carried back some distance, but was finally abandoned, as there were no means of taking him along.

Subjoined is the official report of Col. Browne, of the part taken by the 7th in the expedition to West Point, and battle of Okolona:

HEAD-QUARTERS SEVENTH INDIANA VOL. CAVALRY,
CAMP GRIERSON, TENN., MARCH 12, 1864.

Lieut. A. Vezim, A.A.A.G.

In submitting the following report of the part taken by this regiment in the late cavalry expedition made to West Point, Mississippi, I have to regret the absence of Col. J. P. C. Shanks, who was, during all the time, in command, but who is now absent in consequence of illness induced by the hardships and exposures incident to the march. Having, however, been constantly with the command myself, I hope to be able to give the material facts with reliable accuracy. Nothing of interest transpired on the march in which this regiment was concerned, independently of the brigade, until its arrival at the first camp beyond Okolona. On the morning of the 19th of February, the 2d battalion, consisting of Companies B, F, D and H, in command of Maj. Simonson, was detailed to return to Okolona and destroy the railroad, depot, &c., at that place and north of it. Pursuant to his instructions he destroyed a bridge on the Mobile and Ohio railroad of about 300 feet in length, five miles north of town, burned the depot, fifty barrels of salt, a warehouse containing a large quantity of Confederate corn, and destroyed a locomotive at Okolona and after capturing about fifty horses and mules, rejoined the command on that evening.

On the evening of the same day, Capt. Elliott with companies M and A under instructions, destroyed twenty-three large cribs, containing Confederate tithe corn, which had been placed for shipment, by the side of the railroad near Egypt Station. The quantity of corn thus destroyed was immense, but I could not venture an opinion as to the number of bushels. On the same day Capt. Elliott destroyed three bridges of considerable size, on the Mobile and Ohio railroad between Egypt and Prairie Stations.

On the 20th, being advised that the advance was en-

102

gaged with the enemy near West Point, the regiment was ordered rapidly forward, and arriving on the ground immediately formed in line of battle, in good order, upon the right of the road. Remaining in this position for nearly an hour, it was ordered still further to the right, in support of the 4th regiment of regulars for the purpose of ascertaining the position of the enemy, who were reported to have been recently seen in that direction. A march on the double-quick of five or six miles, brought us at dark to the place selected for the night's bivouac, without our having discovered the enemy in force.

On the 21st, on the return to Okolona, the regiment was placed in the column of march at the rear of the 1st brigade, the 2d battalion constituting its rear guard. Toward evening the enemy appeared in considerable numbers on our right flank and made a demonstration upon our rear guard, but two companies being promptly thrown out to meet them, they retired without attacking. At this time the regiment was ordered to the rear to the assistance of the 2d brigade, which had been, during much of the day, engaged. It was countermarched, and proceeded rapidly to the rear, when the enemy was discovered upon the right, marching in a direction parallel to our column. Maj. Beck fired upon and drove in their flankers, when they retired to a safer distance, but a more vigorous attack for which we had prepared was prevented by the character of the intervening ground. The 2nd brigade arriving in the meantime, we were ordered to rejoin our brigade. On this day, Capt. Elliott, in command of a small detail of foragers, was attacked near the roadside by an equal number of the enemy, when he charged upon them with so much spirit that he killed one, wounded two severely, captured six prisoners with their horses, arms and equipments, bringing them safely to the command, he not having lost a man.

On the 22d, the regiment was again placed in the rear of the brigade and of the train of contrabands, and captured horses and mules. Upon arriving near Okolona, the enemy was discovered upon the right in the open prairie moving in the same direction with ourselves, but keeping the embankment of the railroad between them and us.

By General Grierson's order the regiment moved to the right deploying company H as skirmishers, which soon became engaged with those of the enemy. Moving rapidly forward through the centre of the town to the north side, it formed in line of battle, the enemy forming in its front to the east, and still hugging closely the railroad embankment. The first battalion had a brisk skirmish of a few minutes duration with their skirmishers, driving them rapidly back upon their line. Other regiments were now brought and formed in our rear. Artillery put in position, and everything seemed to indicate that an engagement was at hand. This regiment having been withdrawn from the brigade, left the rear of the train exposed and measurably unprotected, therefore after occupying the above position for some time, we were, by Gen. Grierson's order, relieved by another regiment, and directed to resume our place in the column of march. This order was being executed, but we had moved but a few miles from Okolona before a portion of the force left in our rear, came forward in the wildest imaginable disorder and confusion, having been attacked and driven back by the enemy. The 1st battalion was immediately thrown in line across the road, the 2d and 3d forming for its support in its rear. Our officers now used every reasonable exertion to rally and re-form the panic stricken and flying troops that came pouring upon our lines. To accomplish this was impossible. Very soon the forces of the enemy made their appearance, and sharp skirmishing at once ensued between them and the 1st battalion. They were held in check until we were directed to retire by order of Gen. Grierson. The regiment then fell back slowly and in good order, by alternate battalions, for some distance and then resumed its march in column. We had not proceeded far before the avalanche of stampeders again came rushing upon and past our column, when we again formed in line and again met the enemy who was at this time pressing the rear closely and in considerable force.

The fighting at this time was short but brisk. The command charged, drove the enemy back, but becoming exposed to a severe flanking fire, and being unsupported we were compelled to fall back. Here we lost several men in killed and wounded, among them Lieut. G. R. Kennedy of Co. C, who fell, gallantly leading the charge. He was left on the field. Here we also inflicted considerable punishment upon the enemy. Falling back but a short distance, we again halted, and held our position till ordered back. Passing through the line formed in our rear by the other regiments of the 1st brigade and a portion of the 2d brigade, Maj. Beck was ordered with two companies of the 1st battalion, and companies L and M by Gen. Smith, to the left to protect that flank. After going a considerable distance and encountering no opposing force, he rejoined the regiment with his command at Ivy Farm.

It was now near sundown, and the enemy was pressing closely upon our rear. The regiment formed in line of battle, a portion of it dismounted and sent to the support of the battery of the 4th Missouri regiment, which was in position. The dismounted men were soon afterwards ordered to their horses, and being again mounted, Gen. Smith gave the order "charge." No sooner had the command been given than Maj. Beck with companies A, E, and G, and Maj. Febles with companies I, K, and M, rode rapidly and gallantly forward to the very lines of the enemy. The nature of the ground prevented an effective use of the sabre, but the pistol was substituted and did most excellent service. By this charge the enemy was driven back, many men killed and wounded and several taken prisoners. In it this command lost heavily, sustaining here the larger portion of its losses during the expedition. At this point and in this charge Lieut. John Donch of company A, was mortally wounded [a mistake, he was not *mortally* wounded], and Capt. John R. Parmelee was either killed or fell a prisoner into the enemie's hands. His fate is not certainly known.

On the 23d we were ordered back from the crossing of the Tallahatchie to the support of the 2nd brigade and took position, but the enemy having discontinued the attack, our services were not required. We quietly crossed the river, the bridge in our rear was burned and the ford obstructed. Nothing more of interest occurred until the ensuing day. On this day the 1st brigade in charge of the trains marched on a different road from the balance of the division, our regiment being in the rear of the 1st brigade. We arrived without molestation nearly to the crossing of the Tippah river, when a small guard, thrown out to protect the rear, was suddenly attacked by a considerable force of guerrillas. In this attack we lost one man killed, two wounded, and one taken prisoner. As soon as information of the attack reached the column, the regiment was marched back and put in position for their reception, but they made no further hostile demonstrations, withdrawing quickly to the woods and the rear. The number of this force we could not ascertain with certainty, but a captured contraband who had been the servant of one of its officers, put their number at 200. This ended the exciting and interesting part of this expedition so far as this regiment was concerned. From this point we marched without interruption to our present camp, at which place we arrived on the evening of the 27th of February.

Our losses in killed, wounded and missing was *eighty-four*, a list of whom has already been furnished.

In conclusion allow me to say that under the most trying and disheartening circumstances by which the command was surrounded, both officers and men behaved themselves admirably. To the officers, both field and line, much credit is due for the coolness and alacrity with which they executed every order. Notwithstanding the disorder and confusion many times about it, the regiment was at no time disorganized or demoralized.

Respectfully submitted,

THOS. M. BROWNE,
Lt. Col. Comd'g.

CHAPTER IV.

GUNTOWN EXPEDITION.

Invasion of West Tennessee by Forrest—Gen. Grierson makes a recognizance in force at Raleigh, Tenn.—Skirmish and capture of color bearer—Return to camp—Forrest concentrates at Tupelo, Miss.—Gen. S. D. Sturges marches against him with eight thousand men—Reviews the regiment—Heavy skirmishing at Ripley—Col. Browne dislodges the rebels by a flank movement— Col. Karge surrounded on an Island in the Hatchie River—Col. Browne goes to his relief—Gen. Grierson discovers Forrest in position at Brices-Cross Roads—Battle commenced between Forrest and Grierson's cavalry—Heroic conduct of Col. Browne and the 7th Indiana—Holds its position for two hours, and repulses repeated attacks of the rebels—Infantry arrives and the regiment withdrawn—Sturges overwhelmingly defeated—Retreat—Desperate fighting of the Colored troops—Fight at Ripley —Return to Memphis—7th Indiana complimented by Gen. Grierson.

The regiment on its return from the expedition to West Point, was greatly exhausted by the fatigues and dangers it endured and met. Many of the men became sick and were sent to the hospitals. The horses, from incessant marching, and for want of forrage on the expedition, were broken down, and scarcely fit for service, and many of them died. Not more than one-fourth of the men were mounted. Those who were, were almost constantly employed on scouting duty, and in chastising the guerrillas who infested the woods and bottoms of the Nonconnah creek and the Coldwater. These pests, principally under the command of the notorious "Dick Davis," lurked about the picket posts, watching for opportunities to capture and kill the pickets, and lay in wait in ambush for scouting parties, the country about those two streams affording them ample facilities for that mode of warfare.

Emboldened by his success over Gen. Sooy Smith, Gen. N. B. Forrest, in March succeeding, began the invasion of West Tennessee, in which he attacked Fort Pillow, and put the garrison to the sword. A portion of his command approached Raleigh, a small town twelve miles north-east of Memphis.

Gen. Grierson with the 1st brigade, to which the 7th Indiana was attached, made a recognizance in force in that direction. He left camp near Memphis on the 2d of April and marched to Raleigh and camped for the night. On the 3d, he proceeded several miles on the road to Lagrange, Tenn., and met the advance of the enemy. The regiments took the positions assigned them in line of battle. The 7th Indiana, under the command of Maj. Simonson, dismounted and formed on the right of the road in a barnyard, the log stable and corn-cribs therein, answering the purpose of block houses. A skirmish line was advanced in the field in front, and a slight fire occurred between it and a few rebel scouts, on an opposite hill. After that had ceased there was perfect quiet for a while, when unexpectedly, a body of about fifty rebels, with yells, charged boldly down the hill into the federal line on the left of the road, took a color-sergeant and the colors he was bearing, out of the ranks and marched off with him. It was a cool audacious proceeding, and was so unexpected that the line attacked was taken by surprise. But the rebels were sufficiently punished for their temerity. They left on the field one man mortally wounded and carried away on their horses three others who were wounded. They were permitted to escape. After lingering there for an hour without seeing anything more of the enemy, the brigade began falling back by regiments, and camped on the same ground it occupied the night previous. The next day it returned to camp in the vicinity of Memphis. After the massacre at Fort Pillow, Forrest returned with his army to Mississippi, and in May succeeding, began massing at Tupelo, a force for some other enterprise.

General Washburn organized, at Memphis, an expedition to march against him, and placed it under the command of Brigadier General S. D. Sturges.

General Sturges had the usual reviews preceding a campaign. As he won an unenviable reputation in the expedition about to be mentioned, a description of the manner in which he reviewed the 7th Indiana, and the effect it had on the men, may not be out of place. Contrary to the usual custom, he reviewed it, by riding in a cab, in front of the regiment. The most that could be seen of him was his prodigious black mustache, occasional glimpses of which were had through the windows of the cab. Derisive remarks about him were made by the men, before he was scarcely out of hearing. On their return to camp, the men freely expressed their opinion, that under such a general the expedition would prove another failure.

His force consisted of nine regiments of infantry, some of them Colored, twenty-four pieces of artillery, and two brigades of cavalry, the latter under the command of Brigadier Gen. B. H. Grierson. The entire force numbering in the aggregate eight thousand men.

The 7th Indiana, numbering three hundred and fifty men, that number being all that could be mounted on serviceable horses, under the command of Maj. S. E. W. Simonson, joined the expedition at White Station on the morning of the 1st of June. Both Col. Shanks and Lieut. Col. Browne were sick when the regiment started, and unable to go with it. The latter, however, overtook and assumed command of the regiment at Salem, Mississippi.

From White Station, the army marched eastwardly along the Memphis and Charleston railroad to Lafayette, where it took a south-eastwardly direction, and passing through Lamar and Salem, arrived at Ripley, Miss., on the evening of the 7th of June.

At Ripley the 4th Iowa cavalry having the advance, encountered a body of rebels, and in the skirmish that ensued, drove them through the town, and south of it two miles, where the rebels took a position on the crest of a hill, that could be reached by the road, only by crossing a bridge, covered by two pieces of artillery and a skirmish line, in close range in the woods on the hill. A heavy fire took place between the 4th Iowa and the rebels, but the efforts of the former, failed to dislodge the enemy.

The 7th Indiana, which was in the extreme rear of the division, was ordered to the front to the assistance of the 4th Iowa.

It moved forward on the trot, the troops in front moving to either side of the road to allow it to pass. On arriving at the bridge, Gen. Grierson, ordered Col. Browne to form his regiment on the left of the road, and carry the hill by assault. The ground, over which the regiment had to pass, was a low creek bottom, cut up by ditches, and covered with logs and fallen timber. It was impossible to advance mounted. Col. Browne, therefore dismounted the regiment and marched it forward on foot. It was now dark, and the men in advancing, were constantly falling into ditches and stumbling over logs. They, however, reached the hill, and the rebels, finding themselves flanked, withdrew without firing a shot. Col. Browne informed General Grierson of the fact, and by his order retired, to near Ripley and went into camp. On this day Col. Karge, of the 2d New Jersey cavalry, was ordered to take four hundred men and proceed to Rienzi and destroy the railroad at that point. He encountered the enemy beyond Ruckersville and was driven on an island in the Hatchie river, and surrounded.

On the morning of the 8th, a courier, who managed to get through the rebel lines, brought intelligence of Col. Karge's critical situation. The 7th Indiana, under Col. Browne, and the 4th Missouri, were immediately dispatched to his assistance. They met Col. Karge and his command, a few miles beyond Ruckersville, he having effected his escape by swimming his command across the river at a point not guarded. The two commands returned to Ripley.

On the 9th, the march was continued on the Tupelo road. No enemy was seen by the army on this day. The scouts, however, reported having seen in the evening, a brigade of rebel cavalry a few miles to the east. From the starting of the expedition up to this time, it rained every day. Some days the water fell in torrents. The roads were so very muddy, that the artillery and baggage trains could advance but slowly. This condition of the roads, undoubtedly contributed, in a measure, to the disasterous defeat on the next day.

The morning of the 10th of June was clear and pleasant. The cavalry division pushed on in advance. The advance guard as a matter of discipline, was watchful, but no one suspected that Forrest, with his entire army, was a few miles ahead on a carefully selected field, awaiting the advance of Sturges' army. And no one dreamed that on that day a bloody battle was to be fought. The advance guard arrived at *Brices Cross Roads*, a few miles from Guntown, on the Ohio and Mobile railroad. Here the roads were cut up by fresh tracks, which indicated that a force had recently passed over them. This was all that was seen that would lead one to suspect the presence of the enemy. The column was halted, and a courier swept to the rear to find Gen. Grierson. The General, a moment afterwards, dashed to the front and carefully inspected the road. He immediately dispatched strong scouting parties on the different roads to find the enemy.

A scouting party of fifty men from the 2d New Jersey, went on the road running north, and found the enemy in position half a mile from the cross-roads.

Captains Shoemaker and Branham with fifty men from the 7th Indiana, went several miles on the Tupelo road. Hearing cannon-ading at the crossing, they returned and took their position in the regiment in line of battle. When within half a mile of the crossing, a body of rebels attempted to cut them off, but Capt. Shoe-maker ordered a charge, and put them to flight. The battle that ensued is generally known by the name of "Guntown," a small place on the Mobile and Ohio railroad, three or four miles from the place where the battle occurred. But in the official reports it is known as the battle of *Brices-cross-roads*, the name given to the crossing of the road running south-east from Ripley to Gun-town, and the one laying nearly parallel with, and to the west of the railroad.

The ground from the crossing sloped gradually north to a small creek, less than a quarter of a mile distant, that ran nearly par-allel with the Ripley road. Beyond this creek, the ground was low and marshy. The fighting principally occurred on the north side of the Ripley road.

The 1st brigade (cavalry) was formed in front of the enemy, and the 2d to its right to guard the Tupelo road. The 7th Indi-ana was dismounted and formed in line of battle on the crest of the hill on the right of the road running north and south behind a rail fence. The hill was covered with timber and a thick under-growth of shrubs. A skirmish line was advanced to near the mid-dle of the marsh in front of the line, and awaited the attack of the enemy. The position occupied by the 7th Indiana was a strong one. If it had not been, it could not, unaided, have held it as long as it did.

The enemy were formed on an opposite hill in the edge of the woods. For them to advance, they would be obliged to cross the open swamp between the two lines, and be exposed to the fire from the Federal lines concealed in the woods. General Grierson would have had to encounter the same hazard, had he advanced to the attack.

The batteries of the 14th Indiana and 4th Missouri, were placed to the left of the 7th Indiana, and did good execution in the ranks of the rebels. Speaking of the batteries, Col. Browne said: "I passed up to the batteries and watched with delight the effect of the bursting bombs. They made the rebels scatter delightfully."

A brisk fire from the hostile skirmish lines broke out, which lasted some time. A loud cheer rose from the rebels, and almost immediately massed columns emerged from the woods occupied by the rebels, and began crossing the open space. Col. Browne ordered his men to reserve their fire till the enemy were in close range. When but a few rods distant, the regiment from behind the fence, poured such a well directed fire into them that it caused them to break in confusion, and retreat to the hill. They soon rallied, however, and again marched to the attack. They were welcomed in the same manner, and again fell back before a withering fire. They formed in the open space, and opened a terrific musketry fire, which had but little effect on the 7th Indiana as the men were concealed behind the trees and fence. Notwithstanding they had to face a destructive fire not only from the lines, but also from the batteries, yet the rebels steadily advanced till they were almost at the line occupied by the 7th Indiana. Probably there was no braver fighting done during the war, than occurred at this point and at this time. Col. Browne, by orders, was compelled to weaken his line by sending Capt. Moore with his company H to reinforce a portion of the line to the left. He had but 280 men with which to hold his position. One-fourth of these were employed in holding horses, leaving but about 200 men to resist the attacks of the enemy. The feats of valor performed by the regiment on this day, will be fully appreciated, when it is remembered that it was dismounted cavalry, drawn up in the single rank formation, to oppose massed columns of infantry, out-numbering it four to one. The muzzle of carbine or musket was placed against the body of the assailants or the assailed, and discharged. In many instances, the men not having time to re-load their carbines, used them as clubs over the heads of the rebels, and even clinched and pounded them with their fists. The rebels on getting over the fence were either shot, and

112

fell on either side of it, or were knocked off either with the butts of the carbines, or with the fist. It was impossible for the regiment to much longer withstand the assault of such overpowering numbers. The fence being carried, the contest was continued from bush to bush and from tree to tree. In this mode of fighting, the navy revolvers, of the 7th Indiana, proved formidable weapons. Many a rebel in feeling his way through the heavy foliage of the bushes, found the muzzle of a navy in his face and bid goodbye to the world. This occurred so often, that it made the rebels cautious, and materially abated the vehemence of their attack.

The rebels were moving a force to flank the regiment on the right. Col. Browne informed Col. Waring, Commander of the 1st Brigade, of his situation, and asked for reinforcements. Col. Waring sent Lieut. Hansen, with information that every man was disposed of and that reinforcements were out of the question, and ordered Col. Browne to hold his position to the last extremity. The flanking movement of the enemy rendered it necessary for Col. Browne to shift the position of the regiment to the rear and right, to prevent its right flank from being turned. He ordered the men to their horses, a few rods to the rear in an open space in the woods. The rebels, seeing the movement, advanced their line through the brush and halted but a short distance from the 7th Indiana and opened a vigorous fire. The regiment, under this fire at short range, mounted as cooly as if they were on parade. War has its comical as well as serious aspects. The lines being so close that the adversaries could speak to each other, they exchanged language more forcible than elegant.

At this juncture, the gallant Col. Browne, who was always found where the conflict was fiercest, received a painful wound in the ankle, and his horse was shot. His orderly was shot dead at his side. Remounting, the Col. retired the regiment a short distance, dismounted the men, and formed them in line, the left wing of the regiment resting in a graveyard near the crossroads. At last a regiment arrived to reinforce the 7th Indiana, and took position on the right of it. For two hours the 7th Indiana unaided, resisted the attacks of the enemy who overwhelmingly outnumbered it. The rebels having paid dearly for their slight success, made no further attempt to break the line at this point. Hostilities were now confined to the batteries. A knot of officers gathered at the battery at the crossroads, to watch the duel.

They smiled with delight to see the rebels scamper from their guns, when a well-directed shell exploded among them. But their serenity was somewhat disturbed, when a shell from the enemy's battery exploded near *them*, and killed two gunners and wounded three others.

The infantry by this time began to arrive and take position on the field.

The 7th Indiana was then ordered back on the Ripley road, about half a mile, and formed in line of battle on the north side of the road, on the extreme left of the federal line.

Col. Browne, owing to his wound, being unable longer to remain with his regiment, turned the command over to Major Simonson.

The ground in front was a field of gentle acclivity. The rebels were formed on its crest, behind a fence at the edge of the woods.

The regiment was dismounted, and advanced half way up the hill, and a skirmish line thrown forward of the regiment. The entire command was ordered to lie down to protect it from the sharp-shooters of the enemy. It occupied this position for some time, no firing occurring except an occasional shot from the rebels.

When the engagement between the enemy and Grierson's cavalry commenced, the infantry and most of the cavalry were miles in the rear, toiling through the mud, under a scorching sun. General Grierson dispatched messenger after messenger to Sturges to hurry on the infantry before he was overwhelmed. As his position grew momentarily more precarious, he dashed back in person to the infantry to hurry it up. He met Col. McMillan two miles and a half from the field, and told him he could not hold his position but twenty minutes longer. The gallant Col. told him he would be on the field in twenty minutes. The Col. started his column on the double quick, which gait it kept till it arrived on the field. Some of his men dropped from the ranks exhausted, some fell in the road with sun stroke, but still the brave men pushed on, intent on saving from annihilation the cavalry, that had fought so gallantly.

When they arrived on the field, they were almost exhausted. The regiments as they came up, took position wherever needed, without reference to brigade organization. The 93d Indiana infantry was formed on the extreme right. The rebels, with their

114

usual perfidy, marched a regiment, bearing the national colors, and dressed in the federal uniform, toward it, and when within a short distance, poured a deadly fire into its ranks. Sixty-five men of the 93d fell under that fire, among them Lieut.-Col. John W. Poole and Adjutant Irving Moody. Forrest, as the different brigades of infantry arrived, hurled his massed columns against them, and defeated and routed them separately. Everything done by Forrest, showed generalship of the highest order, while Sturges manifested nothing but treasonable incompetency.

The scene, witnessed by the 7th Indiana, from its position last mentioned, was probably never before seen on a battle field. Half a mile from the cross-roads, was a swamp between two hills and crossed by the road. The baggage train came down the hill nearest Ripley, and occupied nearly all of the road across the swamp. The lines were driven back from the cross-roads, and were but a short distance from the train. The artillery that was being moved to the rear to save it from capture, could not cross the swamp, because the road was completely blockaded with the wagons, and necessarily fell into the hands of the enemy. To make things worse, the officer in charge of the baggage train, attempted to turn it back, and got a few wagons crosswise with the road, when the mules and the wheels of the wagons on getting out of the narrow road-bed, were mired, and could not be moved.

Maj. Simonson was now ordered to withdraw the 7th Indiana, all the other cavalry regiments having left the field. The Maj. knew, that the moment the regiment began a backward movement, that the rebel line in his front would charge him. He therefore ordered every other man to stand fast, and deliver a fire at the enemy the moment they crossed the fence on the hill, while the rest retreated a few rods, faced about, and in like manner fired at the enemy till the front line had taken a new position to the rear, when it would retire. The withdrawal of the 7th presented a splendid picture. When it began, as was expected, the rebels were quickly over the fence in pursuit. The two lines were in full view on the open field, one advancing and the other retiring. Blue smoke curled up from the muskets on the one side, and from the carbines on the other.

When within a few rods of their horses, the men of the 7th Indiana made a rush for them, and speedily vaulting into the saddles, wheeled to the left in column of fours, and started to leave the field. The regiment had to cross the creek, by jumping the horses over it. A tolerably good place was found for this purpose, but only one or two men could cross at a time. This caused delay, and compelled a great part of the regiment to sit on their horses in the field, exposed to the fire of the enemy. The rebels were pressing so closely, that there was danger of some of the companies being captured *en-masse*. Maj. Simonson therefore gave the order for each man to get across the best way he could. The men broke ranks, and dashed through the willows that fringed the banks of the creek, and spurred their horses into and over it. Some of the horses being too weak to clear the creek, jumped into it and mired, when their riders were compelled to leave them and save themselves on foot. The crossing was done so hurriedly, that the men got separated from their companies, but it was the only thing that caused confusion in the regiment on that day. But in less than half an hour, every man was in his proper place. The entire army was now in total rout. The infantry was streaming by the wagons in the marsh, beyond the control of its officers, while shot and shell from the enemy's guns plunged through them. The scene that ensued beggars description. The teamsters, the inevitable course of a defeated army, cut the mules loose from the wagons, mounted them and dashed madly to the rear, riding down every one in the way.

Gen. Sturges was on the hill, beside himself with excitement. He ordered Lt. Gleason of company "A," and Lt. Cogley of company "F," of the 7th Indiana, to halt some men and form them across the road, and shoot down every straggler that attemped to pass. These officers, by threats, succeeded momentarily in checking the current, but it soon became so large that nothing could restrain it. It broke through the line and rushed to the rear. It was pitiable to see the colored soldiers, who well knew that they would be shot without mercy if captured, when compelled to halt, some knelt down and prayed, others threw themselves on the ground, and sobbed in the greatest agony of despair.

After the stragglers had gone by, the 7th Indiana was formed on the crest of the hill facing the enemy, and compelled to stand under a furious cannonade, directed at the retreating infantry. The colored brigade was still in the rear, fighting furiously. It saw some of its members shot, after they had surrendered. This nerved them with the energy of despair. The repeated yells of

116

the rebels, told of the fury of the onslaught, and the crashing volleys from the brigade, of the determination of the defence. The poor fellows, after exhausting their ammunition, ran about the field, to get cartridges from the boxes of their dead comrades, and boarded the ammunition train and loaded themselves down with cartridges, and renewed the conflict with unabated bravery. It was the division of the rebel General French, celebrated for its hatred for, and barbarous treatment of the colored troops, that made this attack on the colored brigade. It was a contest of courage between the chivalry of the South and the despised African. The pride of the former was humiliated by the soldierly qualities of the latter.

A body of Colored troops covered the retreat of fifteen hundred white soldiers all the way from the battle field to Collierville. Another body of about 300, that got separated from the army, successfully resisted the attacks of the rebel cavalry, and foiled the guerrillas, and arrived at Memphis a few days after the battle.

The 7th Indiana was soon ordered to withdraw from the position last mentioned, and take its place in the column of retreat. At daylight, the army passed through Ripley. At that place some heavy fighting occurred between Forrest's advance and the infantry, in which both sides lost heavily. From Ripley, the cavalry took the advance, and was constantly annoyed by the enemy till near Collierville. The retreat was continued night and day. The men were completely exhausted, by the fatigues of the battle, and the want of sleep. Nature will assert her demands. Notwithstanding the presence of danger, the men went to sleep in the saddle, and fell from their horses, and were trampled on by them. Even the animals suffered for rest and sleep as much as the men. They staggered against each other, and frequently fell, unhorsing their riders. Many of them unable to travel further were abandoned, and the unfortunate owners compelled to plod along on foot. Many of the men thus dismounted, laid down by the road-side, to sleep, and awoke to find themselves prisoners. Many of them fell into the hands of the merciless Guerrillas and were murdered in cold blood.

The wagon-train, with the supplies of rations, owing to the stupidity of General Sturges, was captured, and as a consequence the men were almost starving. Forrest pursued so vindictively, that there was no time to forage.

117

Frequently, when, a soldier in turning his haversack inside out to empty the crumbs into his hand, dropped a piece of cracker not larger than an inch square, the men in his rear seeing it, would jump from their horses and scrabble for it, and that, too, after it had been tramped into the mud by the horses feet.

Those of the wounded who could not ride on their horses were left behind. Among them, was the brave Capt. Joel H. Elliott, who was shot through the shoulder.

General Sturges in this expedition, suffered a disgraceful defeat, lost his entire wagon-train, and supplies, nearly all of his artillery, and his reputation as a soldier.

In the battle of *Brices-cross-roads*, the 7th Indiana acquired new laurels, and wrung from Col. Waring, commander of the 1st Brigade, the following complimentary recognition of its services:

HEAD QUARTERS FIRST CAVALRY BRIGADE, 16, A. C.
CAMP AT WHITE STATION, JUNE 13th, 1864.
Major:

By my action, proceedings were some time since instituted against several officers of the 7th Indiana Volunteer Cavalry, and they were ordered to appear before a Military Commission for examination, I respectfully but earnestly request that further action in these cases be stopped, and the papers be returned to me. The 7th Indiana Cavalry was in action under my command, on the 10th inst., at Brices-Cross-roads, Mississippi, and for two hours fought most gallantly against superior forces. From Lieutenant-Colonel Browne commanding to the last private, their conduct was brilliant and soldierly in the extreme. I am sure that such brave men can not fail to become, in all respects good officers, if allowed another opportunity under proper control.

Very Respectfully your Obedient Servant,
GEO. E. WARING, JR.,
Col. 4th Mo. Cav. Com'dg.

In instituting the proceedings referred to in the above communication, Col. Waring was aiming at no less a person than Col. Shanks himself, for whom he had a dislike. He pretended

118

that Col. Shanks had a keener eye to his political advancement at home, than to the proper discipline of his regiment. Although, Col. Shanks was, to a certain extent, a politician, and had been in Congress previous to organizing the regiment, yet, the charge that he neglected any of his duties as a soldier, and commanding officer, was without any foundation whatever. From the organization of the regiment, till its return to Memphis from the expedition to West Point, Col. Shanks was almost constantly in command of it.

The fact, that the regiment was shifted from front to rear, or from rear to the front, or to the flanks, to meet threatened danger, shows that not only Gen. Grierson, but Col. Waring himself, regarded it as an efficient military organization, that could be relied on in any emergency. The brilliant conduct of the regiment on the 22d of February, on the retreat from Okolona, under the command of Col. Shanks, relieved Gen. Smith's failure, of a portion of the odium attaching to it, and, in brief, saved the greater portion of his army from capture. A regiment that could fight so well and accomplish so much, must have had an able commanding officer.

Col. Waring's every act showed that he had more confidence in the 7th Indiana cavalry than he had in his own regiment. He was forcibly reminded of it by a private of the 7th who rode up to him, when he placed the regiment in the rear after Sturges' army was routed, and allowed the 4th Missouri to pass to the front out of danger, and asked him, why, he always placed the 7th in positions of danger, and his own regiment in places of comparative security. The Colonel, knowing the truth to be as stated, did not get angry with the soldier or reprove him, but said, as he rode away, that he would send the 4th Missouri back to the rear; but it did not come.

General Grierson recognized the gallant services of the 7th Indiana, in an order, in which the following complimentary language occurs:

"Your General congratulates you upon your noble conduct during the late expedition. Fighting against overwhelming numbers, under adverse circumstances, your prompt obedience to orders and unflinching courage, commanding the admiration of all, made even defeat almost a victory. For hours, on foot, you repulsed the charges of the enemy's infantry, and, again, in the

119

saddle, you met his cavalry, and turned his assaults into confusion. Your heroic perseverance saved hundreds of your fellow soldiers from capture. *You have been faithful to your honorable reputation, and have fully justified the confidence and merited the high esteem of your commander."*

The following is the official report of the casualties of the 7th Indiana cavalry in this expedition and battle:

CAMP WHITE STATION, NEAR MEMPHIS, TENN.,
June 14, 1864.

FIELD AND LINE WOUNDED.

T. M. Browne. Lieut. Col., in the ankle.

J. H. Elliott, Capt. Co. M, in left lung and shoulder severely.

James Sloan, 1st Lieut. Co. E, in right side and shoulder severely.

Company A—Killed, Serg't John Marsh, Private Lyman Temple.

Company B—Killed, Edward Gray, George W. Gray. Missing, George W. Smith.

Company C—Killed, Corp. Josh McCann. Wounded, Geo. W. Knapp in arm, Seth S. Heaton, slightly. Missing, Ferdinand Santz, Philander Underwood.

Company D—Wounded, Thomas Starkey in leg severely.

Company E—Killed, Daniel Vancamp. Wounded, Humphrey Davis slightly. Missing, Thomas J. Updike.

Company F—Missing, Corp. William A. Fink.

Company G—Killed, Timothy Kelley. Wounded. Adam Nelson slightly, Andrew F. Lakin severely. Missing, Serg't Geo. W. Kennedy.

Company H—Wounded, John P. Baker. Missing, Wm. Winfield.

Company I—Killed, Gideon Wing, orderly to Lt. Col. T. M. Browne. Wounded, Lewis Gercean. Missing, James Chery.

Company K—Killed, Valentine Backar. Missing, John J. Collins, Uriah G. Hatley, Julius Oppero, James H. Lewis.

Company L—Wounded, Serg't R. M. Beetly in thigh severely, Corp. Vance McManigal in side severely, Calvin Griton in thigh slightly. Missing, Henry K. Zook.

Company M—Missing, Joseph Walker, Oliver N. Ratts, Rollin W. Drake, Asbury Lunger.

There was only a detachment of some 340 of the regiment in the engagement, the balance being unable to accompany the expedition for want of horses. We succeeded in getting most of our wounded off the field. Capt. Elliott was so severely wounded that we were compelled to leave him some twenty-five miles back, but he will be sent for and brought in under a flag of truce.

Very Respectfully,
John Q. Reed,
Lieut. and Acting Adj't.

The official report of Lieut. Col. Browne is here given:

HEADQUARTERS SEVENTH INDIANA CAVALRY,
CAMP AT WHITE STATION, June 16, 1864,

Lieut. A. Vezin, A. A. A. G:

I herewith respectfully submit the following report of the 7th Indiana Volunteer Cavalry, as to the part taken by it in the late expedition of Gen. Sturges to Brices Cross Roads, Miss., and the engagement that ensued at that place:

The regiment, 350 strong, in command of Maj. S. E. W. Simonson, joined the expedition at this camp on the morning of the 1st inst. It proceeded without serious interruption to Salem, Miss., at which place I overtook the command, on the afternoon of the fourth (4th) inst.

Nothing occurred of particular interest beyond the usual incidents of scouting and foraging until our arrival at Ripley, on the evening of the 7th inst., at which place the advance of Gen. Sturges was fired upon by a small party of rebels, but being charged, fled precipitately through the town, and some two miles to the south of it, where securing an advantageous position on the crest of a hill, which could only be approached by passing over a narrow causeway, they made a stand, and for a short time obstinately contested a further advance. A portion of the 4th Iowa cavalry, having engaged them in a spirited skirmish of an hour's duration, and having failed to drive the enemy, this regiment was ordered forward from the rear of the cavalry division to the front. We moved forward at once, but met the dismounted horses of the Iowa regiment on the bridge coming to the rear, which fact delayed for a few moments our advance. Arriving on the ground we were ordered to take a position on the left of the road and to move thence forward and carry the hill. The ground upon the left was of such a character from marshes and ditches that it was impossible to maneuver the regiment mounted. The regiment was at once formed in line, the men dismounted and moved forward to the hill, occupying it, the enemy retiring at our approach without firing upon us. It was now dark. I sent Gen. Grierson information of the situation of affairs, and by his orders retired.

On the 8th inst., we proceeded with the 4th Mo. cavalry to Ruckerville to the relief of Col. Karge. Meeting the Colonel with his command a short distance beyond that place we returned, rejoining our forces on the same day at Ripley, where we camped for the night.

On the 10th inst. at Brices-cross-roads, Captains Branham and Shoemaker were sent forward, by Col. Waring's order, with fifty men, on the Tupelo road, to ascertain if possible, the whereabouts of the enemy. While they were absent the enemy were discovered in force in position but a short distance from us on the left hand road. The cavalry forces were moved into position. This regiment was placed by direction of Col. Waring, on the right of the road, supporting the battery of the 4th Mo. cavalry, which was upon our immediate left. The position was well selected, being in the edge of a grove on elevated ground in the rear of a fence and having a large open field between us and the enemy. Over this open space the enemy would have to pass to attack us. The regiment was dismounted and placed in the rear of the fence and skirmishers thrown out into the open field in front. The enemy occupied a strong position on a wooded hill, immediately in front of which was a swamp, so that to have attacked them with a cavalry force only, would have been disastrous. We awaited them in our position, our skirmishers and battery, in the meantime, keeping up a very lively fire. Col. Waring instructed me to hold the position occupied by us to the last extremity. The men were directed to lay close to the fence and reserve their fire until the enemy should be at short range. While this was taking place, quite a demonstration was made by the enemy upon the extreme left, and by order of the Colonel Commanding Capt. John M. Moore, with Co. H of this regiment was ordered to that point. Soon after the 2d N.J. cavalry, which were upon our right, was moved to another position leaving this command on the extreme right of the 1st brigade. At half after one o'clock, p.m., and after we had held this position some two hours and a half, the enemy approached our front and right in heavy force. They had two lines of skirmishers and a line of infantry supporting them. In a moment, I discovered that the position could not be long held by us without reinforcements, as they could overwhelm us with numbers. At this time my command only numbered about two hundred and eighty men, one-fourth of whom were holding horses. I dispatched an orderly to the Col. commanding, asking that a force be sent to my right, but was informed in reply that he had already disposed of every available man in the brigade, and that to give me assistance was impossible.

By this time the enemy were advancing rapidly and attempting to turn our right. The regiment was rallied to the right and soon the conflict became desperate. But a few yards intervened between their line and ours, and indeed so close did they approach us that our men in a few instances employed the butts of their carbines in resisting their advance. At this point the enemy suffered severely as we could see many of them fall before our fire. It soon became evident that we were being flanked on the right and that to hold our position much longer would be impossible. We had maintained our ground for near three hours and the enemy's fire at such short range became murderous.

As our infantry were coming up and going into position, we were ordered to fall back, which we did in tolerable order.

While this was transpiring on the right, the force of Capt. Moore which had been sent to the left was by no means idle. He was constantly engaged skirmishing with the enemy until he rejoined the regiment near the wagon-train in the rear of the cross-roads.

Upon leaving the field at the cross-roads, feeling too weak to continue longer in command, I turned it over to Maj. Simonson, to whose judgment, coolness and bravery, both on the field and in the subsequent retreat, I am greatly indebted.

Upon falling back on the Ripley road, Maj. Simonson was directed to take the regiment and rejoin the brigade at the rear. Arriving at the brigade, by Col. Waring's order, two battalions under the command of Capt. Henry F. Wright and Hubbard were dismounted and thrown forward in line on the crest of a hill to the left of the road. The remaining battalion in command of Capt. Ryan was ordered to the left to hold the enemy in check and prevent his passing our left flank to our rear. In this position the command was constantly skirmishing for about an hour, when it was ordered *"to horse"* under a heavy fire. From this it marched about one mile to the rear, and again formed by order of General Grierson, on the left. It remained in this position until the infantry came up when it was ordered to fall back. It then took up the march in the rear of the brigade and arrived at Ripley at daylight the next morning. Halting there a short time to rest, it was placed in the advance and moved for Memphis. With the residue of our forces it marched all the day and night, the rear being constantly harassed by the enemy, and arrived safely at Collierville on the morning of the 12th inst.

I can not speak in terms of too high commendation of the conduct of the officers and men of this command in this regiment. To name some when all did their duty so well, would be unjust. Of the line officers Capt. Elliott of Co. "M," and Lieu't James Sloan of Co. "E," were seriously wounded while gallantly engaging the enemy. I regret deeply that we were unable to bring Capt. Elliott back to camp, but hope he may yet be brought safely to the command.

Our loss is as follows: killed, 8; wounded, 16; missing, 17;—a list of whom I have heretofore forwarded.

Very Respectfully, your Obedient Servant,

THOS. M. BROWNE,
Lt.-Col. Com'd'g.

CHRISTIAN BECK, Major, Co. F, S

126

CHAPTER V.

The Regiment goes to Vicksburg by Steamboat—Then Marches to the Big Black—Skirmish at Utica—Rebels Driven through Port Gibson—7th Indiana has a Running Fight to Bayou Pierce Wirt Adams Repulsed at Grand Gulf—Regiment Returns to Memphis.

About the 1st of July, 1864, Gen. A. J. Smith organized an expedition to march against Forrest, at Tupelo, Mississippi. On the 14th, he encountered the rebels under Forrest at that place, and defeated them.

As a co-operative movement, the 1st Brigade, including the 7th Indiana Cavalry, was sent down the Mississippi river in transports to Vicksburg, and from there marched against Wirt Adams in the neighborhood of Port Gibson.

At twelve o'clock on the 4th of July, the regiment broke camp at White Station and marched to Memphis, where it embarked on steamboats.

On the morning of the 5th, the expedition started down the Mississippi. On the evening of the 7th, the command disembarked at Vicksburg and immediately started for the Big Black River, where it camped at midnight. The next day, the entire force under Gen. Slocum, crossed the Big Black, marched to Raymond, and from there to Utica, where the advance encountered and drove a small body of rebels through the town, soon after, the rest of the force arrived and camped for the night. The next day about two hundred rebels attacked the picket lines, and a spirited skirmish of about an hour's duration resulted, when the rebels were put to flight, losing several killed and a few prisoners. From Utica, the command marched to Port Gibson, defeated a small force of rebels, and went into camp near the town.

The next day Gen. Slocum, leaving the 7th Indiana and the

127

2d New Jersey Cavalry regiments under the command of Col. Shanks, as a rear guard, marched with the remainder of his force to Grand Gulf.

About ten o'clock in the morning, the rebels attacked the picket lines, and a skirmish lasting for near an hour took place. Col. Shanks withdrew his force through the town, and had scarcely quitted it, when the rebels were informed of his departure by the ringing of the church bells. Soon after, the rebel cavalry were seen marching through the town in pursuit. The 7th Indiana Cavalry was placed in the rear, and slowly retreated by companies. When the rebels approached near enough, the company in the rear would fire a volley into them, and retire, the next company would form face to the rear, and in like manner deliver a fire at the rebels when they pressed too closely.

In this manner, the retreat was conducted for several miles to Bayou Pierce, without the slightest disorder in the ranks. At the Bayou, the rebels, hoping to cut off the rear companies and capture them, charged with yells upon the rear. All the command had crossed the Bayou, except company "F" of the 7th Indiana. It was formed near the banks of the stream, faced to the rear, and when the rebels made their appearance around a bend in the road, fired a volley into them at short range, which caused them to halt. It then crossed the Bayou, and the regiment proceeded to Grand Gulf and camped.

After the 7th had crossed the Bayou, a regiment of Colored troops were formed in an ambuscade, into which the rebels run, losing several in killed and wounded. The next morning, the rebels attacked and drove in the pickets, but were soon met by the First Brigade of Cavalry, and after losing thirty killed and wounded, and a number of prisoners, withdrew. The prisoners reported, that Wirt Adams, thinking that the most of Slocum's force had departed for Vicksburg, determined to attack and capture the remainder of Grand Gulf. Contrary to his expectations, Gen. Slocum was present with his entire force, and Adams was compelled to hastily retreat. The regiment, with the rest of the command, embarked on transports and went to Vicksburg.

From Vicksburg, the regiment went up the Mississippi, to Memphis, where it disembarked, and marched to its old camp at White Station, arriving there on the 24th of July.

CHAPTER VI.

Fight at Tallahatchie river—Gen. Hatch pursues the rebel Gen. Chalmers to Oxford and returns to the Tallahatchie—1st brigade of cavalry returns to Holly Springs—Capt. Skelton with thirty men attacks six hundred rebels at Lamar Station, in the night, and runs them through the town—Forrest's raid into Memphis—Gen. Washburn barely escapes capture.

In a few days after the return of the regiment from Vicksburg, Gen. A. J. Smith, with ten thousand men, consisting of infantry, cavalry and artillery, started once more in search of Forrest. He marched to Holly Springs and camped three or four days, while a detachment pushed on to the Tallahatchie river, on the Oxford road, to repair the railroad bridge at that point. The rebel Gen. Chalmers was there with his brigade, and interrupted the work on the bridge with a battery planted on the south side of the river.

The 7th Indiana cavalry with the 1st brigade marched rapidly from Holly Springs to the river. When several miles distant the boom of cannon was heard, and it was expected that an engagement would take place at the river. The regiment arrived there in the middle of the afternoon. Two companies, F and another, its letter the author is not able to recall, immediately crossed to the south side, and forming in skirmish line, advanced cautiously, and compelled the rebel sharp-shooters to take position further from the river, where they could not so effectually annoy the pioneers at work on the bridge.

A lively skirmish was kept up all the afternoon. But notwithstanding, the work on the bridge progressed rapidly, and, by night, it was so far completed that troops could cross on it. During a continuous fire from the rebels, directed at the pioneers, only two were slightly wounded. The skirmish was of a comical character. A rebel sharp-shooter would fire at the men on the

129

bridge, and exclaim, "How is that Yank?" The pioneers would defiantly retrort, "You have got to do better than that!" The skirmishers would watch for the smoke from the gun of a sharp-shooter, posted in a tree, and fire at it, and shout, "How do you like that, Reb?" The rebels, if no damage was done, would rejoin, "Oh, what shooting!" However, a sharp-shooter was seen to descend from a tree as if a ball had passed uncomfortably near. The rebels then withdrew to a safer distance, and the *serio-comic* fight was ended. The companies of the 7th Indiana recrossed the river and went into camp with the main army on the north bank.

Early the next morning, the cavalry, under the command of Gen. Hatch, crossed the river and started in pursuit of Chalmers. The latter was posted at Abbeyville, a small town two miles from the river. On the approach of the cavalry, the rebels opened fire with their artillery, and after a brief skirmish, abandoned their position and retreated on the road to Oxford.

Occasionally through the day, when their rear was hotly pressed, the rebels faced about with their artillery and opened fire, but soon limbered up, and galloped off the field, on discovering preparations for a charge.

In the evening about an hour before sunset, one mile from Oxford, the rebels posted their cannon on a hill, opened a brisk fire, and seemed determined to oppose the entrance of Gen. Hatch into the city. The 7th Indiana cavalry was ordered to the front and formed for a charge, but the rebels did not wait for it, but hastily limbering up, left Oxford to their left and started south. The 7th Indiana and another regiment passed through Oxford, and two miles south of it, but discovering nothing of the rebels, returned to the main column and *bivouacked* for the night.

Further pursuit of Chalmers was abandoned, and the next day Gen. Hatch returned to the Tallahatchie river. The 7th Indiana, with the 1st cavalry brigade returned to Holly Springs. From there, Capt. Wright of company D, with a battalion of the 7th Indiana cavalry, was sent north on the railroad to recognoiter, and to disperse any Guerrilla parties that might interfere with the railroad. Capt. Wright marched to Hudsonville, where he halted, but sent Capt. Skelton with company F to Lamar Station on the railroad.

Capt. Skelton with but thirty men, arrived at Lamar about sundown, and *bivouacked* half a mile north of the town in a grove of young oaks. About ten o'clock that night, a scout, sent out by Capt. Skelton, discovered a body of rebels entering the town, and conveyed the intelligence to the Captain. Capt. Skelton, believing it to be a Guerrilla party, mounted his men, and started in pursuit. He encountered them at the railroad crossing at the edge of the town, and charged them so vigorously and unexpectedly, that the entire force, numbering six hundred, was put to flight and driven pell-mell through the town and a short distance beyond it. This rebel force was Gen. Forrest's old regiment, that he recruited and commanded when a Colonel, and was composed of picked men. It was always relied upon by Forrest in a dangerous enterprise. Col. Kelley was in command of it. It was afterwards learned that this force was intended to dash into Memphis, and at the time of its surprise, was on its way there; thus, Capt. Skelton had the honor of defeating, for a time, the plan of Forrest to capture that place. The Captain lost the Author, wounded and taken prisoner, and another man wounded. The rebels lost several killed and wounded, and at one time nearly one hundred prisoners were taken; but the rebels rallying, Capt. Skelton was compelled to let them escape. The full particulars of this daring enterprise will be given in the sketch of Major Skelton.

Col. Kelley retreated to Okolona, Miss. Gen. A. J. Smith, with the greater part of his army was at the Tallahatchie river, waiting for the repair of the railroad bridge and for the arrival of supplies, after which he marched to Oxford.

While at Oxford, Forrest, by a dextrous movement, slipped his army to the rear of Smith and suddenly appeared at Memphis, dashed into the city, killed a few soldiers and captured 200 prisoners. His stay was very brief—about twenty minutes. The federal troops, soon recovering from their surprise, rallied and drove him from the city as rapidly as he entered it. Colonel Browne was in the city at the time and in a letter to a friend, gives the following facetious account of it: "I was in the city when Forrest took it, saw the whole affair, was shot at and had to vacate my position to save my 'bacon.' I was quietly sleeping in our court room on my cot, when I heard the firing commence. I put on my clothes and hurried into the street to see what was up. I had gone but two squares before I discovered rebel cavalry charging on almost every street. It was just at daybreak, and they got quite near me before I discovered who they were. Having on my uniform and being unarmed, I thought 'distance would lend enchantment to the view' and I mizzled, but not until a few stray bullets admonished me that I occupied a position, that in a military sense, was wholly untenable. One bullet took out a window pane a few feet from me. The rebels just then were being kept very busy. Our guards were rallying in every part of the city and sending volley after volley into them. Our officers, who were in the city temporarily, were cracking at them from the windows of the buildings. Dead horses and men were soon visible on every street. The rebs did not stay long; they took some two hundred prisoners, killed about ten of our men in town, and took two hundred horses, robbed a cigar stand at the Gayoso House and then run like the devil. There were probably eight hundred rebs in town, and from two thousand to three thousand at the outskirts. Our forces soon rallied and pursued, and a very spirited fight took place from three to five miles from the city. The rebs were whipped with a loss of fifty or sixty killed and an equal number of prisoners. Taking it all together, they did not make much money in the operation, and will probably not try another raid on Memphis soon. Our forces were nearly all away under Smith, and our Generals were taken by surprise. Washburn (Gen. Washburn) came very near being captured. He had to run to Fort Pickering minus his breeches."

There remained at White Station, when this expedition started, and were there at the time of the capture of Memphis, a part of the 7th Indiana cavalry and of some other regiments, and would have fallen an easy prey to Forrest, if he had turned his attention to them. The fact that they were not molested shows the haste Forrest was in to get away from Memphis.

Aside from the complete surprise, this dash of Forrest's was devoid of any military results; while it must be conceded that a practicable joke was played on Gen. Washburn, by compelling him to flee the city *dishabille*, yet the laugh comes in against Gen. Forrest, who was compelled to quit the city in equally as undignified haste, without time to eat his dinner at the Gayoso House, where he registered his name. Gen. Smith received intelligence at Oxford of the capture of Memphis, and began his return by forced marches. On the 29th of August the cavalry arrived, and, two days later, the infantry and artillery.

CHAPTER VII.

March to Brownsville, Arkansas, thence to Cape Girardeau, Missouri, up the Mississippi and Missouri Rivers, into the Interior of Missouri, Chase of Price—Attack on the Rebel Rear-guard at Independence—Seventh Indiana Fights for the Possession of a Corn field, at Big Blue, and Wins—Battle of the Little Osage, Brilliant Sabre Charge—Pursuit of Price to the Marmiton, Attacked and Driven Across the River, Retreats to the Arkansas River—Cavalry Returns to St. Louis.

The junction of the rebel forces, under Gen. Price and Shelby, at Batesville, Arkansas, about the middle of September, 1864, threatened both Little Rock, held by the federal Gen. Frederick Steele, and the State of Missouri. It is probable that the authorities at Memphis, believed Little Rock was the objective point of Price, for on the return of Gen. Smith to Memphis, the cavalry was ordered to Brownsville, Arkansas, and before it arrived there, Price revealed his intentions by starting northward toward Missouri.

With an army of about fourteen thousand men, and a good supply of artillery, Price entered the State of Missouri about the 22d of September, on his last invasion, that proved disastrous both to his army and the rebel cause in Missouri. He marched to Bloomfield, thence to Pilot Knob. On the 26th of September, he failed to carry the latter place by assault, but, by occupying Shepherd Mountain, he compelled Gen. Ewing to evacuate Fort Ironton, near Pilot Knob. Gen. Ewing retreated to Harris Station, followed by Price. After marching to Richwood's, and threatening St. Louis, Price started toward Jefferson City, the State capitol.

A division of infantry under Gen. Joseph A. Mower, and the

cavalry under Gen. Winslow, of the Fourth Iowa Cavalry, crossed the Mississippi near Memphis, and began their march for Brownsville, Arkansas.

Five hundred men of the Seventh Indiana Cavalry, under the command of Maj. S. E. W. Simonson, joined this expedition. The men supposed they were going on a five days' scout toward Little Rock, but they did not return to camp at Memphis, until they had marched over the greater part of Missouri, and into the Indian Territory in pursuit of Price.

On the second day's march from the Mississippi, the command crossed Black Fish Lake, on an old ferry, and *bivouacked* on its west shore. This lake is about a mile in width and very deep. Col. Karge, in his hurry to cross his command, over-loaded the boat with men of the Second New Jersey, and when near the centre of the lake, the boat sunk, and twelve men and horses were drowned. Proceeding on the march, the command reached St. Francis river, where it expected to meet transports with supplies, but the river being low, they had not arrived. The supply of rations being nearly exhausted, the command pushed on rapidly. The march for the next two days was through a desolate country, that yielded nothing in the way of food for the men. At White river, some cattle that had been picked up on the line of march, were slaughtered and distributed to the men, who had to eat the meat without salt. The command crossed the river at Clarendon in a steamboat, and marched to Brownsville, twenty-five miles from Little Rock, where it formed a junction with the army under Gen. Frederick Steele, and got supplies of rations and clothing. Gen. Frederick Steele, thus reinforced, started north in pursuit of Price.

The cavalry under Col. Winslow, marched to Cape Girardeau, Missouri where it embarked on steamboats, sailed up the Mississippi, to the Missouri river, and up it, to Jefferson City, where it disembarked.

Gen. Price, finding Jefferson City too strong for him to attack, marched upon Boonville, Missouri on the Missouri river.

Gen. Pleasanton arrived from St. Louis and assumed command of the cavalry. He started Gen. Sanburn, reinforced by Winslow's cavalry, in pursuit.

At Independence, Price's rear-guard was overtaken, and a skirmish ensued. The Seventh Indiana Cavalry was in the advance, and Lieut. William H. Crane, of company "F," had command of the extreme advance guard. On coming in sight of the enemy, Lieut. Crane ordered a charge, and put the rebels to flight, and captured a few prisoners.

At the Big Blue, the Seventh Indiana Cavalry had a spirited fight with the rebels in a cornfield for the forrage, in which the rebels lost heavily in killed, and were driven from the field.

At Little Osage, Price crossed one of his divisions, and formed the rest of his army on the east side of the river, to oppose Pleasanton, who was in hot pursuit.

The country was a large prairie. Every man in both armies was in plain view. Gen. Pleasanton formed his regiments for a charge.

Winslow's brigade was formed in front of the key of Price's position, at the crossing of the river.

At the command, six thousand sabres gleamed in the bright sunlight, and six thousand cavaliers swept down on the rebel lines, with irresistible power. They dashed through the lines, doing terrible execution with the sabre. Col. Winslow charged through the line in his front, wheeled, and charged it from the rear on coming back. The rebels, unable to withstand the onset, broke and fled to the river, the federals pursuing, and fighting them into, and across it.

The rebels were cut from their horses with the sabres, or knocked into the river with revolvers.

The Seventh Indiana was led in this battle by the intrepid Maj. Simonson. The regiment captured two pieces of artillery, and three hundred prisoners. The brigade to which it was attached (Winslow's) captured five pieces of artillery, and a large number of prisoners. Price lost in this battle twenty-five pieces of artillery.

His retreat now became a disorderly flight. At the Marmiton river, he was overtaken, attacked, and driven across the river, losing a large number of prisoners. The Seventh Indiana, with Winslow's brigade, made two brilliant charges at that point. The pursuit continued into Indian Territory, when it was abandoned and the cavalry returned, a part of the Seventh Indiana to St. Louis, and a part to Louisville, Kentucky. Price retreated rapidly across the Arkansas river, shorn of his former prestige. In this brief but brilliant campaign, the detachment of the Seventh Indiana Cavalry participating, saw hard service.

Leaving Memphis, it marched into the interior of Arkansas, thence to Cape Girardeau, Missouri, thence by water to the interior of the State, where it entered on an active chase of Price, traveled to the western border of the State, thence across the Marmiton into the Indian Terriory, and returned to St. Louis, having traveled over a great part of the State of Missouri. It participated in three battles, and by its bravery added glory to its already proud reputation as a fighting regiment. It was complimented by Gen. Alfred Pleasanton, for its bravery and efficiency, and authorized by him to inscribe on its banners the names of the battle of Independence, Big Blue and Osage.

Gen. Pleasanton, not satisfied with the compliments he had already bestowed on Col. Winslow's brigade, issued the following complimentary order, which did not reach the regiments of the brigade until they had returned to Memphis:

HEAD-QUARTERS CAVALRY DIVISION,
WARRENSBURG, MO., Nov. 3d, 1864.

General Order,
    No. 11

Winslow's Brigade of Cavalry, commanded by Lieutenant-Colonel Benteen, being about to leave for another department, the Major-General commanding takes this occasion, not only to express his regret in separating from such glorious troops, but also to recall more especially than was done in General Order, No. 6, from these Head-Quarters, the splendid manner in which this brigade fought at the Osage, capturing five pieces of artillery from the enemy, with a large number of prisoners, and carrying by a daring charge the most important and conspicuous position on that brilliant field.

No troops could win for themselves a prouder record than they have done, and the best wishes of their commander in the late campaign will accompany them wherever their services may be required.

By command of
MAJOR-GENERAL PLEASONTON.

CLIFFORD THOMPSON,
    1st Lieut. and A. A. G.

136

The detachment of the Seventh Indiana Cavalry, that remained at Memphis during the Missouri campaign, was constantly employed in performing picket duty, and in scouting in the neighborhood of the Nonconnah creek and Coldwater. It was under the command of Major Carpenter, who was untiring in his efforts to clothe, arm and equip his command, having become destitute of nearly everything, in its frequent and trying campaigns.

It seems to have been reserved for the Seventh Indiana to accomplish results of incalculable benefit to the forces about Memphis.

As already stated, the country around the Nonconnah creek was infested with guerrillas, under the command of the notorious "Dick Davis." This man was a blood-thirsty human monster. He lurked about the picket posts and shot the pickets. He lay in wait, in ambush in the thickets about the Nonconnah, for scouting parties, and poured deadly volleys into them, while he was protected by his concealed position. A brave man can fight without concern, as long as he can see an adversary to fight, but when the attack comes from an unsuspected quarter, and from an unseen foe, the highest order of courage is put to the severest test. It was understood that the guerrillas murdered all their prisoners; and with a secret dread, scouting parties approached the Nonconnah. "Dick Davis" inspired more fear than Forrest himself.

On the 3d of October, Capt. Skelton, on returning after dark from a scout, and when about six miles from camp lost some horses, that fell into a ravine. Owing to the darkness of the night, and the steepness of the banks, they could not then be got out. In the morning, the Captain sent Corporal Archibald F. Inglish, with privates Charles Fennimore, Henry Gabler, Hiram Iseminger, Herman Kile, John L. Redding, Ashbury Ritter, of Company "F," to recover the horses. Corporal Inglish stationed one man as a *vidette*, to watch in the direction of Coldwater, while the rest, laying aside their arms, went to work to get the horses out of the ravine. While thus employed, "Dick Davis" with his men, coming from the direction of the federal camp, and who had probably watched them all the way there from the picket line, and knew full well their purpose in going out, when near them, with a fiendish yell, dashed upon, and surrounded them. Being taken by surprise, and unarmed, they could not offer the slightest

137

resistance, and all were captured. Davis marched them rapidly to Coldwater creek, went up the stream a few hundred yards in the heavy timber, seated them in a row, on a log across the creek, and had them shot, their bodies falling into the stream. To render his cowardly act the consummation of wickedness, he fastened a written warning over his own name, to a tree, threatening the same fate to any who should bury them.

There is no doubt but this was the fate of these men. A few days after the outrage, a young lady called on Maj. Carpenter, at his head-quarters, and gave such accurate description of them, that they were readily identified as the missing persons, besides, she had letters taken from their bodies, that established their identity beyond a doubt. Capt. Skelton had a cousin, a Mrs. Jennie Smith, who resided at Cockrum's crossroads, a few miles from Coldwater, who visited the bodies, and caused them to be taken out of the water and buried. She gave the Captain such an accurate description of them, that he recognized all as being the members of his company sent after the horses.

The manner of their death, the Author learned from two of the band, who were present at the shooting, whom he captured a few miles from Cockrum's-cross-roads, while on a scout in that direction, in the summer of 1865.

The Author had command of the advance guard. Several prisoners had been captured during the day. In the afternoon quite a force formed in line across the road on the crest of a hill. The advance guard was ordered to charge. The guerrillas did not wait for the advance to close with them, but broke and scattered in all directions in the woods. The guard dashed after them and succeeded in capturing two prisoners.

While marching along the road, the advance met a Negro, who well knew the prisoners, and that they belonged to "Dick Davis's" band. He told who they were, and that they were concerned in the murder, not far from there, of seven soldiers.

The prisoners at first pretended not to know the Negro, and denounced his story as false. The Author had the Negro confront them and make his statement. He told all about them in such a straight-forward and convincing manner, that they did not dare to dispute him, and when he said there would be plenty of people at Cockrum's, to corroborate him, they held out no longer, confessed to being members of Davis's band of guerrillas, and to being present at the shooting of the members of company "F."

At that time it was reported, that the secretary of war had issued an order, that all persons captured with arms, should be deemed guerrillas, and should be shot. Although the Author had not seen it, yet he believed such an order existed, and determined to execute these men. The advance went into camp that night at Cockrum's crossroads, where further evidence was found against the prisoners. The Author had preparations made to hang them, the end of a rope was placed around a limb of a tree, and one of the prisoners mounted on a horse under it, but still he disliked to assume the responsibility, and while hesitating what to do, Capt. Skelton arrived, who being the superior officer, the Author was relieved of the disagreeable duty. The Captain, after hearing all the facts, decided that the lives of the prisoners were forfeited under the rules of war, but concluded to defer the executions till morning.

During the night Col. Phelps, commander of the expedition arrived, to whom Capt. Skelton communicated the facts. The Colonel also concurred in the opinion that they ought to suffer death. He, however, decided to have them tried by a drumhead court-martial on the return of the expedition to camp. The prisoners were taken to the farm houses along the rout for their meals. When being taken to dinner, across a slightly wooded field they attempted to escape. The guards fired on them and returned without them, reporting that they had escaped. One of the guards had been a mess-mate and particular friend of one of the men murdered by the band to which these men belonged, and had often been heard to declare that if he ever came across any of the band, he would kill some of them if in his power to do so. It is probable that retributive justice overtook the assassins and robbers.

The seven men not returning as soon as they should, Capt. Skelton and Maj. Carpenter grew alarmed for their safety, and by order of the latter, the former took fifty men and proceeded in quest of them. At the Coldwater he learned that Dick Davis had captured them and was taking them in the direction of Holly Springs. Capt. Skelton believed from this that his men would be treated as prisoners of war, and it being impossible to overtake Davis, returned to camp.

A few days after their capture, Capt. Skelton, with company

F, was scouting near Coldwater, and came upon a small body of Guerrillas, several were captured. The Captain saw two of them running from a house to the woods. He dashed after them alone, and captured them, one of whom proved to be "Dick Davis" himself. The full particulars of his capture will be given in the biographical sketch of Maj. Skelton; and his trial, conviction by court-martial, and execution, in a chapter devoted to that subject.

In the latter part of October, 1864, Capt. Skelton, with a scouting party of about twenty men, early in the morning, while it was yet quite dark, ran into an ambuscade at the crossing of the Nonconnah creek. The first intimation he had of the presence of a foe, was a volley fired into his ranks about fifteen or twenty feet distant, from behind the railroad embankment. Two of his men were killed, three or four wounded, and two captured and shot not far from their place of capture, and left for dead. One of them lived till the relieving party arrived, and told of his being shot after he surrendered.

Capt. Skelton did all he could to rally his men, and charged alone in the direction of the fire, but the men dispersed and the Captain was left alone. Some of them returned to camp with information of the attack. The Author was ordered to take fifty men and go to the assistance of Capt. Skelton.

The men hastily mounted their horses, and left camp on the gallop. The news spread rapidly through the regiment, and the men without orders, saddled and mounted their horses, and before the relieving party had gone two miles, nearly the entire regiment was following.

Capt. Skelton was met about half a mile from the ambuscade, all alone, determined not to return till he learned the fate of his men. The relieving party dispersed in all directions in the woods for miles around, to find the Guerrillas, but so perfect was their mode of dispersing, that not one of them could be found.

The Guerrillas were sometimes beaten at their own game, as the following incident will show: On one of the roads leading out of Memphis was a picket post, so situated, that the pickets stationed at it, were an easy target to the Guerrillas who crept through the brush within ten rods of them and picked them off. This occurred so often, the men were afraid to be stationed at that point. Corporal Adam H. Shoemaker of company F, was detailed for picket duty, and placed at that post. The Corporal knowing that two or three times a week a picket was killed there, took the responsibility of moving the post into a yard near a large house but a few yards distant, where the picket could watch as well, and at the same time be concealed. Early the next morning before daylight, the Corporal, who was on the alert, heard a rustling in the leaves and bushes on the opposite side of the road. Grasping his carbine and laying flat on the ground, he peered in the direction of the noise, when presently he saw a man with a gun crawling stealthily on his hands and knees, and looking in the direction of the fatal post. The Corporal crawled on his belly a short distance to get in a position to get good aim, when he drew a bead on the Guerrilla and fired. Immediately on the discharge of the carbine, about a dozen mounted Guerrillas dashed up from a bend in the road, to the old post, undoubtedly believing the shot they heard was fired by their comrade with the usual fatal effect, and intending to capture the reserves before they could form, as they had frequently done before. But the reserves were wide awake, and when the Guerrillas made their appearance, gave them a volley from their carbines, a change in the programme the Guerillas were not expecting. They broke and fled in wild dismay. Corporal Shoemaker crossed the road to the object he fired at, and found a mortally wounded Guerrilla officer, who lived long enough to make it known that he was the successor to "Dick Davis." It seems to have been reserved by fate for company F to avenge the death of its seven members, murdered by this band of Guerrillas. The joke was this time on the Guerrillas, who took it so seriously, that they never again disturbed that picket post.

The Presidential election was approaching, and it was deemed as important to win a victory for the Union at the polls as in the field. As many of the regiment as could be spared, were given a ten days furlough to go to Indiana and vote. To prevent this the rebels grew very active, and were continually threatening the lines. This caused the forces at Memphis to be constantly on the alert, and to perform arduous picket and patrol duty.

The regiments were formed in line of battle every morning before daylight, and remained in line till after sunrise, to be ready for any possible attack, and to guard against surprises.

After election, affairs about Memphis assumed their usual aspect.

141

About Christmas, Gen. Grierson began preparing to make another of his famous raids into Mississippi, in which the 7th Indiana took a conspicuous part, an account of which will be given in the next chapter.

CHAPTER VIII.

GRIERSON'S RAID THROUGH MISSISSIPPI.

Gen. Grierson marches to Harrisburg—Capt. Elliott, with the 7th Indiana Cavalry, captures Verona, a large number of prisoners, and destroys a large quantity of rebel army stores—Railroad and bridges destroyed—Gen. Grierson captures a rebel stockade and its garrison at Egypt, rebel Gen. Gohlson killed— Chases a railroad train and captures a large number of cars, and rebel prisoners—Tears up the track and prevents the arrival of rebel reinforcements—Capt. Elliott, with one hundred men, attacks three hundred rebels—Capt. Beckwith captures Bankston and burns a cloth and leather factory, surprise of the superintendent of the works—Capture of hogs—Col. Osborn defeats the rebels at Franklin—Grenada captured—Arrival at Vicksburg and enthusiastic reception—Capt. Moor's expedition in Arkansas—Capt. Skelton captures three prisoners—Breakfast in the rebel camp.

In December, 1864, the rebel Gen. Hood marched his army in proud defiance, to Nashville, Tennessee, where he encountered that sturdy warrior, Gen. Geo. H. Thomas, and his army of veterans. In the battle there on the 15th, Hood sustained a terrible defeat, that sent his broken columns flying in dismay towards the Tennessee river. At different points on the Mobile and Ohio railroad were collected supplies for Hoods army, and trains were constantly transporting more from the interior of Mississippi.

Gen. Grierson organized a cavalry force at Memphis, to destroy the Mobile and Ohio railroad, to prevent the transportation of supplies to Hood's army, and to capture and destroy the supplies accumulating at Verona, Okolona and Egypt on that railroad. His forces, numbering in the aggregate three thousand three hundred men, composed three brigades of cavalry. The 1st com-

143

MAJ. GEN. BENJAMIN H. GRIERSON

144

manded by Col. Joseph Kargé of the 2d New Jersey cavalry, was composed of the 2d New Jersey, 4th Missouri and a detachment of one hundred and sixty men and seven officers of the 7th Indiana cavalry, under the command of Capt. Joel H. Elliott, of company "M," and the First Mississippi Mounted Rifles. The detachment of the Seventh Indiana, was divided into three squadrons, commanded respectively by Capt. Joseph W. Skelton, Capt. B. F. Bales and Lieut. John F. Dumont. The 2d brigade, commanded by Col. Winslow of the 4th Iowa, was composed of the 3d and 4th Iowa, and 10th Missouri regiments. The 3d brigade, commanded by Col. Osborn, composed of the 4th and 11th Illinois, 2d Wisconsin and 3d U. S. colored, and a pioneer corps of fifty men commanded by Lieut. Lewis, of the 7th Indiana cavalry.

Ten days rations and the extra ammunition were transported on pack mules. On the 21st of December, Gen. Grierson with the 2d and 3d brigades, took a south-eastwardly direction from Collierville, and proceeded to Ripley, Mississippi, arriving there at noon on the 24th, without interruption. At that place, a detachment of one hundred and fifty men were sent to Boonville to cut the Mobile and Ohio railroad at that point, and having done so rejoined the main command at Ellistown, twenty-five miles south of Ripley; and a detachment of two hundred men went to Guntown on the railroad, and rejoined the command at Ellistown.

The First Brigade proceeded along the Memphis and Charleston railroad to Lagrange, Tenn., where it left the railroad, passed through Lamar and Salem, Miss., to Harrisburg, arriving at the latter place on the evening of the 25th of December. After a brief rest it proceeded in the direction of Verona on the Mobile and Ohio railroad. After having gone about four miles, the advance met the enemy, who fired upon it and then retreated. After pursuing them about a mile, the brigade halted and the 7th Indiana was ordered forward to reconnoiter and capture their camp. The detachment of Capt. Skelton had the advance during that day, and had captured many prisoners, who represented that the rebel force at Verona was from three thousand to seven thousand men. It was raining and the night very dark. The detachment ran into an ambuscade and was fired upon, but owing to the extreme darkness, no harm was done. Gen. Grierson had arrived with the other brigade and decided to camp for the night

145

with the main force, but ordered Col. Kargé to move forward as far as he could with his brigade. The colonel proceeded about three miles and concluded to camp till morning, but ordered Capt. Elliott to advance as far as he could with the 7th Indiana. An aid of Col. Kargé, questioning the propriety of sending the 7th Indiana forward alone, the Colonel, who was a German, showed his confidence in the regiment by exclaiming: "Mein Got, when the 7th Indiana comes back, wes all come back." Capt. Elliott had proceeded but a mile and a half when suddenly there burst forth in front of his detachment a solid sheet of flame from the muskets of the rebels. It was so unexpected, that the men were thrown into confusion, and fell back in disorder about two hundred yards, when they were halted and reformed, and again moved forward. They had gone but about half a mile when they were fired into again. Capt. Skelton, who commanded the advance guard, ordered a charge, and the men dashed forward into a clump of black-jack oaks, the road at that point making an abrupt turn to the left towards the town. Nothing more serious resulted from the charge, than the loss of some hats and a few scratched faces.

Capt. Skelton then rode back to Capt. Elliott for instructions. The latter was undecided what do, and asked the former, as the second in command, what course to pursue. Capt. Skelton, who was always ready for emergencies, advised Capt. Elliott to dismount the rear guard, without letting the rest of the command know it, and send them across a field to make a feigned attack on the enemy's left, by discharging their revolvers, whooping, yelling and making all the noise they could.

Capt. Elliott liked the plan, but still thought there was a possibility of it failing. He however, told Capt. Skelton if he would assume all the responsibility in case of a failure, he would give him permission to try it. Capt. Skelton readily agreed to do so, and accordingly, sent Serg't Grey with eight men to make the feigned attack. The Sergeant executed his orders to the letter, and when his party commenced firing, the rest of the command, led by Capt. Skelton charged with yells down the road towards the town. The rebels supposing that Grierson's entire force was upon them, abandoned their camp, of which the 7th Indiana took possession, and also of the town. Capt. Skelton wanted the rest of the command to believe that the attack on the left was made by Gen. Grierson, so they would readily obey the order to charge when given. While pondering how he could best accomplish that purpose, a Lieutenant rode up to him and said, "Captain, don't you think we have got into a hell of a tight place?" The Captain ordered him back to his place, saying he would hear something on the left pretty soon. The Lieutenant asked if Gen. Grierson was advancing from that direction, and the Captain said yes. It was whispered through the ranks that Grierson was coming up on the left. When the firing commenced in that direction, the men believing reinforcements had come up, cheerfully obeyed the command to "charge." A prisoner reported their numbers at seven hundred, two hundred of whom were old soldiers, and the remainder conscripts.

A large amount of Quartermaster and Commissary stores, four hundred and fifty new English carbines and rifles, a large amount of artillery ammunition, a train of fifty cars, and two hundred and fifty wagons were captured. The most of the wagons were the same captured from Gen. Sturges, in June, 1864, at the battle of Brice's-cross-roads. Col. Kargé, learning of the capture of Verona, marched the rest of the brigade to that place and ordered the buildings containing army stores to be fired. All of the buildings except two or three, contained stores for the rebel army, and all except three were burned. The wagons were placed beside the buildings and destroyed with them. The shells, when the fire reached them, began exploding, the noise of which sounded like a furious cannonading. Gen. Grierson, several miles distant, hearing it, and believing Col. Kargé was engaged with the enemy, formed and kept the other brigades in line of battle till morning, when he moved to the town and learned the real state of facts.

After burning all the Confederate Government property, and destroying the railroad for several miles, Grierson, with his entire force, returned to Harrisburg.

While Col. Kargé was moving on Verona, Lieut. Col. Funk, with the Eleventh Illinois, went to Old Town, and burned the bridge and a long trestle-work over the creek.

On the morning of the 26th, Gen. Grierson marched from Harrisburg for Okolona, the Third Brigade following the railroad, burning the bridges and trestle-work, and tearing up the track, and cutting the telegraph wires, to Shannon, where it captured a train of cars, containing one hundred new wagons, and a large

147

quantity of quarter-masters' and commissary stores, intended for Forrest's army, all of which were burned. The First and Third Brigades took the usual road to Okolona, crossed the Tombigbee river at night and camped near it.

At Shannon, the Third Brigade was relieved by the Second, which proceeded along the railroad, destroying it as they went; while the other brigades, following the public road, passed through Okolona, and camped four miles beyond at Chawappa creek.

At Okolona a small body of rebels were encountered and some skirmishing ensued, in which the rebels were compelled to retire.

A messenger was captured with a dispatch to the commander of the post, stating that he would be reinforced by thirteen hundred infantry from Mobile. A telegraph operator, accompanying the expedition, cut the wire, and applying a small instrument, intercepted dispatches from General Dick Taylor and Maj.-Gen. Gardiner, to the commanding officer at Egypt station, ordering him to hold that post at every hazard.

Gen. Grierson rightly conjectured from the dispatches, that reinforcements were being hurried forward to that point, and early on the morning of the 28th, marched rapidly toward Egypt, where he opportunely arrived, and captured a rebel stockade just as a train with the expected reinforcements came in sight. It devolved on the First Brigade, it being in the advance, to capture the stockade.

The Second New Jersey was formed in front, and the Seventh Indiana in its rear in supporting distance, with orders to shoot down any officer, or man, who attempted to run. The Second New Jersey moved toward the stockade, and when at short range, the rebels opened a severe fire on them. They halted, afraid both to advance or retreat, and for a brief time they sat on their horses, helpless targets fort he rebels to shoot at. An Aid of Gen. Grierson rode up, and ordered them to dismount, which they did, and led by the Aid, charged on the stockade.

The officers in command of it, seeing that reinforcements were cut off, surrendered.

When the attack on the stockade commenced, there was a train of fourteen cars, and a platform car with four pieces of artillery, that had come from the north, standing on the track. There were indications that it was about to move. Gen. Grierson, taking the

Seventh Indiana and Fourth Missouri, charged upon it, and pressed it so closely, that the engineer was compelled to detach the fourteen cars, and make his escape with the locomotive and platform car of artillery.

Lieut. Dumont, with his squadron, by order of Capt. Elliott, burned the detached cars, that were heavily loaded with clothing and other army supplies, and pursued and captured the rebels who were attempting to escape from them to the woods.

The detachments of the Seventh Indiana and Fourth Missouri, led by Capt. S. L. Woodward, Gen. Grierson's Adjutant General, pursued the retreating locomotive and artillery; the latter throwing shells, which were replied to by the carbines and revolvers of the former.

After an exciting chase of about a mile, two trains of cars, loaded with reinforcements under General Gardiner, were seen approaching from the south, the fugitive engine and artillery from the first train, backing up in front of them. Capt. Woodward was ordered to tear up the track, to prevent the approach of the trains. There was nothing with which to obstruct the road, and the hatchets carried by the men were not sufficient to break the spikes. Capt. Skelton, therefore, ordered all the men to get on one side of the track, and taking hold of the rails succeeded in wrenching a portion of it loose, and threw it off the embankment, just as the train with reinforcements came up.

The rebels got off the train, and formed behind a fence, in a cornfield.

Capt. Skelton was sent forward with a skirmish line to ascertain their numbers. As he was advancing, the rebels opened a brisk fire on his lines.

One of his men had a part of the brim of his cap shot off. He cooly took it off, and holding it up, said, "that was pretty d—m close." Another man, hearing the remark, and having his hat-band shot off, held up his hat and said, "that is a d—m sight closer."

Capt. Skelton reported that the rebels were at least three hundred strong. The two detachments of the Seventh Indiana and Fourth Missouri participating in the attack, numbered but one hundred men. Notwithstanding, Capt. Elliott ordered a charge. After proceeding but a short distance, Capt. Henky, of the Fourth Missouri, fell, when it was discovered that there was a ditch in

149

front of the rebels, which rendered it impossible to proceed further. The rebels opened a severe fire, and killed two men of the Seventh Indiana, and shot down twenty-eight horses. Capt. Elliott then withdrew his command, and succeeded in getting away all of the wounded and dismounted men.

The entire loss of the Seventh in the affair, was two killed, eleven wounded, and twenty-eight horses killed and disabled.

The squadron of Lieut. Dumont burned a train, and captured forty-seven prisoners, among them a Lieut. Colonel.

Gen. Grierson, in this engagement, captured a stockade and its garrison, numbering eight hundred men. Brig. Gen. Gohlston, the commander of the post, was killed, also a Colonel, whose name was not learned. The federal loss was fifteen killed, and seventy wounded.

Gen. Grierson, before leaving Egypt, cut the telegraph wire, and sent false dispatches, that caused the rebels to send troops to points he did not intend to visit.

After burying the dead, and making provisions for the care of the wounded, who could not be taken along, the entire command left Egypt on the same day of the engagement, marched westward, and camped for the night near Houston.

On the morning of the 29th, Gen. Grierson dispatched a detachment in the direction of Pontotoc, and another toward West Point, on the Mobile and Ohio railroad, for the purpose of deceiving the rebels as to the real course he intended to take.

On the return of the detachments, the Seventh Indiana burned the bridges across the Hulka river, and the entire command taking a south-westwardly direction, toward the Memphis and Jackson railroad, camped that night at Hohenlinden.

Early on the morning of the 30th, the command continued its march, and camped at night at Bellefontaine.

During the day, a wretch by the name of Capt. Tom Ford, whose business for two years had been to hunt down Union men with blood hounds, was captured, and confessed to having hung several Union men. He managed to escape from the guards.

From Bellefontaine a detachment was sent in the direction of Starksville to threaten the Mobile and Ohio railroad, and Capt. Beckwith, of the Fourth Iowa Cavalry, with one hundred and fifty men, went to Bankston, arriving there at midnight and taking the inhabitants completely by surprise.

At this place the rebel government had a large cloth and leather manufactory, that gave employment to five hundred men. This factory turned out one thousand yards of cloth and two thousand pairs of shoes, daily. Its destruction would materially affect the resources of the rebel government. The torch was applied, and the establishment, with a large amount of clothes and shoes, destroyed. The following anecdote will show how completely the town was taken by surprise: After the factory had been fired, the superintendent of the works made his appearance in night attire, and seeing the soldiers sitting around and making no effort to stop the conflagration, and taking them to be the operatives, he threatened to arrest the night watches, and wanted to know "why in h—l they made no effort to stop the fire." Capt. Beckwith, seeing his mistake, quietly remarked, that as it was a cold night, he thought he would have a little fire. "H—l and damnation," exclaimed the superintendent, in a towering rage, "would you burn the factory to make a fire to warm by?" Then, for the first time, noticing the Captain's uniform, and that the supposed operatives were armed men, the fact that the "Yanks" had arrived, broke on his mind, and his utter amazement on making the discovery, was as comical to witness, as it had been a moment before to see his anger.

On the 31st, at 9 o'clock in the morning, Capt. Beckwith rejoined the main column, that had been on the march since 6 o'clock in the morning.

At 11 o'clock in the forenoon, the command reached Lodi. At that place two thousand bushels of wheat were burned, and eight hundred and ninety fat hogs, intended for Hood's army, were captured. They were driven in front of the army for several miles, and were the occasion for an infinite variety of jests and remarks, in which Gen. Grierson participated. It being found that they impeded the march, they were driven into a large pen, constructed for the purpose, and killed by the men with their sabres. Rails were piled on them and set on fire.

Col. Kargé, with the First Brigade, preceding the main column, reached Winona, on the Memphis and Jackson railroad, where he cut the telegraph and intercepted a dispatch, making inquiries respecting the movements of Wirt Adams, at Canton.

From Winona, the entire command, excepting the Third Iowa Cavalry, marched to Middletown and camped.

The Third Iowa, commanded by Col. Noble, went north to Grenada, with orders to destroy all the rebel government property at that place, and rejoin the command at Benton.

On New Year's Day, 1865, the main column marched south on the Benton road, and camped at night at Lexington, while the Third Brigade moved down the railroad, with orders to destroy it, burn the bridges, and rejoin the command at Benton.

On the 2d of January, Gen. Grierson passed through Lexington and took the road to Ebenezer, through which place he passed at noon. Some skirmishing occurred in his front, in which a rebel Lieut. was captured, who stated that there was a rebel force of eleven thousand men at Benton, awaiting Gen. Grierson's approach. This information served only to quicken Grierson's march for that place, which he reached at six o'clock in the evening without opposition, and found that the place was not occupied by the rebels.

The Third Brigade destroyed the railroad as far as Goodman's, from which place it marched to Franklin, where it encountered six hundred of Wirt Adams's cavalry, under Col. Woods. A spirited fight occurred, in which the rebels were defeated, and retired, leaving on the field twenty-five killed, among them a Major and a Captain, and twenty prisoners. The loss of Col. Osborn (Commander of the Third Brigade) was five killed and fourteen wounded. After the engagement, Colonel Osborn continued his march, and reached the main command at Benton, at ten o'clock at night.

Col. Noble had been equally successful in his march on Grenada. He destroyed twenty-five miles of railroad, dashed into the town, taking it completely by surprise, captured and destroyed fourteen engines and a large machine shop, set fire to several buildings containing quarter-masters' and commissary stores, twenty cases of Enfield rifles, intended for the arming of the militia, and a large amount of fixed ammunition. The Col. visited the printing office of the "Greanada Picket," and glancing over the columns of the previous day's issue, read an article, stating that Grierson's army had been defeated on the Mobile and Ohio railroad, and his columns were flying in dismay back to Memphis. The Colonel ordered the establishment to be burned. He then joined Gen. Grierson, in safety, at Benton.

On the 3d, Gen. Grierson marched to Mechanicsburg, arriving there at dark.

On the 4th, he reached Clear creek, at five o'clock in the afternoon.

Here, at sundown, the evening gun at Vicksburg, was heard, and elicited from the weary command hearty cheers. At this point, the command was met, pursuant to request of Gen. Grierson, sent by a couple of scouts a day or two before, with rations and forage from Vicksburg.

The next day, the command marched through a cold, drenching rain, to Vicksburg, arriving there about two o'clock in the afternoon, where it was welcomed by hearty cheers from thousands of persons gathered by the road-side, who had heard of its safe arrival.

Thus terminated one of the most successful raids of the war. The damage done to the rebels by destroying their supplies was incalculable, and contributed materially to the dismemberment of Hood's army.

Gen. Grierson displayed military talent of a high order. He moved rapidly, and by having portions of his command appear at different points at the same time, so confused the rebels, that they did not know where to concentrate against him.

At Brice's-cross-roads, with dismounted cavalry he resisted infantry; but in this expedition, he accomplished feats with cavalry, in charging and capturing a stockade, heavily garrisoned, and in chasing away railroad trains, with large reinforcements, the possibilities of which had never been dreamed.

His marching was so rapid, that he frequently reached places in advance of rebel couriers carrying information of his movements. At other times, messengers had but given information of his approach, when his columns would be charging through the town. His humane treatment of his prisoners was equal to his courage. He compelled rebel citizens to contribute clothing and blankets, to protect them from the inclemency of the weather.

In this raid, the Seventh Indiana bore an honorable part, and was complimented by Gen. Grierson for its bravery and efficiency. On the 8th of January, the squadrons of Captains Skelton and B. F. Bales left Vicksburg on transports, and reached Memphis on the 10th. The remainder of the detachment left on the 10th by steamboats, and arrived at Memphis on the 12th of January.

The guerrillas were getting troublesome on the west bank of the Mississippi, in Arkansas. The rebel Colonel, McGee, had quite a force at Mound City.

The commanding officer at Memphis determined to break up the rendezvous at that place.

Accordingly, Capt. Moore of the Seventh Indiana Cavalry, in command of detachments from the Seventh Indiana, First Mississippi Rifles and Second Wisconsin Cavalry, numbering in all two hundred men, pursuant to orders, embarked on a steamboat, a little below Fort Pickering, on the evening of the 20th of January, and steamed down the river a few miles, when the boat put about, passed Memphis and went up the river several miles, and stopped on the Arkansas side of the river.

At day-break the next morning, the command disembarked and marched for Mound City.

Capt. Skelton, who accompanied the expedition voluntarily, or, to use his own language, "just for fun," took command of the advance guard.

The advance was dressed in rebel uniforms, and on arriving at Mound City, dashed through the town, yelling, "Yanks! Yanks!"

When a mile or so from the town, they slackened their speed to a slow walk. They were soon overtaken by rebels from the town, who were pretending to be citizens, and believing Capt. Skelton and his men to be genuine rebels, had no hesitancy in coming up with them. As they did so, in squads of three or four, they were captured and their concealed revolvers taken from them. In this manner thirty prisoners were taken.

From the prisoners, Capt. Skelton learned the location of the rebel camp at Marion. Sending his prisoners to the main command, he pushed on rapidly toward that place, and soon arrived at their camp without being discovered. He galloped back to Capt. Moore and asked for twenty additional men, with which to charge the rebels. This was refused. Capt. Skelton then asked for ten men, and that also, was refused. Capt. Moore then gave command for his force to form in line, in so loud a voice that the rebels heard it; and that was the first intimation they had of the presence of an enemy.

Capt. Moore, although a brave man, and a good officer, lacked the dash, so essential to the successful operations of cavalry, but which was possessed in so high a degree by Capt. Skelton.

The latter, disgusted with the course of Capt. Moore, dashed back to the advance guard, and with only ten men, boldly charged into the enemy's camp. The rebels, thrown into the greatest confusion by their complete surprise, broke and fled in all directions, Capt. Skelton and his men hotly pursuing. Capt. Skelton after following a squad of five rebels for a mile found none of his men with him but "Jimmy" Graydon, as he was called, a small boy of fifteen years of age, but with courage equal to any man. His full name was James Wier Graydon. The rebels separated into two squads, three going in one direction and two in another. Capt. Skelton followed the three, and "Jimmy" the two. The mud and water thrown by the horses in the mad chase through a swamp, almost concealed the riders from view. The horse of one of the rebels, that Capt. Skelton was pursuing, stumbled and fell, and threw its rider completely under the mud and water. This one proved to be a rebel pay-master, with a large amount of money. Capt. Skelton kept on after the other two, who stopped and surrendered after going a short distance further. The Captain disarmed his prisoners, before they discovered that he was alone, and took them back to the pay-master, who was emerging from the mud and water. The latter, seeing the Captain was alone, started to run, but an ominous movement of the Captain's arm, decided him to surrender. After going a short distance, one of the prisoners asked Captain Skelton where his men were. The Captain replied that he saw all there were. "Hell!" exclaimed the prisoner, "I thought the woods were full of Yanks." After traveling about a mile, Captain Skelton met Jimmy Graydon, coming through the woods, crying, because, by firing his revolver at too long a range, he had allowed the rebels he was pursuing, to escape. The disappointment of not getting them vexed him sorely.

Capt. Moore's command took possession of the rebel camp and partook of breakfast, already prepared, when the rebels were so unceremoniously driven from it. The exercise of the morning gave the men a good appetite, and their relish for the breakfast was not lessened by the variety of jokes cracked at the expense of the "Johnnies."

After destroying the rebel government property, the command returned to Memphis, having been eminently successful.

LEE ROY WOODS, 1st Sergeant, 1st Lieutenant, Co. E

156

CHAPTER IX.

Louisiana Expedition.

The Expedition goes down the Mississippi River to Grand Lake —March Through the Swamps to Bastrop, La.—Negroes Flock to the Command, and Perish of the Cold—A Negro Mother Throws away her Child—Sufferings of the Soldiers—March to Hamburg, and Gains Landing—Return to Memphis.

In a few days after the return of the regiment from the expedition mentioned in the last chapter, another cavalry expedition was fitted out at Memphis, and placed under the command of Col. Osborn. It consisted of detachments from the regiments of two brigades.

The First Brigade, including five hundred men of the Seventh Indiana Cavalry, under the command of Major S. E. W. Simonson, was commanded by Colonel J. P. C. Shanks.

On the 26th of January, 1865, the expedition embarked at Memphis, on transports, and steamed down the Mississippi river. It disembarked a few miles above Grand Lake, Arkansas.

The extra rations and ammunition were strapped on Pack mules, and everything being in readiness, the command started toward the interior over the low, flat country.

On the first day's march, it reached a small stream. It was reported that the crossing there was held by a considerable force of rebels. To surprise and capture them, the column marched from the road through the timber and advanced toward the crossing, with extreme caution, and after an almost breathless march of a mile, the 7th Indiana having the advance, arrived at the stream in time to see two men on the opposite side gallop away.

The stream was crossed by means of an old rickety ferry, which was on the opposite bank. A Negro, soon appearing at the ferry, in obedience to orders, brought it across.

157

When the crossing was effected, the command pursued its march through a dreary, uninhabited country to Bastrop, Louisiana. From that place it marched north, crossed Bayou Bartholomew River, and went to Hamburg, in Arkansas. Between these points the country was execrable. Human beings could not and did not inhabit it, except in an occasionally dry spot. It was given over by Nature, and Nature's God, for habitation, to frogs, lizards, snakes and alligators. In such a country it was impossible to get subsistence for man or beast. Nearly all of the extra rations transported on the pack mules, were lost with those animals, as they sank out of sight in the mud and water of the swamps. The ammunition was lost in the same way. But that did not amount to anything as there was no enemy to use it on. It was pitiable to see the poor animals try to extricate themselves while they were all the time sinking deeper in the mire. They would cast appealing looks at the men and utter piteous groans.

At Hamburg the country was better. Some forage for the horses and food for the men were obtained. At this point the Negroes began flocking from the plantations, to the command, and as it advanced, hundreds of them were following in the rear and on the flanks. They were half clad wretches, indeed, many of them were almost entirely destitute of clothing. Men, women, and children, without a moment's consideration or preparation, left their huts and the plantations, and followed the command not knowing where they were going, or what they were to do. They were of the most ignorant and degraded of their race. Having lived all their lives in a God-forsaken country, they had not the means of gaining the information of others of their race in more favored portions of the South. When asked where they were going, they invariably replied, "Donno, Massa." When asked what they intended to do, they gave the same laconic answer. For the privilege of following the command, they cheerfully rendered menial services for the officers and men. Nearly every private had a servant. Even Negro women, with sucking babes trudged along by the marching column. Many of them finding their infantile charges burdensome, left them by the road-side to die. The soldiers had taken pity on a wench with a young babe, and placed her and the child on a mule. In crossing a muddy creek, the mule stumbled and threw the mother and child into the mud and water. The mother fell on the child and buried it beneath the water. Hastily rising, and lifting it up, she saw it choking and gasping, and after looking at it a moment, threw it back into the water, and exclaimed: Dah, go to yar Jesus, yar better off in his hands, than yah'r in mine," and abandoned it. A soldier sprang into the water, but before he could recover it, it drowned. Many of the women were advanced in pregnancy and gave birth to children by the roadside. After a short time they would be seen with the command, but without their offspring. What they had done with them was easily guessed. Some of the Negroes perished of the cold and exposure. Their dead bodies were found in the morning where they had lain down the night before, without blankets, to sleep, but not to wake in this life.

The ground most of the way was exceedingly treacherous. The surface looked firm and solid, but underneath a thin crust was quick-sand and mud. While riding along in fancied security, the horses broke through the crust, and precipitated their riders over their heads.

The horses, by the excessive labor of traveling through such a country without forage, were reduced to skeletons, and many of them were abandoned, the unfortunate riders being obliged to walk until they captured a mule.

From Hamburg the command marched to De Bastrop, crossed the Bayou Bartholomew on a steamboat, and marched to Gain's Landing on the Mississippi river, where it embarked on steamboats and returned to Memphis.

It is impossible to divine the purpose of this expedition. The projector of it must have been utterly ignorant of the nature of the country through which the command passed. No armed force ever had, and never could have occupied it. It was utterly worthless from any possible military point of view.

JAMES A. PRICE, Adjutant, Co. F, S

CHAPTER X.

GUARDING RAILROAD AND SCOUTING.

The regiment moves along the railroad to Lagrange—News of the assassination of President Lincoln—Death of Lieut. Skirvin—Mass meeting of citizens and soldiers—Speech of Col. Browne.

The rapid succession of victories attending the federal arms, in the Spring of 1865, foretold the speedy overthrow of the rebellion. Sherman had accomplished his famous "march to the sea," captured Savannah, and marched north into the Carolinas; Fort Fisher had fallen, and the rebel army of the West and South, under Joseph E. Johnston, was cooped up at Raleigh, North Carolina; Gen. Robert E. Lee had surrendered with his entire army.

At Memphis the only enemy to be encountered were the Guerrillas, who were still troublesome. The cavalry at Memphis was distributed along the Memphis and Charleston railroad, to guard and repair it.

The 7th Indiana cavalry was at LaFayette Station on that road, when the intelligence of the surrender of Gen. Lee was received. The news was hailed with the wildest delight by the soldiers. It was known that negotiations were pending for the surrender of Gen. Joseph E. Johnston's army to Gen. Sherman. The soldiers were already forming their plans for the future on being mustered out of the service, which event they expected would occur in a short time. Discipline was relaxed and the camps were given up to rejoicings. The sutlers were permitted to bring beer into the camp for the men.

In the midst of their jollification, the news of the assassination of President Lincoln was received. A thunder-clap from a cloudless sky could not have produced greater consternation. The terrible intelligence passed rapidly from person to person, and the smile of gladness, playing on their faces a moment before, was supplanted by looks of amazement and horror. The merry-making was instantly stopped, and the men separating into small groups, talked in undertones of the great calamity that had befallen the country. Tears trickled down the faces of men who had never been known to weep before. The camp wore a funeral-like appearance, and, an unnatural stillness crept over it. There was great solicitude as to the effect of the death of the President would have on military operations. Would it prolong the war, and necessitate more bloody battles?

There was in Northern Mississippi a semi-guerrilla chieftain, by the name of Capt. Fort, who made it his business to attack railroad trains and scouting parties. He operated about North Mt. Pleasant in Mississippi. Two or three times a week a scouting expedition was sent to that place to look after him.

On the morning of the 3d of April, 1865, Lieut. Jacob Skirvin of company D, with about thirty men, consisting of details from the various companies of the regiment, left camp at Lafayette Station, and proceeded towards Mt. Pleasant. He came upon the camp of Capt. Fort, a mile southwest of the town. The two parties discovered each other at about the same time. Lieut. Skirvin at first thought the rebels were a party from his own regiment, that left camp at about the same time he did. He, a moment afterward, discovered his mistake, but the slight delay gave the rebels time to make some preparations for defense. He then, with the advance guard, consisting of only five or six men charged into the camp of the rebels, and was received with a volley from behind the trees, to which the rebels sprang, not having time to mount their horses. The Lieutenant was struck with two balls in the breast and mortally wounded. Those who were with him said, he with difficulty kept his saddle, and spurred his horse up to the tree where Fort himself was, and reeling from side to side in the saddle, his eyes almost closed in death, put his revolver around the tree and tried to shoot Fort, but before he could discharge his pistol, Fort shot him with his revolver in the face, when he dropped dead from his horse. Two of the men with him were killed and another badly wounded. The main command came up, but on seeing Lieut. Skirvin and two of the men with him fell, broke away and fled. Some stragglers returned to camp with the news of the disaster, when Capt. Moore hastily mounted and went to the relief of Skirvin's party.

Before the Captain arrived at the scene of the fight, Fort and his men had withdrawn. Some citizens had taken Lieut. Skirvin's body to a farm-house, half a mile distant, and carefully washed the blood and dust from his face and person. He was a fine looking man, and so recent and sudden had been his death, his face wore nearly its usual ruddy appearance, and it was difficult to realize that he was dead.

The bodies were placed in a wagon and taken to camp. Lieut. Skirvin's was sent to Memphis and buried in the military cemetery, with the honors of war.

Lieut. Skirvin had participated with the regiment in all its expeditions and battles, and in every instance had proved himself a good officer and a brave man. He was wounded in the sabre charge, on the evening of February 22d, 1864, at Ivy Farm, on Sooy Smith's raid to West Point, Mississippi. His loss was deeply regretted by the entire regiment. George Patrick and Hiram J. Kail, of company D, were also killed.

About the first of January, the regiment went to Lagrange, Tennessee.

All of the Confederate armies had at that time surrendered. Paroled prisoners were constantly passing through the town, on the way to their homes in Tennessee and Kentucky. The members of the regiment were jubilant with the expectation of soon being mustered out of the service and being permitted to return to their homes.

Gen. Washburn had resigned, and was succeeded by Gen. Smith.

On turning over the command, Gen. Washburn accompanied Gen. Smith to Lagrange, where an impromptu meeting assembled, composed of Federal and ex-Confederate soldiers, ladies and gentlemen from Memphis and Lagrange, and, Negroes. The assemblage was quite large and reminded one of old times.

Gen. Washburn addressed the meeting in a speech of an hour's duration. In his remarks he predicted that the Negroes would be given the right of the elective franchise, and to hold office. His prophecy came true. He was followed by Gen. J. P. C. Shanks, in a brief speech.

Next, and last, Col. Browne was called out, and appeared on the stand amid a storm of applause. He delivered the following extemporaneous little speech, which was received by the listeners with delight:

163

My Fellow Citizens: It was the custom of the ancients to preserve the best of the wine to the last of the feast. But that order has been reversed to-day, as you have called me out to throw my little speech in the shade of the distinguished ones who have preceded me. If it had been left to my own judgment, I would have been commanding every one in this country for thirty years past. I left the South thirty years ago, and have been living in the North ever since, but I speak to you as an American citizen. I left you in boyhood; I came back to you in the full vigor of manhood, and found you in arms against your brothers, against those who never entertained one unkindly feeling against you in the world. I inquired why it was. Because, I was informed, we had elected a sectional President; and, that we proposed to interfere with your domestic institutions; that you were going to whip us, and play the devil generally. Now, suppose Mr. Breckenridge had been elected, and the North had rebelled. I do not think there was an abolitionist in the North who would not have rallied around the banner of our country and said to those discontents: "you must submit to the Constitution and the Government," and we would have been with you in that controversy.

When the leaders of the rebellion started to go out of the Union, they went very much as the dog which tried to jump the well in two jumps—he took one jump and then caved. You took one jump and then went under. The result is, that the institution of slavery has gone clean under, and you need not attempt to hunt up the fossils. Our Government did not use the war as a measure for destroying slavery, but they used slavery as a means of destroying the rebellion. You sent your sons and husbands to the war, and asked God to protect them while they were fighting to destroy the Government. The North did the same thing for the purpose of rescuing it.

I must say a word to the Negro. You have got to work, and if you expect to be respected, you must respect yourselves. If you commit murder, you will be hung the same as any other man. This war has disclosed a few facts; one of them is that this continent is ours, that the

164

American Union must grow and extend from the frozen seas to the Gulf of Mexico—until it takes in the Western Continent.

The ludicrous parts of the speech were vociferously cheered. The Negroes were delighted with the remarks addressed to them and promised to do everything the Colonel recommended.

The men, in their hopes to be speedily mustered out of the service, were doomed to disappointment.

The regiment soon after entered upon a long and tedious journey by water and land to Texas, the history of which will be given in the next chapter.

EDWARD CALKINS, Sergeant, 1st Lieutenant, Co. B, H

Chapter XI.

By Land and Water to Texas.

Trip Down the Mississippi, and Up the Red River to Alexandria—Amusement of Shooting Alligators, Southern Etiquette—Military Execution for Desertion—Departure for Texas—A Long, Dreary March Through the Wilderness—Snakes, Bugs, Toads, Lizards, and all manner of Creeping Things— Arrival at Hempstead—Brutality of Gen. Custer—Consolidation of the Regiment.

The regiment marched from Lagrange to Memphis, where it embarked on four steamboats, on the evening of June 17, 1865.

On the 18th, in the morning, the boats swung loose from the wharf, and steamed down the broad Mississippi river.

Aside from being somewhat crowded, and being obliged to halt occasionally to assist a boat off a sand bar, the trip down the river was a pleasant one.

The fleet passed Helena, Arkansas and Napoleon, the latter situated at the mouth of the Arkansas river. Both of these places had been almost entirely destroyed by the war, and were, during hostilities, places of resort for bands of guerrillas, that occasionally interrupted the navigation of the river, by firing on passing boats. It steamed by "Millikin's Bend," the scene of a bloody conflict, fought June 6, 1863, between the Colored troops and the rebels, in which the latter were defeated. The overflowings of the river were rapidly washing away the earthworks, which the Negroes so gallantly defended.

The fleet arrived at Vicksburg in the evening. Its high hills rose gloomily in the darkness. Two years before, on the approach of such a fleet, they would have blazed from base to summit, and would have been rocked as in a cradle, from the furious cannonade that would have belched from the guns of the fortifications; but now all was peaceful and quiet.

167

The boats lay at the wharf during the night, to take in coal. Before daylight the next morning, they were pursuing their journey down the river.

At Natchez, the fleet stopped awhile, and the men availed themselves of the opportunity to mail letters to their friends.

From Natchez it proceeded to the mouth of the Red River, where it lay at anchor through the night, the pilots being afraid to continue the journey in the dark, they not being acquainted with that stream. Early the next morning we were again under way toward the headquarters of that great river.

The monotony of the journey was relieved by the alligators that abound in the river. They wallowed in the mud on the banks, sometimes looking like old logs, or swam across the bow of the boats and along side of them. They were of all sizes, from old ones ten or twelve feet in length, to young ones just commencing the world on their own responsibility. They were very dignified in their deportment; when one had occasion to cross the river, he managed to pass ten or twenty feet in front of the boat, the near approach of which would not accelerate his speed a particle. They swam without making a ripple on the water, with their heads only above the surface. It occurred to some genius among the men, to try what affect lead would have on the mailed denizens of the river, and he *accidentally* discharged his carbine at one, and was astonished to see the ball glance from the scaly body without attracting, in the least, the attention of the alligator.

This little incident suggested to the rest of the men the idea of making similar experiments. Accordingly they got their carbines and kept a sharp lookout for alligators. They did not have to wait long. Ahead a short distance, a tolerably good sized one was crossing to the opposite bank, and passed in front of the boat but a few feet from it. The men commenced cracking away at it. It was struck several times, but the balls glanced off harmlessly; the alligator acted as if nothing unusual had occurred, and did not so much as wink when the balls struck it. One day, when all was quiet, someone exclaimed, "Alligator!" "Where, where?" responded a dozen voices. "Yonder in the mud on the bank" was the answer. Every eye was strained in the direction indicated, but nothing could be seen but an old log as it was supposed to be. But by watching it closely, it was seen to slowly roll from side to side. At first it was believed to be a log, and that the motion

168

was given it by the flowing of the river; but a nearer approach disclosed the outlines of the villainous looking head of a mammoth alligator. Nearly every man was firing at it with his carbine or revolver. It was probably struck fifty times before the boat was out of gunshot range, but so far as any outward manifestations were concerned, it was totally oblivious to the presence of a steamboat loaded with soldiers. It kept on rolling, as if rendered too blissfully happy by a meal on dog, with a young Black for desert, articles of diet of which alligators are said to be extremely fond, to notice worldly things.

Even shooting alligators became stale, and would have been entirely abandoned had not an order been made prohibiting it. After that, it was astonishing how many carbines went off by pure accident, when an alligator was in sight.

There was little in the appearance of the country on either bank of the river to cheer the traveler. The country to within fifty miles of Alexandria is low and flat, covered with timber, and a large part of it overflowed with water.

On approaching Alexandria, the prospect improved. The ground rises in places to gentle elevations, and plantation residences dot the country. On the evening of June 23, 1865, the fleet landed at Alexandria, Louisiana, and the troops disembarked, and went into camp on a sugar plantation at the edge of town. The sun beamed down on the shadeless camp terribly hot. Awnings, both for the men and horses, were constructed of poles and brush brought from the woods, which measurably relieved the suffering caused by the intense heat.

Alexandria, before the war, was a small city of about five thousand inhabitants. It acquired some historic interest by being given over to the torch, and the greater and best portion of it destroyed by fire, by Gen. Banks, when he left it on the 14th of May, 1863, on his retreat from his disastrous expedition to Shreveport. At the time the regiment was there, it contained but about five hundred inhabitants.

Old chimneys not yet fallen, and ruined walls, marked the site of former business blocks, or of palatial residences.

But the greatest interest that centers there is the fact, that only three miles from the town, was located the military academy of which Gen. W. T. Sherman was President, on the outbreak of the war. As Gen. Sherman acquired a fame as lasting as history itself, any institution with which he was connected will always attract a lively interest.

Above the city a short distance, were the Red river rapids, which were damned up to make the water deep over them so the gunboats, that accompanied Gen. Banks, on his Red river expedition, and had gone above them, could get over them, after the defeat of Banks at the battle of Mansfield.

Opposite Alexandria and across the river is Pineville, a small village, deriving its name from the groves of large pines that surround it.

There, also, were two forts constructed by the rebels, when they had possession of the country.

The country around Alexandria is the finest and most fertile in the State of Louisiana, and was known as the sugar and cotton region.

The planters were wealthy and haughtily aristocratic, as the following incident will show. Some officers, one day, called at a splendid plantation residence, to pay their respects to the proprietor. They were met at the door by a Negro servant, whom they told to inform the master that some officers called to see him. The servant soon reappeared with a silver salver, and bowing profoundly, held it out. The officers did not know the meaning of this kind of etiquette, and looked inquiringly from one to another for an explanation. One of them said afterwards that he thought the Negro wanted to take up a collection, and was mortified to think he had not a cent to contribute, not having been paid for several months. The spokesman of the party explained to the Negro that they had *simply* come to make a friendly call, and directed him to so inform the master of the establishment, and to say that they were waiting.

The servant disappeared, and soon an angered gentleman appeared at the door, and said, he was not surprised that Northern men were not sufficiently well bred to know that they were expected to send up their cards when they called on a gentleman. Of course the officers pretended to have understood all the time that cards were expected from them, but explained that not having been near a printing office for a long time, their supplies of cards were exhausted.

There were concentrated at Alexandria, destined for Houston,

170

Texas, about three thousand cavalry under the command of Maj. Gen. George A. Custer.

The time was spent at Alexandria, in drilling in the hot sun, fishing in the Red river, and in catching alligators. The men occasionally caught catfish weighing one hundred pounds and upwards.

Occasionally a baby alligator, from a foot and a half to two feet in length, got on dry land and was taken prisoner by the men. There were several such pets in the Seventh Indiana. Even full grown alligators, in making raids in search of food, got quite a distance from the water, and were attacked and killed by the soldiers.

Like all monsters, that seem invulnerable, they have their weak points, which when known, make them an easy prey to the hunter. These points are the eyes, and a certain spot in the back of the head. A ball entering either of these places will instantly kill them. As already stated, they have a peculiar fondness for dogs and Negroes. A bark of a dog near a bayou, will bring to the surface the heads of all the alligators in it. They leave the water, and crawl up behind Negro children, and by a peculiar stroke of their tails, knock them into their jaws.

A short time after the troops disembarked at Alexandria, a Negro laid down and went to sleep on some baggage near the brink of the river, and an alligator was discovered crawling out of the water, but a short distance from him, evidently intending to make a meal of him. The soldiers drove the alligator back into the river and awoke the Negro, who was seized with an almost mortal terror, on being informed of the danger he had so narrowly escaped.

There was a growing discontent among the soldiers at being sent further south, when, as they supposed, the war was over. This led to numerous desertions, in fact, the men deserted in squads and platoons. On several occasions nearly the whole command was called out at night, to prevent the threatened desertions of companies and of a regiment. Some of the men on this duty deserted, when attention was directed elsewhere. The dissatisfaction of the men was increased by the cruel treatment of General Custer. That General had won a good reputation in the east, as a fighting general. He was only twenty-five years of age, and had the usual egotism and self-importance of a young man.

171

He was a regular army officer, and had bred in him the tyranny of the regular army. He did not distinguish between a regular soldier and a volunteer. He did not stop to consider that the latter were citizens, and not soldiers by profession—men who had left their homes and families, to meet a crisis in the history of their country, and when the crisis was passed, they had the right to return to their homes. He had no sympathy in common with the private soldiers, but regarded them simply as machines, created for the special purpose of obeying his imperial will. Everything about him indicated the fop and dandy. His long yellow hair fell in ringlets on his shoulders. Everything in the regulations, that was gaudy, and tended only to excite vanity, he caused to be scrupulously observed.

His wife accompanied him on the march to Texas, and he compelled soldiers to perform menial services for her and himself, which was an express violation of the law.

A sergeant of the Second Wisconsin, and a private of the Fifth Illinois Cavalry, were court-martialed for desertion and sentenced to be shot. Gen. Custer, disregarding the earnest appeals of all the field officers of his command, determined to carry the sentence into effect.

The army was formed on three sides of a hollow square, faced inwards. Two coffins were placed near the center of the square, and fifteen feet apart.

Gen. Custer and staff took their positions in the center of the square, facing the open side. The provost guard that was to do the shooting, was formed about thirty feet in front of the coffins, facing the open side of the square.

The condemned men were placed in a cart, with their hands pinioned behind them, with each a white bonnet on, that was to be drawn over their eyes when the execution took place, entered from the open side at the right, and passed slowly around the square in front of each regiment, to the tune of the dead march. No one can know till they witness it, the feelings of horror, a military execution imposes!

Language, aided by the most vivid imagination, cannot portray the agony of mind, the condemned must suffer. Each step, and each roll of the muffled drum, admonish them that they are surely approaching their doom.

After reaching the left of the square, the condemned were

172

taken out of the cart, and each seated on a coffin, facing the provost guard, their legs lashed to the coffins, and the bonnets drawn over their eyes. The law requires that one gun fired by the provost guard shall be loaded with a blank cartridge. The guard are informed that one gun of the lot has no bullet in it; and, of course each man hopes that he has that gun. The provost marshal cautions the guard to take accurate aim, that the condemned may be saved unnecessary suffering by not being killed. He further has a selfish motive, for it his duty, should the condemned not be killed, to step up to him and complete the work with a revolver.

Gen. Custer had concluded to commute the punishment of one of the condemned to imprisonment for three years at the Dry Tortugas, Florida, but he kept it a secret from all except his provost marshal.

A moment before the execution, the provost marshal stepped up to the one whose sentence was commuted, to lead him away. He clapped his hand on him rather roughly, and the poor fellow, thinking he was shot, swooned away, and died a few days afterwards from the fright he received.

The provost marshal then gave the command: "Ready!" the click of the guns, as they were cocked, was heard by the entire command, who almost held their breaths, and who could hear their hearts throbbing against their bosoms. "Aim!" was the next command, and the guns were leveled at the condemned. After quite a pause, to enable the guard to get accurate aim, the command: "Fire!" rang out, and simultaneously the report of the rifles were heard. The blue smoke from the guns curled away, and the soldier who had such a longing to return to his wife and children, after an absence of years, that he braved death, in attempting to get home, pierced by several balls, fell back on his coffin, dead!

Each regiment was marched past the body, so every man could see it, and then returned to its quarters.

The execution was pronounced by the officers to have been barbarous. The frightening the soldier to death, under the pretense of commuting his sentence, was the refinement of cruelty.

The crime of which these men were guilty cannot be excused, and, in time of active war, they should have suffered death. They ought to have been punished as it was, but not with death. There is a vast difference in desertion in the face of an enemy, and desertion after a war is over, where soldiers are kept in the service simply to retain dandy officers like Custer, a little longer in authority. An officer who cannot distinguish between grades of crime is not fit to have authority over his fellow men.

The most horrible part of this proceeding is, the execution was in violation of law. Article 65 of the Articles of War, required, that before the death sentence could be carried into effect, the proceedings of the court martial should be submitted to the President of the United States for his approval. That was not done.

After waiting in vain to be paid off, previous to resuming the march, General Custer, on August 8, 1865, with his command, left Alexandria for Texas.

We give the history of this march in Gen. Browne's own language, as copied from his journal, which is well worth reading on account of the rich vein of humor that pervades it.

"*Tuesday, August 8th*:—All things being ready, we started on the morning of August 8th, on our ever-to-be-remembered expedition as an "army of observation" to Texas. Day had not broken, and the full, clear-faced moon threw out a resplendent shower of bright silvery light over the world. Its radiance danced "fantasies most beautiful" upon the muddy waters of the old river. Even burned and dilapidated Alexandria looked proud and majestic, but desolate amid her ruins. As I started I cast a look "behind me," to the old sugar field where our camp had been, but no tent stood upon its bosom. Our village of tents had melted from the face of the earth, like "snow flakes" beneath a "summer sun." A hearty shout went up from three thousand throats, and in a moment a long line of mounted cavalry, with sabres and carbines threaded through the sleeping town, and passed out of it forever. Farewell, Alexandria! Farewell, land of bayous, alligators, bugs, flies, mosquitoes, and graybacks.

Our route for the first few miles lay almost parallel with Red River, and over large level and abandoned cotton and sugar plantations. We then "tacked," in sailor phrase, "sou-west." Here, the road was for several miles, skirted on either side with hedges, resembling the wild rose of the north. In height, these hedges were full twelve feet, reaching far above our heads as we rode along. They were thickly matted, and I suppose neither bird or beast could pass through.

It looked beautiful, indeed, to see these long narrow aisles between the growing fence, and to see the banks of green on

174

either side, with here and there a modest white flower peeping half reluctantly from beneath the foliage. The weather was hot, the roads about one foot deep in fine dust and sand. We got dust in our eyes, dust in our mouths, dust in our ears, and, in fact, we were well nigh transformed into living sand-heaps.

Fifteen miles from Alexandria, we struck a bluff rising abruptly at the edge of the level plain. Up to this point we had scarcely seen a tree, or bush, but now we suddenly entered a thick and unbroken forest of pines; which grew upon a soil so barren, that ten acres of it would not raise a hill of beans. On this day we made a march of some twenty-five miles, and went into camp at 4 o'clock p.m., in a beautiful pine grove.

We had plenty of water, although it was taken from bayous and from a creek. But for millions of vermin, that were constantly fighting us, we slept well.

Wednesday, August 9th, 1865:—Reveille at two o'clock. We marched at four o'clock in the morning, and having made eleven miles, went into camp on a delightful little knoll, in a forest of tall and thrifty pines. Here we found the first good water in Louisiana, and it was in a little and nearly stagnant creek. The country, so far, is still flat, and has nothing but sand and pines. Deer, and other wild game, are abundant, and it is nothing uncommon to see an old buck scampering through the road by the side of our marching column. Once in ten miles we find a little cabin standing in a small clearing of a half acre. This patch is planted in melons, and sweet potatoes, or yams, and this cabin is occupied, as I observed in passing it, by a "lean, lank and bony" woman, of the color of clay, and by a half-dozen dirty and sickly-looking children.

Women and urchins stand about the door as we pass, and seem to be utterly bewildered. They can't imagine "whar in the devil all the 'Yanks' come from."

In the evening, inasmuch as we had made so short a march, I had regimental dress parade. It was, perhaps the only "Yankee parade" those old forests ever witnessed; as for me, it will be the last.

Thursday, August 10th:—Marched on the same time as yesterday, passed through the same kind of country. Pines before us, pines behind us, pines on each side of us, nothing but pines. Weather very hot. Water very scarce and bad. The little water we got was brackish and unfit for any use, except to be drank by soldiers. We made sixteen miles today, and pitched our tents again in the pine woods, (excuse me for writing so much about pines, sand, dust, bad water, and bugs, for this country affords no other subjects for the pen, and in other respects is so unpoetic, that to make a draft on imagination would totally ruin the brain of an ordinary man.)

Friday, August 11th:— Had no sleep last night. Was up till midnight drawing rations and forage, then went to bed to be bitten and stung, and scratched and kicked until 2 o'clock a.m., when the bugles blowed me out of bed, high and dry, by the morning reveille. The morning was pleasant, as every morning always is, but, oh, Lord! the noon of day blistered us delightfully.

Camped at noon at Annacoco creek, which afforded abundance of clear, running water. I dipped my canteen full of its "liquid," and took a good "swig" of the beverage with a keener relish than ever toper took his whisky toddy. I felt like serving out the balance of my time there.

Saturday, August 12th:—As on the previous days, we were up at 2 o'clock and started on the march at 4 o'clock a.m. The country was still "pine woods and sandy roads," without variableness or shadow of turning. This day we arrived, after a march of fifteen miles, at the Sabine river, which is the boundary between Texas and Louisiana. This river is navigable during six months of the year for a hundred miles above the point at which we struck it, although at this time it was not more than fifty yards wide, and the water is not more than ten feet deep at the deepest point. By looking at the map you will see the place at which we made the crossing; it is marked, "Bevil's Ferry," which is at the northeast corner of Newton county. At this place, (which is no place at all, but a river crossing), the rebels threw up a large and formidable earthwork to stop our forces, in the event they should have undertaken to cross into Texas. They had their "labor for their pains," as no Yankee was ever so foolish as to undertake to march an army through such a God-forsaken country as that between Alexandria and the Texas line.

Sunday, August 13th:—Lay quietly in camp on the Annacoco, until 4 o'clock p.m. The forenoon was employed in putting a pontoon bridge across the Sabine. On this day, at about 10 o'clock a.m., I crossed the river on horseback and stood for the

176

first time on the chivalric soil of the "Lone Star" State, Texas. I went some three or four miles through the woods to the nearest farmhouse, and found an original Texan. He had come to Texas in 1829, and fought in the Texan war of 1836, and in the war with Mexico in 1845. He was now too old to engage in the pastime of shooting men, and was, therefore, not engaged in the past rebellion, but I enjoyed more than two hours in hearing him relate, in the true backwoods style, the history of his earlier fights and escapes.

For nearly thirty years he had lived in the woods, exiled from civilized life, in a great measure, and today he is so far removed from everybody, that he stands a good chance of dying without his neighbors knowing him to be sick. I bought a bushel of excellent peaches and a melon or two from the old man, paid him in "greenbacks," and bid him a goodbye. He had never seen such money before, and seemed very anxious to know whether such currency would pay his taxes. Being assured that it would, he was happy, and so we left him.

On Sunday afternoon, we struck tents and were again on the march. We crossed the Sabine immediately, with our whole command, and unfurled, for the first time in four and a half years, the "Star-Spangled" banner in northeastern Texas. After crossing the river, we struck a low, flat and sandy country, with only an occasional patch fit for cultivation. The soil is starvation poor. The timber is oak, birch, pine, and magnolia. After traveling through this kind of country for some five miles, we suddenly struck the pine hills again, and on one of these ridges, at 9 o'clock p.m., we went into camp for the night.

Monday, Aug. 14th:—Started as usual at 4 o'clock in the morning, made some fifteen miles and went into camp near Faris' Mills on Cow Creek. Weather warm, roads dusty, no houses, woods all pine, water very scarce and bad. Pitched my tent in a "yaller jacket's" nest, got stung and swore blue blazes.

Tuesday, Aug. 15th:—Marched early again. Passed through the same kind of country, and camped on a very considerable sized frog-pond near the county seat of Jasper county, Texas. The country is almost an uninhabited wilderness. Land wretchedly poor and the people too poor to be wretched.

Wednesday, Aug. 16th:—Marched before daylight, and just as the sun was rising passed through the town of Jasper. This night we camped among the "Pines" again, near the Angelina river and about fifteen miles from its confluence with Neches river. At this place Capt. Moore of Gen. Custer's staff, left us, and went on rapidly to report for orders at Houston.

Thursday, Aug. 17th:—On this day we crossed the Angelina and Neches rivers. The first we forded and the latter we had to bridge with our pontoons. No good country yet. Pines and deer, bugs, snakes and gallinippers inhabit the whole face of the earth. The two rivers run through boundless pine forests, and have no good land about them. The whole face of the country to-day looks as if it was uninhabited by man, and as if even God himself had abandoned it. We camped in the woods after a short march, and enjoyed the usual luxury of being bitten almost to death by the infernal bugs.

Friday, Aug. 18th:—Marched out of the woods, into the woods, and through the woods, and camped, God only knows where. I could not find anybody during the whole day to inquire of where I was, so I can simply say that I was in the woods all day, and camped in the woods at night.

Saturday, Aug. 19th:—Marched a long, dry and weary march today. For twenty-seven long miles we were without water, and after making a march of that distance, we had to camp on a little dry run, and dig holes in it to catch water enough to fill our canteens—miserable water it was after we got it. This was the hardest day of the march, as our men and horses were nearly famished for water. They came very nearly pegging out. I thought a dozen times that I would have to take an ambulance, but I stuck it through. Just before going into camp, we struck a very fine farming country of four or five miles in width. One or two farms were indeed handsome. In any other part of the world, I could have lived on one of them, but there, I would not have taken one as a gift. I can say this of Texas generally. It is a very mean State.

Sunday, Aug. 20th:—Marched as usual in the morning at 4 o'clock, and made a distance of seventeen miles to Swartwoutz's Ferry on Trinity river. We forded the Trinity, and camped shortly after noon, immediately on its western bank. I put up my tent just at the edge of its steep bank, and about thirty feet above its waters. The river banks are very steep indeed. The water was very low when we crossed, but much of the year large sized side-wheel steamers pass for hundreds of miles above the Ferry.

178

This camp was named by the boys, "Camp Rattlesnake," as we killed several dozen of the largest size there. One could scarcely put his foot down without waking up some old rusty looking snake.

These snakes are generally very large, and were the most dangerous of all the various tribes that fill Texas. I killed one old fellow myself, with thirteen rattles on his tail, showing him to have been fourteen years old. His snakeship was near six feet in length and was *very large for his size*. Dr. Roether pulled out his teeth, and has them for a Texan keepsake. We had a snaky time of it while in camp, you may be sure. Swartwoutz Ferry is a little known town as well as a river crossing, but the town, part of it, is too little to mention. We remained in this camp over night and dreamed of snakes; and on

Monday, Aug. 21st:—at 4 o'clock we were in our saddles and off again. Here the country began to improve very decidedly. Passed by some fine plantations and here and there a very commodious farm-house. We made another long march of twenty-seven miles without water, and camped for the night on a little dried up run, that afforded but little to drink for either man or beast. On this day we also passed through two beautiful villages, Cold Springs and Waverly, the only towns worth the mentioning, I had yet seen in Texas. They were not large, but showed both thrift and taste. I noticed also in each, neat churches, and a neat schoolhouse, neither of which had I before seen in Texas, although up to this time I had traveled some one hundred and fifty miles in the State. We spent at this camp another terrible night, with the bugs and other vermin, which ruined my sleep, and got me up at an early hour in the morning.

Tuesday, Aug. 22d:—Marched at the old time. The country still improves. This morning we struck the eastern fork of the San Jacinto river. We crossed it and camped, after a march of some fourteen miles, on the middle branch of the stream. The San Jacinto has three forks to it. The eastern, middle and western, all of which come together and form the river proper. These forks are but small streams where we crossed them, but the river itself is of some size where it enters Buffalo Bayou near Houston. This river is particularly noted for having the battle of San Jacinto fought on its bank on the 6th of April, 1836.

This battle was fought between the Texans under Sam Houston,

179

and the Mexicans under Santa Anna, and was the battle in which the Texans won their independence.

Our camp was about fifty miles above the battlefield. Again in this camp we waked up some of our old enemies, the rattlers and we slew them without mercy. Nothing of interest occurred here. We had plenty of water, and we enjoyed it. It now became apparent that our rations were running short, so the order was to live on half rations, and go fast, as we could get nothing until we reached Houston.

Thursday, Aug. 23d:—We were in our saddles again, and moving, before daylight. We came to the flourishing town of Danville, Montgomery county, at about sun up. The country about this place is beautiful, it being small, rolling, but fertile prairies. From Danville we struck near Montgomery, the county seat, and again camped on a small stream of good water. Today we passed through a large prairie twelve miles in width, in which we saw but one house. The prairie was as level as a floor, and we could see for miles from side to side.

Hundreds of cattle were herding upon the tall prairie grass, but I cannot imagine who owned them, and nobody appeared to live within miles of it. Water was reasonably plenty, and being very much fatigued, I went to bed (that is, I laid down) early and enjoyed a sweet, refreshing sleep. The bugs bit me in vain for once.

Friday, Aug. 24th:—The bugles sounded *reveille* at 2 o'clock, and again the camp was in motion. Three thousand camp fires could be seen in the dark of the morning, with the boys about them, busily engaged in preparing a hasty cup of coffee. That taken, we were in the saddle again and on our way. We soon struck a large prairie and at once the column (which had been marching south) turned directly west. It soon became known that we were making for the railroad, and that we were not to go to Houston at all. We had marched two hundred and fifty miles to see the city, and then had to turn our backs upon it after having come within twenty miles of it. At noon we struck Cypress Creek, near the little town of Cypress City, and once again pitched our tents. We were surrounded upon all sides by prairie. No trees to be seen except a few cypress that stood lonely sentinels on the banks of the creek. Here we were to await rations and then march toward Austin. We were now at the Texas Central railroad, and on this afternoon I saw the first locomotive I had seen since I left Memphis. The sight of it made me feel as if I were almost at home again, but a moment's reflection taught me that I was leaving home and friends farther and farther behind me every day. At sundown we learned that we could not get supplies before reaching Hempstead, some twenty-seven miles distant. We were ordered to march at midnight. The very idea of marching at midnight made me sleepy.

Saturday, 25th:—Promptly at midnight we were up and off. Passed through Cypress City. Passed into a big prairie and haven't got out of it to this day. For twenty-seven miles we had prairie on every side of us. Cattle, prairie hens, and an occasional deer, were the only things animate or inanimate that lent variety to the scene. A long prairie is at first a beautiful sight, but it soon grows tame and dull. At noon on this day, after a tedious march of eighteen days, in which we made some three hundred miles distance, we arrived at Hempstead.

During all this time I did not average more than three hours of sleep in each night, although we made but short marches each day. To sleep in the daytime was impossible, I was broken out with heat as thickly as ever one was with measles, from the 'bottom of my feet to the crown of my head,' and during the warm part of the day, I felt like I was being constantly pricked with a million of pins, or was being sprinkled on the bare skin with hot ashes. The itch isn't a circumstance to the heat. In addition to this, lay down when you might, in the pine woods, and you were alive with bugs and all manner of creeping things in a moment, and each one of this army of vermin could bite, scratch, sting and gnaw you all at the same time.

Then notwithstanding we were in immense forests of pines, we never had any shade. These pine woods are open, without underbrush or small trees. The pines had small, slim trunks, growing up fifty to eighty feet without a limb. At the top they are crossed with a few short limbs, but not larger in whole circumference than a cotton umbrella. They therefore throw out no shade but that of the trunks alone, and its shade has about the width of a gate-post. Lay down in it, and in five minutes it runs away from you and leaves you, high and dry, in the sweltering sunshine." The Colonel's experience on this march was the experience of every man in the command.

181

The regiment, on its arrival at Hempstead, was almost destitute of clothing, and I was nearly starving. Owing to the incompetency or rascality of the quartermaster's department, no stores had been accumulated for the command.

One day word got out in camp that some soldiers, with a pontoon train, had killed a beef, and had left a portion of it. Some men from the 7th Indiana, and other regiments went out to get the refuse meat. The soldiers from the other regiments got it before the men from the 7th Indiana arrived. Sergeant Carr and Corporal Gereau and James E. Arnold of company I, 7th Indiana, were of the party. Greatly disappointed at not getting any of the meat, and being nearly starved, they killed a runty calf worth about one dollar and brought some of the meat into camp. Of course the rebel owner of the calf made complaint to Custer, who, anxious for an opportunity to exercise cruelty, lent a willing ear to his statements. The next morning, while the regiment was at roll-call, an Aid from Custer dashed up with orders for the regiment to remain in line till the quarters were searched. The Aid went through all the tents of the men, and in the tent of Corporal Gereau found some of the meat. The Corporal and all of his messmates were arrested and sent to Custer's headquarters. Contrary to his promise to Col. Shanks, to have the men tried in a legal way by court-martial, Custer ordered his Provost Martial, a brute perfectly willing to do his dirty work, to go through the farce of an examination. Gereau and James E. Arnold confessed in a manly way all they had done. Custer ordered their heads to be shaved, and that they receive forty lashes each, and afterwards, be marched in front of the regiment on dress parade.

Against the protest of Colonels Shanks and Browne and Maj. Carpenter, the brutal and illegal order was carried out to the letter. By act of Congress approved Aug. 5, 1861, flogging in the army was abolished and prohibited. This outrage won for Custer the lasting hatred of every decent man in his command.

Corporal Gereau had been in the service since the commencement of the war. He was severely wounded in the battle of Antietam, and discharged on account of his wounds. He sufficiently recovered to be able to enlist in the 7th Indiana cavalry.

He had always been a true and reliable soldier. He would not lie to save himself from punishment. Maj. Carpenter, who knew him well, put the utmost reliance on his truthfulness; he was too manly to expose Sergeant Carr, who was with him and assisted in killing the calf.

But poor Gereau came to a sad end. After the war, he was tried and convicted in Indiana, of the crime of rape. The details of the offense, as stated by the prosecuting witness, were horrible in the extreme. He was sent to the Jeffersonville prison. Maj. Carpenter was passing through the prison one day and saw a convict rapidly approaching him. When in front of him he discovered the convict to be Gereau. The Major learned from him the cause of his imprisonment. He also learned from him that he was innocent of the crime. Major Carpenter says, that as soon as Gereau told him he was innocent, he knew he was, for Gereau would not lie. After Gereau had been in prison about four years, the prosecuting witness was taken sick and died. Before dying she confessed to her priest, that Gereau was innocent of the crime, and that she had perjured him into the State prison for revenge. The Priest took down her statement, and, laid it before Gov. Baker, who immediately pardoned Gereau.

When informed of his pardon, he was so overjoyed by his unexpected good fortune, that it threw him into brain fever, of which he died a day or two afterwards.

By the usual casualties of the service, the number of the regiment had been reduced to five hundred and fifty men.

In some of the companies the commissioned and non-commissioned officers were in excess of the privates.

It was, therefore, decided to consolidate the regiment into six companies, and muster out the supernumerary commissioned and non-commissioned officers. The opportunity of getting home, was eagerly embraced by those lucky enough to be mustered out of the service.

The reorganization of the regiment and its operations, thereafter, will be given in the next and last chapter of this History of the Regiment.

JOSEPH F. McCARTHY, Co. C Sergeant, Private, Co. D

CHAPTER XII.

The Regiment Begins its March for Austin—Passes Through Benham and Bastrop—The Mayor of Bastrop Extends to Col. Browne the Liberty of the City, in a Speech in German, that Knocks the Poetry all out of him—"Colonel, you ish a German, I Understant"—Arrival at Austin—Final Muster Out.

The following commissioned officers of the regiment, were mustered out of the service, on its consolidation: Col. J. P. C. Shanks, Maj. James H. Carpenter, Capt. John R. Parmelee, of company A; Captain Sylvester L. Lewis, and 2d Lieut. Cyprus B. Polly, of company B; 1st Lieut. Lewis F. Braugher, D; 1st Lieut. Lee Roy Woods, of company E; 1st Lieut. Thomas S. Cogley, of company F; 2d Lieut. James Dundon, of company G; Ezekiel Brown, as 1st Sergeant of company H, was commissioned 2d Lieutenant, but did not muster. 1st Lieut. John W. Longwell, and 2d Lieut. Thomas J. Howard, of company I; Captain Samuel M. Lake, and 1st Lieut. Charles T. Noble, of company K; Captain Benjamin F. Dailey, and 1st Lieut. George W. Stover, of company L.

These officers, together with some enlisted men, who were mustered out at the same time, went by railroad to Galveston, and from there by steamer on the Gulf of Mexico to New Orleans, thence by steamboat and railroad to their homes in Indiana.

The evening before their departure from the camp at Hempstead, the regiment assembled at headquarters, and listened to parting speeches from Colonels Shanks and Browne, and Major Carpenter. Although those who were going home were delighted with the prospect of soon being with their families and friends in Indiana, yet when the hour for parting came, the recollections of the common dangers and privations they had shared, caused the tears to course down the cheeks of the war-worn veterans, as they grasped each other by the hand and said "goodbye."

The field and regimental non-commissioned officers of the regiment as reorganized, were: Colonel, Thomas M. Browne; Lieut.-Col. Samuel E. W. Simonson; Majors, Joel H. Elliott, John M. Moore, and Joseph W. Skelton; Adjutant, Charles H. Gleason; Quartermaster, Aaron L. Jones; Commissary, 1st Lieut. Nathan Garrett; Surgeon, Joshua Chitwood; Assistant Surgeon, Daniel B. Roether; Sergeant-Major, George W. Spicknell; Veterinary Surgeon, Lysander F. Ingram; Quartermaster-Sergeant, William H. Eldridge; Commissary-Sergeant, William A. Dynes; Hospital Steward, John Cook; Chief Bugler, George F. Andrews; Saddler Sergeant, Samuel B. Henderson.

Company A was composed of companies H and I of the old organization. Officers: Capt., Robert G. Smither; 1st Lieut., William H. Crane; 2d Lieut., Max Schoen.

Company B was composed of companies L and M. Captain, John G. Meyer; 1st Lieut., Barton B. Jenkins; 2d Lieut., Thomas W. Gibson.

Company C was composed of companies A and F. Captain, John Donch; 1st Lieut., James C. Barnes; 2d Lieut., Rufus H. Norton.

Company D was composed of companies B and D. Captain, John L. Reid; 1st Lieut., George W. Shreeve; 2d Lieut., George W. Baxter.

Company E was composed of companies K and E. Captain, James E. Sloan; 1st Lieut., Elijah S. Blackford; 2d Lieut., John D. Longfellow.

Company F was composed of companies C and G. Captain, George R. Kennedy; 1st Lieut., Andrew J. Thompson; 2d Lieut., Charles R. Jones.

At 3 o'clock, on the morning of the 30th of October, 1865, the regiment broke camp at Hempstead, and started on its march to Austin, the capital of the State. It crossed the Brazos river about 8 o'clock a.m., on a pontoon bridge, and at 4 o'clock p.m., camped two and a half miles from Brenham, on the Texas Central railroad.

On the evening of November 2d, the regiment camped one-half mile northeast of Bastrop, a town on the Colorado river. At this place Gen. Custer perpetrated a joke upon Col. Browne. The General, with the main command, preceded the Seventh Indiana. In passing through Bastrop, Gen. Custer told the Mayor of the city that Colonel Browne was coming, and that he was a German. On arriving at the edge of the city, Colonel Browne, and Lieut.-Colonel Simonson, who were in advance of the command, were met by the Mayor of the city, a tall, gaunt man, whose accents betrayed his teutonic origin.

Col. Browne was pointed out to the Mayor, who inquired for him. The Mayor then introduced to the Colonel, a man with a speckled face, short legs, and a bay-window abdomen, as the "Chief Justice." His Honor, the Mayor, then proceeded to inform Colonel Browne, that they came on behalf of the people of Bastrop, to extend to him the Liberty of the City. Here was an event in the life of the Colonel. It was an occasion that required the highest order of oratorical powers on the part of the recipient of such extraordinary honors. The Colonel quickly took in the whole range of ancient history, and remembered that in olden times, the citizens, to conciliate conquering heroes, went forth to meet them, and extend the liberty of the cities.

The Colonel closed his eyes, in an effort to invoke the aid of the muses. Just as he had stumbled on a choice quotation from Shakespeare, and was about to accept of the hospitalities, etc., the poetry was knocked out of him, and the muses banished to their shaddowy realms, by the Mayor remarking: "Colonel, you ish a German I understand," and proceeding to address him in the German language, which was as unintelligible to the Colonel as Chinese or Cherokee Indian. The Colonel was compelled to acknowledge his ignorance of German, and pleading pressing official duties, bade the Mayor adieu. As the Colonel and his attendants proceeded on their way, Lieut.-Colonel Simonson was heard to say, as if talking to himself: "Colonel, you ish a German I understand."

From Bastrop, the command marched to Austin, arriving there on the 4th of November. The permanent camp was established at "Seiders Springs," two and one-half miles north of the city.

The regiment was mustered out of the service on the 18th of February, 1866, pursuant to special orders No. 20, Department of Texas.

It then proceeded to Galveston, where it embarked on a steamer and crossed the Gulf of Mexico to New Orleans. From there it went by steamboat up the Mississippi to Cairo, Illinois, and from thence by railroad to Indianapolis.

187

At the latter place, the ladies prepared a dinner for the regiment.

Gov. Baker and Gen. Shanks, the former Colonel of the regiment, were present, and made speeches, to which Colonel Browne responded.

After being paid, the men dispersed to their homes.

Here ends the history of the Seventh Indiana Cavalry. Indiana sent no better regiment to the field during the great rebellion. It was the last Indiana Cavalry regiment mustered out of the service.

CHAPTER XIII.

BURNING OF THE SULTANA.

The burning of the splendid steamer, *Sultana*, is connected with the history of the Seventh Indiana Cavalry, because at the time of that terrible disaster, there were aboard of her, and lost in the calamity with hundreds of other soldiers, from thirty to forty of the members of the regiment.

The *Sultana* was one of the largest size steamboats. She had been running but three years, and was valued at eighty thousand dollars.

The quartermaster, at Vicksburg, was guilty of criminal carelessness in overloading the boat. About two thousand soldiers were on board, most of whom had but recently been released from Andersonville and other prisons, where they had been imprisoned for months, and suffered the tortures devised by the rebel government, and were at the time of the disaster, on their way to their homes in the North. Besides these, there were a large number of passengers consisting of men, women and children, and the boats crew, and a large quantity of freight, principally sugar.

With her freight of precious souls, the *Sultana*, on the 6th of April, 1865, arrived at Memphis, where she lay till midnight, to unload one hundred hogshead of sugar. Having discharged her freight, the bell summoned passengers "on board," and warned visitors to go ashore. Parting friends shook each other by the hand, and said "goodbye," little dreaming that that was the last time they would ever clasp hands, or exchange words of friendship this side of the grave. The gangplank was drawn in; the engines of the boat put the ponderous wheels in motion; and the proud *Sultana* swung out into the current of the Mississippi, and was soon hurrying on to her terrible doom. The passengers retired to their berths:

"To sleep, perchance to dream,"

189

Cogley: Original Edition

THE SULTANA

190

of home, friends and loved ones, thinking that when they awoke in the morning they would be many miles nearer their destination. Sixteen hundred of them were destined to awaken soon after, to find themselves, not only nearer, but at their great final destination. Before the sun, on the morrow, illumined the east with its golden flood of light, sixteen hundred human beings, who left Memphis a short hour before, bouyant with hope, were doomed to enter upon—

"That bourne whence no traveler ere returns."

When about seven miles above Memphis, the boilers of the *Sultana* exploded, hurling the pilot-house and a portion of the cabin high into the air. They came down on the deck a complete wreck, and buried many of the passengers in the debris, who, being unable to extricate themselves, were burned to death. Men, women and children, rushed from their berths in their night attire, and with the most heart-rending screams, plunged into the river, preferring death by drowning, to the more horrid one of burning. Mothers, with their babes pressed to their bosoms, jumped into the water and sank to rise no more. One heroic mother cast herself and babe into the river, and by means of a mattress, managed to keep afloat till both were rescued by a boat, several miles from the scene of the disaster. Husbands threw their wives into the water and plunged in after them, and after a brief struggle, found their last resting place beneath the waves.

The explosion occurred in the widest part of the river, where none but the most expert swimmers could reach the shore. Some sank never to rise when they had almost reached the banks. Some who had reached them, and succeeded in catching hold of the limbs of the bushes, unable longer to sustain themselves above water, relaxed their grip, sank out of sight, and were never seen again. Some floated down past Memphis, and by their cries, attracting the attention of the boats at the wharf, were saved.

Immediately after the explosion, the flames, spreading rapidly, enveloped the *Sultana* in a sheet of fire. The scene presented by the light of the burning vessel was horrid beyond the power of language to describe. Two thousand persons were in the water engaged in a desperate struggle for life. The screams and cries for help, when there was no arm to save, was enough to curdle

191

the blood with horror. Amid the babble of screams and shouts, were distinguished the cries of children and babes. In that sea of drowning humanity, were bride and groom on their wedding tour; families consisting of fathers, mothers and children, returning from or making visits to friends; and soldiers who had fought gallantly on many a hard contested field of battle, and had suffered the tortures of the damned in rebel prison pens in the South.

Such disasters bring out prominently the strongest and weakest traits of character. With the women and children the conflict was soon over. The most of them immediately sank on reaching the water and never again came to the surface. But hundreds of the men kept up for hours a gallant battle for life. Soldiers who had often defied death on the field, were not to be vanquished in a moment—not even by the great Mississippi. Such as managed to keep afloat, were picked up by boats hastening to the rescue.

The steamer *Bostona*, on her way down the river, and about a mile distant at the time of the explosion, hurried to the scene, and succeeded in saving many who otherwise would have perished.

The iron-clad gunboat, *Essex*, left the wharf at Memphis, on hearing of the catastrophe, and steamed rapidly toward the wreck. The morning was so dark that it was possible to see but a few feet ahead. The gunboat was guided to the spot by the cries of those struggling in the water. She saved sixty persons from a watery grave.

The *Sultana* burned to the water's edge, and sank on the Arkansas side of the river.

All of the twenty-two hundred persons, except six hundred, who thronged the decks of the *Sultana* the day before, with visions of a happy and prosperous future of life before them, slept at the bottom of the great Mississippi, while over their quiet bodies, its floods rolled, on their ceaseless journey to the sea.

The following are the names of the members of the Seventh Indiana Cavalry, lost with the *Sultana*, that we have been able to get.

Daniel W. Doner, John Q. Paxtcn, and Costan Porter, of company E; William S. Corbin, of company G; William Barrick and Elisha Swords of company I; Augustus Barrett and Francis M. Elkins, of company K; William M. Thomson, of company M.

Robert B. Armstrong, of company I, was the only member of the regiment who escaped.

CHAPTER XIV.

DICK DAVIS, THE GUERRILLA.

Nature of Guerrillas—Dick Davis, his early life—He enters the Confederate service under John Morgan—Captured in Ohio, while there as a spy, steals a horse to effect his escape—Captured and put in jail and indicted for horse stealing—The case dismissed on condition that he enlisted in the Union army—He avails himself of the first opportunity to desert—Turns up as a Guerrilla Chief near Memphis—Captured and confined in the Irving Block at Memphis, but escapes—His field of operations and mode of warfare—Captured by Capt. Skelton, and again confined in the Irving Block—Attempts to escape by the assistance of his sweetheart, but is foiled by the vigilance of the officers and guards—His personal appearance—His trial and conviction—The murder of Capt. Somers and men—His death sentence—He bravely meets his fate—The Charges and Specifications on which he was tried, and findings of the Court.

We give in this chapter an interesting account of the trial and execution of "Dick Davis the Guerrilla," as written by General Thomas M. Browne, soon after their occurrence. As General Browne was President of the Military Commission that tried Davis, the following may be relied upon as authentic:

"It is an old maxim, that occasions make men, and taking it to be true, what an opportunity this war has afforded to almost every man, to write his name in the world's history! But comparatively few have 'snatched the golden moment,' and yet it has been prolific in the development of the various traits of human character. It has become a stupendous tragedy, in which every cast and type of actor may have his *role*, and play his part. It has made its Alexanders who have fought but to conquer; its heroes, who, like Themistocles, have risen from obscurity to renown; and it has had its martyrs, who, like Marco Bozarris, have sacrificed their lives freely and willingly upon the altar of their country, to secure the nation's triumph, and liberty of its people.

"This giant political convulsion has not only brought General and Statesman to the surface, but it has exhibited another phase of human nature, which, although daring and adventurous, will perhaps, seldom find its place in the history of these times. I refer to a class of Banditti, who, taking advantage of the universal chaos into which society has been thrown by this war, are now committing crimes of robbery and bloodshed all over the southwest. They take 'Dick Turpin' as their model, possessing his courage to do wrong, but none of his eccentric magnanimity. Possessing none of that high-toned chivalric feeling that desires foemen worthy of their steel, they wage warfare upon the unwary and defenseless. Stimulated by no feeling of honor, they fight for no flag, no nationality, but solely for booty. They seek no open battlefield upon which, on equal terms, to break a lance with their foe, like the ancient Knights-Errant, but hide themselves in ambush and entrap their victims like savages. In times of peace they are guerrilla bullies, thieves and loafers, and in war, not having sufficient manhood to espouse either side of the quarrel, they take advantage of circumstances and turn highwayman and freebooters. Notwithstanding all this, the lives of these men are more or less exciting and romantic. Frequently they pass through dangers that would try the courage of the stoutest heart. Of the Guerrilla Chiefs who have spread consternation and alarm in Western Tennessee, none have acted so conspicuous a part as he, a sketch of whose life I propose to give.

"Dick Davis was born in the city of Maysville, Kentucky, I should judge about a quarter of a century ago. His baptismal name was John B. Bollinger, but his father dying while he was yet a chi¹d, and his mother marrying a man by the name of Davis, he subsequently was given or assumed the name of his step-father, and went by the name of 'Dick Davis.' It is said that his step-father, mother and a sister reside at this time in the city of Cincinnati. At the breaking out of this rebellion, he was a resident of Mason county, Kentucky, and engaged in buying and selling stock, in which business he was accumulating some property. Naturally of a wayward, unsettled and nervous disposition, he was not slow in gratifying his desire for adventure by engaging in the war. He joined a Confederate cavalry regiment in Kentucky, under the command of that chivalric raider and horse-thief, John Morgan. By his reckless daring and unscrupulous cunning, he soon secured the confidence of that partisan chieftain. He participated in most of Morgan's raids in Kentucky, accompanied him in his mad-cap tour through Indiana and Ohio, in the summer of 1863, and was one of the few of that command that managed to escape and recross the Ohio at Buffington Island. He was an expert scout, knew the country thoroughly, and was much of his time employed in that service. Morgan sent him several times into the States north of the Ohio as a spy, and he never failed to return with information valuable to the rebels. Just before that grand scare—the demonstration of Kirby Smith on Cincinnati— Dick had been in that city and reported its defenseless condition to that General. With this information the Confederate General thought the Queen City an easy prize, and such, indeed, it would have been had not unexampled promptness and energy been displayed in the preparations for its defense. That the city was not sacked and burned is almost wholly owing to the rapid and numerous response made by the 'squirrel hunters and minute men' of Ohio and Indiana, who rallied to its rescue. While on one of his secret missions into Ohio, he was suspected by some of being connected with the rebel army. Hearing of these suspicions, and fearing arrest, he concluded to return South, and putting into practice the lessons he had learned so well from his leader, helped himself to a fine horse belonging to a friend in the neighborhood, without even thanking the owner. He was pursued, captured, thrown into jail, indicted by the grand jury, and was about being brought to trial, when, at the insistance of friends, the prosecutor was induced to enter a *nolle prosequi* in the case upon condition that he would enlist in the Union army. Upon being released from *durance vile*, he volunteered in an Ohio regiment, accompanied it to the field, but soon afterwards deserted and returned to the rebels. He was present and participated in Van Dorn's attack on Corinth, at the time the lamented Gen. Hackelman was killed. Shortly after this, Dick turned up in the vicinity of Memphis, as the leader of a guerrilla band. He was subsequently captured by the Federal forces, and confined on the charge of being a robber and a spy, in the military bastile, Irving Block, in the above named city; but, before he was brought to trial, he managed to escape, through the complicity of the guard who was placed over him. Having escaped from prison he rejoined his fellow marauders and resumed his old occupation of highwayman.

"His field of operations extended from the Coldwater on the south to the Wolf and Hatchie rivers on the north, and from the Federal picket lines near Memphis eastward to the junction of Memphis and Charleston with the Mississippi Central railroad. This area embraces the villages of White Station, Germantown, Moscow, Lagrange, and Grand Junction, on the line of the first named railroad, and the base of all the traveled roads leading into the Bluff City. He was continually changing the rendezvous of his band, but generally kept it in the bottoms of Nonconnah creek or Wolf river. His strategy was so admirable that he out-witted and out-generaled every scout or party sent to capture him. For months he lived, robbed and murdered with impunity, almost within the Federal lines, and within earshot of the Federal army. He was enabled the more effectually to elude his pursuers, by the fact that he so managed it as to secure the silence of the citizens in the country infested by his band. The friendship of some he secured by acts of kindness, others were silent because of their sympathy with him and his occupation of butchery, while the majority feared to disclose the hiding place of one who pos-sessed the power and the will, when provoked, to inflict upon them the most hellish cruelty. To incur his indignation was equiv-alent to losing their property, and perhaps their lives. His band consisted of from fifteen to twenty men—young, active, and as reckless as himself. They were all well mounted, armed with a pair of revolvers each and a carbine. His men were principally deserters, some from the rebel and some from the Union army. Of the many incidents of his chequered career, but few that are well authenticated, have reached me. All I know is that he fre-quently relieved citizens coming into and going out of the city of their money, watches, jewelry, horses and other valuables. His men and himself had strong bartering proclivities, and frequently indulged in trading their old hats, shoes and coats, with some city gentleman who might happen to be caught with articles of that kind superior to their own. It is said in these exchanges they al-ways got the better end of the bargain.

"In his exploits as highwayman, he made no distinction be-tween loyal and disloyal, white and Black, nor did he respect age, sex or condition. Secreting himself and band in the bushes, in some well-selected spot by the roadside, he awaited the approach of his victim, and suddenly appearing before him, would greet him with that blood-chilling banditti salutation, 'your money or your life,' at the same time, adding force to the suggestion, by thrusting into the face of the bewildered and astonished traveler an enlarged and improved edition of Colt's six-barreled 'persuader.' In this way he armed, mounted and equipped, and subsisted his band. One thing may be said to his credit, he seldom, if ever, disturbed private houses. The most desperate of his enterprises, and the most daring of his exploits, were directed against the Union army and soldiery. He would creep on a dark night through the picket lines, and steal mules and horses from under the very noses of the guards. He would ambuscade and kill patroling parties—steal upon and shoot down a vidette or a picket. At times he was as wary and stealthy as an Indian—then again he would dash upon an outpost or reserve, with the recklessness and audacity of a Mamaluke or Cossack. In firing upon railroad trains he seemed to take a peculiar pleasure. His men, from some hiding place, would deliver a volley, upon a passing train well filled with unsuspecting troops, and before it could be stopped and the men put in position for action, the guerrillas would be on their horses and scampering speedily away to their coverts in the bottoms. In this way they killed three and wounded some ten Federal soldiers at one time, between Germantown and Colliersville, during the summer of 1864. I shall not now recite particular instances of crime as it would make this sketch much too voluminous.

His Capture.

"He was captured by Capt. J. W. Skelton and a detachment of the Seventh Indiana Cavalry, near the Coldwater, Mississippi, some twenty miles southeast of Memphis, on the 2d of October, 1864. The Captain, in command of some forty men, was sent on a scouting expedition in the direction of Holly Springs, and when near Anderson's plantation, his advance guard was fired upon. He immediately ordered a charge, taking the lead himself, and as he passed out of the woods into the open ground beyond, a man dressed in the grey jacket of the Confederate army was discovered making the best possible time across the fields toward the ad-

197

joining woods. The Captain gave immediate chase, leaping his horse over the intervening fences, and was soon upon him. Before, however, he was overtaken, he had slackened his pace, and was rapidly reloading his carbine. The Captain putting his pistol in uncomfortable proximity to the fellow's head, demanded his surrender, to which he coolly replied, 'I guess I will have to surrender, but d---n, it I thought I could load and kill you before you came up, but you was too quick for me.' He was armed with a navy revolver, and a Spencer's breech-loading eight-shooting carbine. While Captain Skelton was engaged in making this capture, his men had pursued and taken three others of the band. The first of these captives gave his name as Rogers, and subsequently as J. W. Smith, and professed to be a private soldier in the 2d Missouri rebel cavalry. These prisoners were delivered on the same evening, to the General commanding, the Captain little thinking at the time that he had captured the veritable 'Dick Davis,' whose name was a terror to all travelers and scouting parties, and who had successfully eluded the vigilance of the United States forces for months and almost years. Yet such was the case. When he was sent to his old quarters in the Hotel DeIrving, he was at once recognized by several officers who had become acquainted with him during his previous confinement.

HE ATTEMPTS TO ESCAPE.

"A prison cell was a narrow abode for one like 'Dick Davis,' who had been accustomed to live 'with heaven for a canopy, and a whole wide world for a habitation.' Although pinioned to the floor with irons, in a strong prison, surrounded by a strong and ever-wakeful guard, and environed on all sides by an army picketing the whole circumference of the city, he did not despair, but deliberately and adroitly planned an escape. No sooner had he matured his plan, than he attempted to put it into execution. Amongst those who had been summoned as witnesses to Dick's defense, was the daughter of a planter, living near Colliersville, a Miss Anna T------, who, dame rumor whispered, was his affianced bride. She was indeed a beautiful and captivating woman, of about twenty summers. If I were writing romance, I might indulge in a more particular description of the bandit's affianced, but for the purposes of this sketch, it is quite sufficient

198

for the reader to know that she was, in common parlance, pretty. Being allowed, under the circumstances, to have an occasional interview with the prisoner, she became his confident, and cheerfully offered her assistance in forwarding his effort to escape. He wrote his plans with the minuteness of a general detailing a plan of campaign, and placed them in her keeping. She was to be the chief instrument in procuring the means by which he hoped to relax the federal grasp. As a starting point, she must procure an introduction to a soldier on guard; her grace and beauty were to captivate and bind him, until submissive to her will, he would gladly do her every bidding. Next in the order of preparation, she was to get the means and procure to be made, two small saws, from watch-spring steel, two saw bows, and buy a small mirror and an overcoat. The saws and bows were to be secreted between the glass and back of the mirror, the mirror to be placed in the overcoat pocket, and the beauty-smitten guard was to be induced to pass in the overcoat to the prisoner. In addition to this, Miss T—————— was directed to purchase two bottles, one to be filled with pure whisky, the other with whisky drugged with laudanum. His object in directing the purchase of the 'pure whisky,' was not stated in his letter of instructions, but the adulterated article was to be administered to the soldiers on guard, to make 'sleep peaceful and their slumbers more profound.' The project went swimmingly on—the introduction was secured, the saws and bows manufactured, the overcoat and other necessaries purchased—but alas! it is as truthful as poetic that 'there's a many a slip twixt the cup and the lip,' for instead of the fair Hebe getting her sundries into the prison, as she anticipated, she suddenly and mysteriously *got there herself.* The officers of the 'Block,' by some means or other, kept track of this embryo conspiracy, and 'nipped it in the very nick of time.' The imprisonment of his sweetheart shattered his last hope, and without another effort 'to flee the wrath to come,' he meekly and submissively accepted his fate.

His Personal Appearance.

"On the 10th day of October, 1864, I took my seat as President of the Military Commission at Memphis. The rattling of chains along the corridor, the regular and heavy step of the guard, admonished me that a prisoner was on his way to the courtroom, and in a moment afterwards, 'Dick Davis' stood before me. He was handcuffed—a chain sufficiently long to allow him to take an ordinary step, prevented one leg from running away from the other. To each ankle was attached other chains, a yard or more in length, at the ends of which were fixed twelve pound solid shot, so that wherever he might go, he was compelled to carry with him this immense weight of metal. I have in my time, seen many in irons, but never before had I seen one so thoroughly manacled. His personal appearance disappointed me. From his reputation—from the deeds of savage ferocity attributed to him—I had concluded that he was a giant in stature, and the personation of the very devil in feature. On both points I was mistaken in my conjectures. He was a small man, scarcely five feet seven in height, and weighing only one hundred and thirty-five pounds. He was neatly and trimly built, stood as straight as an arrow, and was evidently an active and muscular man. His foot was small—so small, that a woman might have envied it. The expression of his countenance was by no means disagreeable. His forehead was well developed, wide at the apex, but considerably depressed at the temples. He had a luxuriant growth of hair, of dark auburn, closely cut; wore side whiskers, without mustache or goatee. The most noticeable features in his whole physiognomy, were his eyes and eyebrows, the first of which were large, clear, dark and flashing—the latter heavy and projecting, and extending continuously from the outer corner of one eye to that of the other. Nothing marred the harmony of his face so much as his nose, which was thick and puggish, like that of a bull-terrier, and the basilar portion of his head—his jaws and chin—which were quite heavy, showing a strong development of the animal. His age appeared to be about twenty-six years.

"He was dressed in a grey jacket, brown pants, drab hat, flannel shirt and neat fitting boots.

"During his protracted trial of over two months duration, his deportment in the courtroom was entirely decorous; while, he exhibited none of the accomplishments of the refined gentleman, nor the blandishments of the fop, neither did he display the courseness or vulgarity of the ruffian. His manners were easy and respectful. To the very last, he manifested the utmost confidence in his acquittal. To the evidence of the witnesses he listened attentively, made suggestions to his counsel during their examination, but never moved a muscle, even when the most revolting crimes were attributed to him. His language was generally correct and unaffected, and contained none of the 'niggerisms' peculiar to the Southern dialect. He wrote a neat hand—spelled his words correctly—showing his education to be above the average.

His Trial.

"His trial commenced on the 11th day of October, and was concluded on the 15th of December. The charges upon which he was arraigned were, for 'being a guerrilla, and carrying on irregular, illegal and unauthorized warfare against the Government of the United States.' I shall not attempt to given even a synopsis of the huge mass of testimony given in the case. One instance only of savage and brutal atrocity, abundantly established by the evidence, have I time to give.

The murder of Captain Somers and men.

"On the 10th of June, 1864, it will be remembered, our forces suffered an overwhelming and most humiliating defeat at the hands of the rebels, under the command of Forrest, at Brice's cross-roads, Mississippi. Our army was demoralized and broken into fragments, and fled from the field more like a mob than an organized troop. On the retreat, many of the infantry threw away their knapsacks and cartridge-boxes, and broke their guns, to enable them to make more speedy their flight before a victorious and pursuing enemy. Neither company nor regimental formations were kept up, but to a considerable extent every one thought only of his own personal safety, and sought to secure it by flying speedily to the defenses of Memphis.

"During this retreat, and on the 13th day of June, Captain Somers, Sergeant Mitchell, Privates Panky, Parks, Guernes, and two others whose names are unknown, all of whom belonged to Illinois regiments, had reached a point on the Memphis and Charleston railroad, two miles west of Colliersville, and within twenty-four miles of the city. They were unarmed, foot-sore, almost famished by hunger, and exhausted by a march of over a hundred miles. They had almost reached a place of safety, and hope was buoyant within them. They expected soon, no doubt, to bivouac on their old camping grounds, under the protecting

201

shadows of the guns of Fort Pickering, and there recount with their comrades who had escaped from that bloody and disastrous field, the story of their adventures, their flight and their escape. They little dreamed of the dread doom that awaited them—that five of their little band, in a brief hour from then, would lay dead in the thicket by the roadside, and the sixth be crippled and maimed for life. But I must pass to the sequel. Just before them lay Dick Davis and his band in ambush, and as these weary and worn soldiers passed, they were greeted with a volley and a yell that to them, sounded as if 'Pandemonium had opened wide its infernal gates' and turned loose on earth a hundred fiends. No shot took affect, but they were at once charged upon by the guerrillas. Being unarmed, overpowered by numbers, unable to run, no alternative was left Captain Somers and his men but to surrender. This they did, thinking, doubtless, they had fallen into the hands of a generous and magnanimous enemy, by whom they would be treated as prisoners of war.

"After their capture they were immediately hurried into the woods, robbed of their money, rings, coats and hats. This accomplished, their captors took them by a by-path, to a place in a thicket of wood, two miles south of the railroad, where the party halted. The captives, with the exception of Captain Somers—who laid down on the leaves—took their seats side by side on a log. Here Dick left them under the guard of two men, and with the rest of his band retired a few paces and held a consultation. The brutal purpose of that consultation was soon made manifest. Returning to his prisoners, Dick ordered Captain Somers to take a seat on the log beside his comrades, which was immediately done. Stepping before them he said to them but a few brief words, but they were words of dreadful import. The heartless and piratical words. 'Boys, you must all go overboard,' was the laconic sentence of death passed by the guerrilla chief upon these helpless and defenseless men. The protestations, piteous supplications, and entreaties of the poor soldiers failed to touch any chord of sympathy in the robber's heart. An elderly man, of his own band—one of those who had guarded the prisoners, attempted to interpose in their behalf, but to no purpose. In a moment, ten grim executioners were in front of the doomed, and with revolvers, at the short distance of three paces, poured a volley of lead into their very bosoms. Somers, Panky, Mitchel, and the two unknown soldiers, fell forward, dead. But He who shapes the destiny of the universe, by a mysterious providence, permitted Parks and Guernes to live, as if it was His divine purpose that they should be instrumental in bringing this inhuman monster to merited punishment. At the moment the command 'fire' was given, Parks threw himself backwards over the log and escaped unhurt, and at the same instant Guernes started to run, but was less fortunate than his comrade, for in his flight he was the recipient of two bullets, one in his side, and the other in his arm—the latter one causing the amputation of his arm above the elbow. They were both pursued some distance and repeatedly shot at without further injury. The tragic fate of their companions in arms, which they had just witnessed, made them forget their fatigue and hunger, and lent a desperate energy to their flight. On the same night they fell in with other fugitives from the battlefield, and subsequently arrived safely at Memphis.

"We must leave the murderers and the slain together, as we can trace them for the present no further. Of the fate of Somers and his men, all that is known beyond what has been stated, is, that about the 1st of July, Lieut. Charles H. Hare, with a detachment of the Seventh Indiana Cavalry, visited the spot, found the bodies of five Union soldiers, stripped, putrid, and unburied. He had these remains removed to a place near the railroad, where they now lie beneath the shade of a little oak, buried in one grave, symbol of the fact that they fell in one cause and in a common butchery.

"Here I must drop the curtain over this tale of blood. For fiendish atrocity, it has scarcely a parallel in the history of these times. It was a cold-blooded and inhuman butchery of defenseless men, against whom, these outlaws, could have no malice—they were strangers, and had done the banditti no wrong.

THE SENTENCE OF DEATH.

"The Commission found Dick guilty of all the charges preferred against him, and affixed the penalty of death by hanging. This was on the 15th of December; on the 19th, Gen. Dana approved the proceedings and sentence of the court, and directed the execution to take place on the 23d of the same month. Truly, it was a brief time in which to prepare to die—but it was much longer than that allotted poor Somers and his men. He received information of his sentence with apparent unconcern, immediately assumed his true name, and commenced preparations for death. He wrote to his friends, instructing them what disposition to make of his property, and in what manner to pay his debts. He made but one bequest, and that was of his favorite race horse, which had been his companion in his expeditions of blood, and that he directed to be given to his friend, Miss Anna T———. To the members of his band he wrote a touching farewell, requesting them not to avenge his death by retaliating upon innocent men. These letters were all read by me, and were subsequently forwarded by the authorities through the lines. He had an interview with one of his counsel, E. B. Woodward, Esq., on the day before his execution, and appeared perfectly calm, talking of his approaching death as a matter of little consequence at most. Of the Court by which he was tried and condemned, and of the witnesses against him, he spoke no word of bitterness or reproach.

THE GALLOWS.

"At a little after noon, on the 23d day of December, Dick Davis was taken from the 'Block,' placed in an ambulance, and conveyed under guard to the gallows within Fort Pickering. He was accompanied by his spiritual adviser, a Catholic Priest, who had remained with him during the preceding night. The day was beautiful, bright and clear. The troops of the garrison and a large assemblage of officers and citizens were present to witness the departure of the noted outlaw to another world. In company with the priest, he ascended the steps of the scaffold to the platform with a bold, firm step. The Provost Martial read to him the charges, finding and sentence of the court, to which he listened attentively, but unmoved. This over, he conversed some moments in an undertone with the priest, and then they engaged in prayer. After prayer he signified to the executioner his readiness to try the fearful ordeal of death. While the rope was being adjusted about his neck, he stood erect, exhibiting no signs of emotion or fear. The cap was drawn over his face, the trap sprung, and the guerrilla hung suspended between heaven and earth. Although he fell full five feet, his neck was not dislocated, as anticipated. For a few moments after his fall there was no motion except a

204

slight pendulum-like vibration of the body, that was soon succeeded by a spasmodic shrugging of the shoulders, then there was a quivering of the limbs, and then—Dick Davis, the Guerrilla Chief, was no more. His spirit had passed from earth and stood before its God. Indeed,

'It is a fearful thing to see the strong man die—
The stripling meet his fate.'

"An execution on the scaffold may be witnessed once, but that man must have a strange taste or a hard heart who would willingly see the second. But I have finished my sketch—Dick Davis has met his reward. 'That measure he meted out to others has been measured to him again.' That his sentence was just—that he deserved to die a felon's death—no one for a moment doubts; but I pray fervently that Providence may so shape my life that I may never again be called upon to weigh justice in the balances against human life."

Below are the charges and specifications on which Dick Davis was tried, with the findings and sentence of the court, and the approval thereof by General Dana:

HEAD-QUARTERS DEPARTMENT OF MISSISSIPPI,
MEMPHIS, TENN., DEC. 19, 1864.

General Court-Martial Orders
No. 1.

1. Before a Military Commission which convened at Memphis, Tennessee, pursuant to Special Orders No. 163, ext. 1, from Head-Quarters District, West Tennessee, dated Memphis, Tenn. October 8, 1864, and of which Lieut. Col. Thomas M. Browne, 7th Indiana Cavalry, was President, was arraigned and tried

DICK DAVIS ALIAS J. W. SMITH.

CHARGE 1ST: Being a Guerrilla.

Specification 1st:—In this, that the said Dick Davis *alias* J. W. Smith, confederating and combining with diverse parties who are unknown, did in and during the months of January, February, March, April, May, June, July, August and September, 1864, levy and carry on irregular and unauthorized warfare upon loyal citizens, and against United States soldiers, and did go about the country armed, and commit diverse acts of crime and violence. All this in and near Shelby county, Tennessee, and Marshal and DeSoto counties, Miss., and within the Military District of West Tennessee.

Specification 2d:—In this, that the said Dick Davis *alias* J. W. Smith, being the leader and chief of a band of guerrillas known and styled "Dick Davis' men," or "band," did levy and carry on irregular and unauthorized warfare against the United States of America. All this during the months and year aforesaid, and in Shelby county, Tenn., and Marshal and DeSoto counties, Miss., and within the Military District of West Tennessee.

Specification 3d:—In this, that the said Dick Davis *alias* J. W. Smith, did levy irregular, independent and unauthorized warfare against loyal inhabitants of the United States. All this during the whole of the year 1863, and in the county of Shelby, Tennessee, and DeSoto and Marshal counties, Mississippi, and within the Military District of West Tennessee.

Specification 4th:—In this, that the said Dick Davis *alias* J. W. Smith, falsely representing himself to be a duly appointed soldier of the Confederate States of America, and confederating and combining with diverse and sundry parties unknown, did levy and wage irregular, independent and unauthorized warfare against the government of the United States—against United States soldiers. All this during the months of January, February, March, April, May, June, July, August, and September, 1864, in the counties of Shelby, Tenn., and DeSoto and Marshal, Miss., and within the Military District of West Tennessee.

CHARGE 2D: Violation of the Rules of Civilized Warfare.

Specification 1st:—In this, that the said Dick Davis *alias* J. W. Smith, confederating and combining with, and assuming to be the leader of diverse and sundry persons, unknown; the whole party being known and styled as "Davis' men," pretending to be in the service of the so-called Confederate States of America, did levy irregular and unauthorized warfare, in this, to-wit: By firing upon unarmed citizens and upon railroad trains, and did violently and willfully murder soldiers of the United States, after they had surrendered as prisoners of war. All this in the months of January, February, March, April, May, June, July, August and September, 1864, and in the counties of Shelby, Tenn., and Marshal and DeSoto, Miss., and within the Military District of West Tennessee.

Specification 2d:—In this, that the said Dick Davis *alias* J. W. Smith, combining and confederating as aforesaid with diverse other parties unknown, belonging to a party styled "Davis' Band," having captured Capt. Somers of the 108th Illinois Infantry, and Private Guernes, 113th Illinois Infantry, and four other Federal soldiers whose names are unknown, during the retreat of the United States forces from Guntown, Miss., and held them as prisoners of war, for about four hours, did without provocation or cause, deliberately, willfully, and with malice, kill and murder the said Capt. Somers and three of the said soldiers. This on or about the 12th day of June, 1864, near Germantown, Tennessee, and within the Military District of West Tennessee.

To each and all of which Charges and Specifications the accused pleaded—Not Guilty.

The Court after due deliberation do find the accused, Dick Davis *alias* J. W. Smith, as follows:

Of 1st Specification to the 1st Charge—Guilty.

Of 2d Specification to the 1st Charge—Guilty.

Of 3d Specification to the 1st Charge—Guilty.

Of 4th Specification to the 1st Charge—Guilty.

Of 1st Charge—Guilty.

Of 1st Specification to 2d Charge—Guilty.

Of 2d Specification to 2d Charge—Guilty.

Of 2d Charge—Guilty.

And do therefore sentence him, the said Dick Davis, *alias* J. W. Smith, *to be hanged by the neck until dead, at such time and place as the Commanding General may direct; two thirds of the members of the court, concur in the above finding and sentence.*

II. The finding in this case are approved, except as to the alleged "firing upon unarmed citizens and railroad trains," and the alleged acts of guerrilla warfare committed prior to June 1864, of which there is not sufficient proof.

The evidence elicited is, however, amply sufficient to sustain the remaining portions of the Specifications as well as the charges. The prisoner, whether his name be *Davis* or *Smith*, is convicted of being a Guerrilla and violating the rules of civilized warfare, and no connection which he may have had with the army of the so-called Confederate States, can screen him from the punishment due his crimes.

The sentence is confirmed; and the prisoner, Dick Davis *alias* J. W. Smith, will be hanged by the neck until he is dead, at Memphis, Tennessee, on Friday the 23d day of December, 1864, between the hours of 10 a.m., and 4 p.m., under the direction of the Provost Marshal General.

By Order of MAJOR GENERAL N. J. T. DANA, T. H. HARRIS, Assistant Adjutant General.

PART III.

Sketches of officers of the Seventh Indiana Cavalry Volunteers.

LIEUTENANT COLONEL SAMUEL E. W. SIMONSON.

At the time the 7th Indiana cavalry was organized, Col. Simonson was a captain in the 4th Indiana cavalry. On account of his known ability and experience as a cavalry officer, he was selected by Governor Morton for one of the majors of the 7th cavalry. His valuable services in that regiment, prove the wisdom of the Governor's choice. With the exception of Grierson's raid through Mississippi in the winter of 1864-'65, he was with the regiment in all its campaigns, raids, expeditions, marches and battles. In the expedition to West Point, and the battle of Okolona his experience as an officer was of incalculable value to the regiment. By his cool, undaunted courage, he inspired the men with his own feelings of confidence. At the sabre charge at Ivy Farm, he commanded a battalion of the regiment held in reserve to support the rest of the regiment engaged in the charge. Although not actually in that part of the engagement, yet he occupied a position of as much danger as if he had been. There was no point on the field at that place, where the balls of the enemy did not reach. Nearly as many men were killed or wounded in the reserve, as there were in the column making the charge.

At the battle of Brice's Cross Roads, Mississippi, June 10th, 1864, he proved himself a hero. He was always found where danger was greatest. In the last of that battle, Col. Browne, on account of his wound, was not able to remain longer with the regiment. The command, therefore, devolved on Major Simonson. He managed the regiment in the remainder of the battle with great skill, and withdrew it from the field without losing a man as prisoner, when the rebels were pushing forward confident of capturing the greater part of it. After the army was in total rout, he held it under a fire from the concentrated batteries of the enemy, directed at it and the flying infantry. On the retreat that followed he maintained perfect order and discipline in the ranks of the regiment.

He commanded the detachment of the regiment participating in the Missouri campaign in the fall of 1864. In the battle of the Osage, the regiment won the enthusiastic admiration of General Pleasanton. The glory it acquired on that brilliant field, was due in a great measure to its intrepid commander who inspired it with his own courage, and led it in the charge on the enemy's lines. Old veterans who were in that battle describe it as the grandest sight they ever saw in war. The field was a prairie, peculiarly adapted to the operations of cavalry. The day was pleasant and the sun shone brightly. The rebels were drawn up in line of battle faced from the river. Opposite them in charging columns were Pleasanton's cavaliers. When with gleaming sabres they dashed on the rebel lines, the scene must have been the sublime of war. To have participated in it as a private was an honor; to have led a regiment in it, that captured two guns and over a hundred prisoners, glory enough for any man of reasonable ambition.

After the reorganization of the regiment, Major Simonson was promoted Lieutenant-Colonel, and served with it as such, until it was mustered out. After the war he returned to Charleston in Clark county, Indiana, where he still resides.

MAJOR JAMES H. CARPENTER.

James H. Carpenter was born in Harrison county, West Virginia, on the 31st day of October, 1822. His father, Lewis R. Carpenter, was a farmer of that county. Lewis R. Carpenter removed with his family to Marion county, Ohio, where he engaged in farming.

James H. Carpenter remained with his father on the farm until 1843. On the 13th of November of that year, he left home and went to Mt. Vernon, Ohio, and began the study of medicine. He remained there until 1845, excepting during the winter months, when he engaged in teaching school, to obtain the means of defraying his expenses, while studying medicine.

In 1845, he went to Goshen, Elkhart county, Indiana, and taught one term of school. On the 24th of February, 1846, he formed a copartnership with Dr. Sutton of Goshen, Indiana, and began there the practice of medicine.

On the 27th of October of that year, he went to Cincinnati, Ohio, to take his last course of medical lectures, and in the Spring of 1847, graduated in medicine.

He continued in the practice of that profession at Goshen, Indiana, until the 15th of April, 1854, when he went to Warsaw, Kosciusko county, Indiana, his present home, and began the study of law, under the instruction of the Hon. James S. Frazer, a very able lawyer, and at this time an ex-judge of the Supreme Court of Indiana.

In the Fall of 1854, he was admitted, at Warsaw, to practice law. He, however, did not enter on the practice of that profession until the Spring of 1855, since which time he has been in active practice, except the time he served in the army during the rebellion, and nearly three years since the close of the war, when he was on the Bench as Judge of the Common Pleas Court.

On the 30th of January, 1849, at Marion county, Ohio, he married Miss Minerva J. Anderson, an estimable lady, by whom he has an interesting family of healthy and intelligent children, consisting of three girls and four boys.

In 1861, after the outbreak of the rebellion, he recruited two companies of volunteers for the 30th Indiana Regiment of Infantry. But on his return home from Indianapolis, he suffered, in a railroad accident, a compound fracture of his right thigh bone, which prevented him entering, at that time, the military service of the country, and which left him a cripple for life.

In 1863, having recovered from this misfortune, he recruited Company I, of the 7th Indiana cavalry, and was commissioned and mustered its Captain. He entered on active duty with the regiment. He was with it in its operations at Union City, and Jackson, Tennessee. He commanded his company in the expedition to West Point, Mississippi, and the battle of Okolona, February 22d, 1864. He led it in the sabre charge of the regiment at Ivy Farm, in the evening. He drove the rebels, and captured several prisoners, and saved from capture, the battery attached to the 4th Missouri cavalry, which had been abandoned by its supports, members of that regiment. He, individually, captured two prisoners and sent them to the rear. Another, whom he pursued, refusing to surrender, he cut down with his sabre. He was about

211

MAJOR JAMES H. CARPENTER

receiving the sword of a rebel officer who had surrendered, when discovering the wing of a rebel regiment but a few feet from him, he was obliged to let the prisoner go, and save himself from capture by a hasty retreat. During the afternoon, while on the retreat, he saw in the road a new currycomb and brush that some one had dropped. Not seeing any good reason why they should be lost, he dismounted and picked them up, and strapped them on his saddle, and coolly remounted; the bullets, in the meantime, were flying about him like hailstones. A rebel prisoner, captured by his company, seeing this performance, remarked that the Captain was the coolest man he ever saw under fire. This little incident illustrated his character for economy. He always guarded government property from loss or waste, with the same care as he would if it had been his own.

He accompanied the regiment, on its expedition to Port Gibson, in July, 1864. He started with the detachment that took part in the Missouri campaign in the fall of 1864, but returned and assumed command of the regiment at Memphis. For meritorious services, he was in October, 1864, commissioned Major of the regiment and mustered as such November 11th, 1864. On the 9th of January, 1865, he was sent by General Dana to Louisville, Kentucky, to bring back a part of the regiment that had gone there, on its return from Missouri. He had permission to visit his home, which he did, staying but two days. On his return to Louisville, pursuant to orders from General Upton, he reported at General Thomas' headquarters, at Eastport, Mississippi, and was sent by the latter to Memphis, with the request that Gen. Dana send the Seventh Indiana Cavalry to Louisville. This request was made on the supposition that part of the regiment was already there, and at the solicitation of Col. Winslow, who wanted to retain the regiment in his command; but, the detachment of the regiment having returned from Louisville, the request was not complied with.

On the 20th of March, 1865, Major Carpenter went on duty at Gen. Dana's headquarters, as Judge-Advocate of a court-martial, but was soon afterwards detailed as Judge-Advocate of the Military District of West Tennessee. He served in that capacity till the 20th of August, 1865, when he was ordered to rejoin the regiment, which he did in due time, at Hempstead, Texas.

On the consolidation of the regiment, which occurred soon

213

after his return, he availed himself of the opportunity to return to his home, and was mustered out of the service.

As a soldier, he was brave—as an officer, efficient—as a disciplinarian, strict but just. He was an officer of good executive ability.

On his return home, he was elected Judge of the Common Pleas Court, of the District embracing the county of Kosciusko, which position he held until the Legislature in 1873, abolished those courts. As a Judge, he was able and upright, and had the confidence of the entire bar.

After laying aside the ermine, he purchased an interest in the *Northern Indianian,* a weekly Republican newspaper of wide circulation, and became its sole editor. He discharged the arduous duties attaching to that position, while at the same time managing an extensive law practice, till after the State and Presidential election campaigns of 1876, commenced, when he sold his interest in the paper to Gen. Rube Williams, and retired from journalism. He now devotes his time exclusively to the practice of law.

MAJ. JOHN M. MOORE

This brave officer, at the time of his enlistment in the Seventh Indiana Cavalry, resided at Plymouth, in Marshall county, Indiana.

He joined the regiment as 2d Lieutenant of company A, but was on the 27th of August, 1863, commissioned Captain of company H, of the Seventh Indiana Cavalry.

He served with the regiment in every expedition in which it participated, except Grierson's raid through Mississippi, in the spring of 1865.

On the expedition to West Point, in February, 1864, at Okolona, he had command of a detachment of the regiment, and pursuant to orders, burned a large amount of property, belonging to the rebel government, and destroyed several railroad bridges. In the evening he was joined by Lieut. Way, of company B, who had gone north on the railroad, with another detachment, on a similar errand. The two commanders were on their way to rejoin the regiment, when they were fired upon by a body of rebels. Captain Moore immediately gave chase, and pursued them about two miles, when they made a stand behind a large white house, a short distance from the road. Captain Moore, with his command, charged up to the house, part going on one side, and part on the other.

The Captain was met at the corner of the house by the proprietor, an armed rebel, who fired his revolver at him. Expecting such tactics, the Captain, just as the rebel fired, threw himself flat on his horse, and the ball passed harmlessly over him. The rebel, thinking he had killed Moore, stepped out from the corner of the house to fire at another man, when Captain Moore, as quick as thought, fired his revolver at him, and brought him down. The rebel, in falling, fired his revolver again at the Captain, but without effect. The Captain's shot proved fatal, and the rebel expired in a few minutes. While this encounter was taking place, a portion of the command, pursued the rest of the bushwhackers a mile or more into the woods.

By the Captain's order the house was fired, and burned to the ground. When it became quiet after the skirmish, a voice from a log building was heard, calling for help. Captain Moore ordered the door broken down, when two members of the regiment, bound and lying on the floor, were discovered. They were speedily released, and stated, that the "bushwhackers" captured and put them there, with the information, that they intended to hang them before morning.

Captain Moore then started for camp, but got on the wrong road, and did not discover his mistake until he got on to the rebel camp at Aberdeen. He rapidly retraced his steps, found the right road, and without further adventure, reached camp at a late hour at night.

He commanded his company in the battle of Okolona, and bravely performed his duty.

At the battle of Brice's Cross Roads, Mississippi, he proved himself a hero. With but a handful of men, he repulsed repeated attacks of the rebels, and held his position until ordered to withdraw. He rendered important services on the retreat that followed that disastrous battle.

He managed with distinguished success, an expedition to Mound City and Marion, Arkansas, an account of which has already been given.

He was in all the battles and skirmishes of the regiment, in the Missouri campaign.

Before the battle of the Little Osage, he was placed, by order of General Pleasanton, in command of the baggage train. This did not suit a brave spirit like his, especially when there was a prospect of a battle. He put the train in charge of a sergeant, and joined his company, and led it, in the glorious sabre charge, in that engagement. He was severely reprimanded by the General, for abandoning the train without orders. Unquestionably the Captain did wrong, but his fault is forgotten when we consider the motive that induced him to incur the displeasure of his General.

He was, on the consolidation of the regiment, commissioned Major of the new organization. He served in that capacity until its final muster out.

He was a genial gentleman, and a kind, noble-hearted man. As a soldier and officer, he had the respect and confidence of his inferior and superior officers, and of all the men.

He returned to his home at Plymouth, Indiana, where he died of consumption, early in the year 1869.

Major Joel H. Elliott.

Joel H. Elliott entered the 7th Indiana Cavalry as Captain of Company M. His residence at the time of his enlistment, as shown by Adjutant-General Terrell's reports, was Centerville, Wayne county, Indiana. No braver or truer soldier ever fought under the starry flag of our country. No member of the 7th can ever think of him but with feelings of respect and sympathy. His military career was an active one. Wherever the 7th Indiana Cavalry marched or fought, there was found the indomitable Elliott. He never failed to win golden commendations from his superior officers for his courage as a soldier and skill as an officer. On the expedition to West Point in February 1864, he was almost constantly detached from the regiment with scouting parties, and many were the examples of courage and ability he set. On one occasion, while with a foraging party near Okolona, Mississippi, and while the most of his men were in a crib, getting corn, a body of rebels, greatly outnumbering his force, dashed upon him, expecting to capture his entire party. Capt. Elliott hastily mounted a few of his men, and charged with them into the ranks of the rebels, and with revolvers put them to flight without the loss of a man. He led his company in the sabre charge on the evening of February 22d, 1864, at Ivy Farm.

In the battle of Brice's Cross Roads, Mississippi, his courage was very conspicuous. For two hours he had command of a part of the line, and repulsed every attempt of the enemy to break it. He exposed himself so recklessly it was a wonder he was not killed. He was a target for the rebel sharpshooters. In the evening when the regiment was leaving the field, he received a severe and painful wound in the shoulder which disabled him. He was carried in an ambulance during the next day, when his wound becoming so painful he could not endure the jolting of the vehicle, he was left at a plantation, where he remained until his wound was sufficiently healed to enable him to be taken to Memphis. In the meantime, he had been paroled by the rebels. He commanded the detachment of the 7th Indiana on Grierson's raid in the winter of 1864-'65. He was invariably placed in positions of danger, and well did he prove himself worthy of the honor. We have already given an account of the manner in which he, in conjunction with Capt. Skelton, captured Verona, Mississippi, and burned a large quantity of army stores. For his glorious services on that expedition he was breveted Major of the regiment.

After the reorganization of the regiment, he was promoted Major, and as such served with it in Texas, until it was mustered out. He was soon after commissioned Major of the 7th United States regular cavalry, recruited by Maj. Gen. A. J. Smith. He went on duty with it, on the frontiers, among the Indians. By their savage hands he was destined to die. There was a tinge of romance in his life, which is given in the following extract from a letter to the Author, from Capt. Will A. Ryan of company G, of the 7th Indiana Cavalry, the friend and confidant of Major Elliott:

"Among the brave men who figured conspicuously in the annals of the Seventh, my mind recalls one—Captain Joel H. Elliott. I, as an intimate and confidential friend of his, was permitted to see and know him, as few, if any, other members of the regiment did or could have done. The Captain's was a quick, open, generous nature, sensitive as a child, yet brave as a lion. The affections were very strong, and were perhaps the guiding star of his destiny. You will perhaps remember the few days' leave of absence granted to our men to go to our homes and attend the

Presidential election in the fall of 1864. The Captain and myself were among the favored ones. He met me on his return to the regiment, in this city (Terre Haute), and we journeyed on together. He was buoyant with hope. Life had new charms for him. He had seen the lady of his choice, and they were betrothed. 'The course of true love never did run smooth' says the poet, and so in his case. Scarcely two months had elapsed when one evening, upon the eve of an expedition into the enemy's country, he summoned me to his tent, and with manly emotion told me 'the story of his life'—gave in my keeping all the little love tokens that he had so highly treasured, with instructions as to their final disposition in case he should 'not return.' The expedition had fruitful results for our arms, and every one who accompanied it, will remember the daring, dashing Captain Elliott, whose exploit in the capture of a town at midnight, scattering the enemy in all directions, and capturing and destroying so many valuable army stores, was flatteringly complimented by his superior officers. Of course, at that time, I attached no importance to this love trouble of the Captain's; but now, ten years after the occurrence, I regard it as the turning point of his life. His determination from that moment seemed bent on the profession of arms. During our subsequent intimacy when discussing the ladies, his conversation ever carried to my mind the remembrance of this 'affair.' There were detached hints of it in his after letters which came to me from time to time. The affairs of civil life possessed no charms for him. He again sought and obtained preferment in the service of his country, and his appointment to a Majorship in the regular army was a flattering recognition of his merits as an officer. I possess letters of his up within a short time of his unfortunate death, and the same sad undercurrent pervades them all. He had not forgotten his first love. It will be remembered that in an expedition against the Indians on our western frontier, under General Custer, that an attack was made upon an Indian encampment and the Indians badly beaten. Major Elliott, with a detachment of sixteen men, was following up one body of the retreating Indians. A few miles from the scene of battle his body and those of his men were found scalped and mutilated. The history of that heroic combat will perhaps never be known—how, after being ambushed, his gallant band fought 'till the last man was slain.' But certain it is, and those who knew him best will unite with me

218

in the belief, that no truer, braver, or nobler life was ever sacrificed in our country's defense."

On the 27th of November, 1868, on the Washita river, in Indian Territory, the brave Elliott fell, fighting to the last. His body rests in an unmonumented grave on the distant plains of the West. Those who knew him, will, in imagination, make a pilgrimage to his tomb, and to his brave spirit chant the lines of the great poet:

"Soldier rest! thy warfare o'er;
Sleep the sleep that knows not breaking;
Dream of battle-fields no more,
Days of danger, nights of waking.
In our isle's enchanted hall,
Hands unseen thy couch are strewing,
Fairy strains of music fall,
Every sense in slumber dewing.
Soldier rest, thy warfare o'er,
Dream of fighting-fields no more;
Sleep the sleep that knows not breaking,
Morn of toil, nor night of waking.

No rude sound shall reach thine ear,
Armor's clang, or war-steed champing,
Trump nor pibroch summon here,
Mustering clan, or squadron tramping.
Yet the lark's shrill fife may come,
At the day-break from the fallow,
And the bittern sound his drum,
Booming from the sedgy shallow.
Ruder sounds shall none be near,
Guards nor warders challenge here,
Here's no war steed's neigh and champing
Shouting clans or squadrons stamping.

CAPTAIN JOHN R. PARMELEE.

At the time Capt. Parmelee entered the service in the Seventh Indiana Cavalry, he was a practicing attorney at Valparaiso, Porter county, in the State of Indiana.

On the 24th day of August, 1863, he was mustered as First

Lieutenant of company A, of the Seventh Indiana Cavalry. On the promotion of Captain John C. Febles to Major of the regiment, Parmelee was promoted to the vacancy caused thereby, and mustered as Captain November 1st, 1863.

As already stated in chapter 3d, he was severely wounded in the sabre charge, at Ivy Farm, on the 22d of February, 1864, and taken prisoner of war. In the charge, he gallantly led his company, A, which suffered severely in killed, wounded and prisoners. From the field at Ivy Farm, he was taken to Okolona, and from there by railroad to West Point, thence to Starksville, Mississippi, and from there to Columbus, Mississippi, arriving at the latter place on the 25th of February, 1864. He remained at Columbus until the 3d of March following, when he, with many other prisoners, was compelled to march on foot to Demopolis, Alabama, a distance of ninety-five miles, arriving there on the 6th of March. The next day, March 7th, he was taken by railroad to Selma, and from there, by steamboat on the Alabama river, to Cahawba, Alabama, arriving there on the evening of the same day. He remained at Cahawba till the 28th of April, when he was taken on the steamboat "Southern Republic" up the Alabama river to Montgomery, the capital of the State of Alabama. From Montgomery, he was taken to Andersonville, Georgia, *via* Columbus and Fort Valley, Georgia, by railroad, arriving at Andersonville on the 2d day of May. On the next day he was taken to Macon, Georgia, where he remained until July 29th. On the 17th of May, the number of prisoners at Macon, were increased, by the arrival of fifteen hundred Federal officers from Libby prison, at Richmond, Virginia.

On the 20th of July, the Captain, together with six hundred other officers, was taken, by way of Savannah, Georgia, to Charleston, South Carolina, arriving there on the morning of July 30th. There he remained till October 6th, when he was removed to Columbia, South Carolina, where he remained until the 4th of November, 1864. On that day, determined to make an effort to regain his freedom, the Captain, in company with Captains George E. King, of the 113th Regiment of Illinois Volunteer Infantry, and Marcus L. Stansberry, of the 95th Ohio Volunteer Infantry, escaped through the guard lines, and traveling across the country, reached Orangeburg, South Carolina, on the Edisto river, on the 9th of November. At that place, the fugitives procured a skiff, and proceeded in it, down the Edisto to its mouth, reaching that point on the 17th of November. In the evening of that day, by the aid of some Negroes, who owned and navigated a small sailboat, they succeeded in getting aboard of the gunboat *Stetten*, of the United States blockading squadron, lying in St. Helena sound, off Otter Island, on the coast of South Carolina. They remained on board the gunboat two days, during which time, they were treated with the greatest kindness and politeness by the officers and men of the vessel.

After the expiration of two days, they were taken in a small boat to Port Royal harbor, and delivered to Admiral Dahlgren on board his flagship.

After a couple of hours conversation with the Admiral, they were taken in a steam tug to Hilton Head, where they were placed in the hands of General Foster, Commander of the Department. The General and his wife, and all the members of his staff, treated them with the utmost kindness.

Gen. Foster gave them a leave of absence for two months. They proceeded on board the *Orago* to New York City, arriving there on the 25th of November, 1864. From there, they proceeded to their homes.

Soon after reaching home, Captain Parmelee was attacked with inflammatory rheumatism, and was unable to rejoin his regiment, until the 26th of January, 1865, which he did on that day, at Memphis, Tennessee.

He was soon after detailed as Judge-Advocate of a military commission, at Memphis, Tennessee, and served as such until the regiment started for Texas. On the consolidation of the regiment, he was mustered out of the service. Since the close of the war he has made Indianapolis his home, where he is engaged in the practice of the law.

MAJ. JOSEPH W. SKELTON.

Joseph W. Skelton was born on the 22d day of January, 1836, in Gibson county, in the State of Indiana. His father was a farmer of that county. Young Skelton remained on his father's farm till he was sixteen years old, when he secured a position as clerk in a store in Princeton, in Gibson county. He remained in the store till he was nineteen years of age, when he returned to his father's

221

farm, and worked on it till he attained his legal majority. He then married, and settled on his own farm, near the family homestead. His wife died in February, 1861. In April of the same year, he enlisted, in a company recruited in his county, for the period of three months, and went to Indianapolis to be mustered into the service. But the quota of three months men was full, and the company organized in a regiment to serve for twelve months. But before it was mustered, the quota of twelve months troops was filled. The company was then mustered into the service for three years, in the Seventeenth Indiana Regiment of Volunteers. He served with that regiment in all its operations in Virginia. He was with it in the skirmish at Green Briar, which was dignified by the name of battle. He went with the regiment in the winter of 1861-62, to Louisville, Kentucky, and from there to Nashville, Tennessee, from there, by forced marches, to Shilo, but did not arrive there till after the battle.

He then marched with his regiment into Mississippi and Alabama, and was with Buel's army, in its pursuit of Bragg, in the march of the latter, on Louisville.

He then returned to Nashville, Tennessee. From that place, his regiment followed John Morgan, into Kentucky, near Louisville, and returned by forced marches, to Murfreesborough, but arrived too late to participate in that battle.

The Major was employed most of the time in scouting. In February, 1863, he was captured by the rebels, near Readyville, Tennessee, and taken to McMinnville. The next morning the rebels were attacked by the Federal troops, and Skelton was sent to the rear, under guard of four men. The weather being cold, three of the men stopped at a house to warm, leaving but one man to guard the prisoner. When the other guards were out of sight, Skelton, to the great surprise of the remaining one, disarmed him and attempted to escape. But he was soon recaptured, and with a squad of other prisoners, placed under a guard of ten men.

The rebels were mounted, but Skelton was obliged to walk. When within about three miles of McMinnville, he attempted a second time to escape. He leaped the fences and ran for the woods, but in dodging around in them, he ran into a different squad of rebels, and was by them turned over to his first captors.

The rebels thought such a slippery fellow was a fit subject to

222

stretch hemp. They struck him in the face, and beat him with their revolvers till tired, then put a rope, with a noose, around his neck, and the other end of it over the limb of a tree, when the commanding officer, of the last party that captured him, at this critical juncture, stopped proceedings. But they stripped him of his clothing, except his shirt and pants, and were about to deprive him of his boots, when the same officer interferred and put a stop to it. The brutal quartermaster ordered Skelton to run the rest of the way to the town, a distance of three miles. He started on the double-quick, and went a short distance, but the road being rough, and being almost exhausted by his efforts to escape, it was impossible for him to keep up. The quartermaster cursed and swore at him, and struck him with his revolver several times over the head. But it was impossible for him to proceed. The rebel then threatened to kill him, but Skelton, sitting down by the roadside, told him not to; that Gen. Rosecrans would hear of it, and would amply retaliate. Finding that his prisoner could not be frightened, the rebel concluded to let him rest for half an hour; at the expiration of which time, he was marched into McMinnville and lodged in jail.

The next day he was taken to Tallahoma, and placed in the guardhouse with a lot of rebels, confined for various misdemeaners. Their rations consisted of a pint of corn meal per day, which was poured out of a sack onto the floor, in a corner of the room, of which, each man got what he could. In addition to this, the prisoners were kicked and cuffed about by the rebels in a most brutal manner. Skelton, unable longer to endure their insults, said to a young Georgian, who was constantly boasting of his worldly possessions, that there was one thing he did not and never would possess, and that was any principle of a gentleman, for no gentleman would abuse a man when he was disarmed and helpless. The rebel was greatly incensed at this remark, and regretted that there was no opportunity to fight a duel with Skelton.

The rebels were principally Missourians and Arkansans, and a duel, above all things, was what they loved to witness. They set to work, to devise means to let the duel come off.

They were imprisoned in a long storeroom, with a smaller room cut off at one end.

One of the rebels suggested that the fight might take place in that small room. The suggestion was favorably received, and the young Georgian had no alternative but to challenge Skelton, which was formally done. Skelton stated to the rebels, that he, in common with northern men, was opposed, on principle, to dueling, but that under the circumstances, he thought that he would be justified in accepting the challenge, and that, if there was one man present who would see fair play, he would accept. A dozen Missourians stepped forward, and said that they would see that the fight was conducted according to rule.

Skelton waved his right as the challenged party to choose the weapons. His adversary chose dirks, with blades fifteen inches in length.

Skelton took his position and awaited the appearance of his antagonist. He came to the door and said he would give half of what he was worth for Gen. Bragg's permission to fight, but that he could not think of such a thing, without such permission. For, he said, he would surely kill Skelton, and if he did, Bragg would have him hung, and that he would not run that risk for any "d---d Yankee."

The crowd interpreted that into a back-down, and greeted him with jeers and derision.

Thus ended the duel. It, however, had a good effect for the Federal prisoners. It won the respect of the Arkansas and Missouri rebels, who afterwards treated them well, and shared with them their rations.

From Tallahoma, Skelton was taken to Chattanooga. There the rebels threatened to make the prisoners work on the trenches. By the persuasion of Skelton, they refused to do so. To the threats of the rebels to kill them if they did not work, Skelton replied that Rosecrans knew how to retaliate.

While at Chattanooga, two Kentuckians, Union men, although in the rebel army, were brought in heavily ironed, and under sentence of death.

One dark night, during a hailstorm, Skelton, with the assistance of some of his fellow prisoners, let these men down from a window in the second story of the building in which they were confined.

As they were not brought back, it is supposed that they succeeded in making their escape. The next morning the rebel officers made great efforts, by threats and offered bribes, to learn the names of the parties conniving at their escape, but utterly failed.

From Chattanooga, Skelton, with other prisoners, was sent to Libby prison, at Richmond, Virginia, and for three months endured the horrors of that filthy bastile.

He was paroled and sent to Indianapolis, where he was placed on duty as clerk at headquarters at Camp Carrington. But lounging around headquarters did not suit such a restless spirit.

He recruited one hundred men, and was commissioned 1st Lieutenant, and assigned to company F, of the Seventh Indiana Cavalry. He immediately entered on active duty with the regiment. He was a brave, daring, and reckless man, and was nearly always selected for enterprises requiring shrewdness and dash. We have frequently, in the preceding pages of this book, referred to his exploits, and will not repeat them here. The particulars of two of his greatest performances have been reserved for this sketch—the rout of six hundred rebels at Lamar Station, Mississippi, with only thirty men—and the capture of "Dick Davis."

In June, 1864, Capt. John W. Shoemaker resigned, and Lieut. Skelton was promoted Captain of company F to fill the vacancy.

In August, 1864, the regiment was with the army of General A. J. Smith, on his expedition to Oxford, Mississippi. On the 14th of August, 1864, Capt. Wright, of the Seventh Indiana Cavalry, with a battalion of that regiment, pursuant to orders, marched from Holly Springs, north to Hudsonville, whence he dispatched Captain Skelton, with company F, numbering but thirty men, to Lamar, on the railroad, a few miles farther north, to disperse any guerrilla parties that might interfere with the railroad. Captain Skelton bivouacked about sundown in the woods, about half a mile north of the latter town. About eleven o'clock, the Captain received information from a *vidette* stationed in the village, that an armed force was entering it from the south. He immediately awakened his men, and mounting them, marched boldly to meet the enemy, who had reached the railroad northwest of the village, and halted. The night being rather dark, Capt. Skelton and his little band got nearly on to the rebels, before they saw the dark outlines of their force. The first intimation the enemy had of the presence of Yankees, was a shot from Capt. Skelton's revolver, and his command to the company to "charge." With a yell, the

225

Captain and his men dashed into the ranks of the rebels, firing their revolvers right and left into them.

They were taken completely by surprise, and were totally unprepared for an attack. Some of their men had dismounted and thrown themselves on the ground to rest, and most of the rest were dozing in their saddles. The front of their column broke in wild confusion, and running through the ranks of the rear companies of their force, stampeded their entire command. They fled in wild confusion through the town, hotly pursued. Indeed, friend and foe were intermingled, the rebels too much confused to do anything but run, and Skelton's men rapidly emptying the saddles of the former, with their revolvers fired at a distance of but a few feet, and in numerous instances, with the muzzles placed against the bodies of their adversaries. At the south edge of the village was a wide, deep ravine, behind which, the rebels made a stand. Captain Skelton, seeing the fearful odds against him, managed to withdraw all his men, except the Author, who was wounded and taken prisoner. When the company dashed through the rebel ranks, those of the enemy left in the rear, surrendered. At one time, Sergt's Aurand and Corporal F. J. M. Titus, had huddled together, and were guarding nearly one hundred prisoners. When the company was withdrawn from the pursuit, Corp'l Titus wanted to know what to do with the prisoners. Lieut. Crane told him to "parole them and come on." Besides the Author, only one other man of the company was hurt. That one was John E. Kelley, who was shot through the right hand and permanently disabled. He came very near being taken prisoner. A rebel had hold of him, but John managed twice to break loose from him; the last time he did so, he left in the hands of his enemy a good portion of his blouse.

On leaving the field, Capt. Skelton's command got separated, a part returning with him to Holly Springs, and a part under Lieut. Crane going to Lagrange, Tennessee. The rebels retreated to Okolona. The next day the men with Crane, not having made their appearance at camp, Capt. Skelton, with fifty men returned to Lamar, to learn if possible the fate of his missing men. He found in the different houses of the town a large number of badly wounded rebel soldiers, and learned that the citizens had buried several dead ones. The force attacked by Capt. Skelton on that night, was the old regiment raised and commanded by the rebel

Gen. N. B. Forrest, when he was a Colonel. It numbered six hundred picked men, commanded by Col. Kelley, and was at that time on its way to Memphis, carrying out a part of Forrest's plan for the capture of that place. Its inglorious repulse and retreat, for the time being, frustrated Forrest's purpose to capture one of the most important depots of supplies on the Mississippi river.

The guerrillas about the Nonconnah creek were bold in their depredations on citizens, and attacks on Federal patrole and scouting parties. Capt. Skelton had recently lost seven members of his company, who had been captured and murdered by Dick Davis, and was burning for an opportunity to capture that guerrilla chieftain. He got permission to take his company and go in quest of him, supposed to be somewhere in the bottoms of the Coldwater. On the evening of October 1st, 1864, a little after dark, the Captain left camp at White Station, and proceeded towards Cockrum's crossroads in Mississippi. He avoided the roads, and marched through the fields and woods. He had made the habits of the guerrillas a study. He knew it was impossible to surprise their camp by following the highways. Some of their band were always along the line of march, lounging about the houses pretending to be citizens, while a command was passing; but when it was out of sight, would mount their horses concealed behind the house, or in the woods close by, and taking the by-paths, with which they were perfectly familiar, get ahead of the scouting party, and warn their comrades in time to escape or to form an ambuscade. Not only that, but the genuine citizens, to save their property or their lives, by conciliating the outlaws, would voluntarily officiate as messengers of warning. At daybreak the next morning, Capt. Skelton, after a difficult march reached the Coldwater, and effected a crossing. At the first house he came to after crossing, he captured four prisoners. Continuing his march some distance further, his advance was fired on, from a house situated quite a distance from the road. The advance immediately charged up to the house, and prevented the guerrillas from getting to their horses tied in the woods several rods from the house. The rest of the command following Capt. Skelton, dashed up on the run. The guerrillas were escaping through the fields to the woods. When Captain Skelton came up, he saw two men running through the garden towards the woods. Without waiting for the bars across the lane leading to the house, to be thrown down, he put spurs to his horse, and cleared them at a bound. But there was still a high fence between himself and the flying guerrillas. He noticed them slacken their pace to load their carbines. He conjectured that their intention was after reloading, to wheel and shoot him. To prevent that he must capture them before they succeeded in loading. To wait for the fence to be thrown down would take too long. There was not an instant to be lost. His only alternative was to leap his horse over the fence and be on them in a moment. Striking the rollers deep into the flanks of his horse, the animal cleared the fence without touching it; and in a minute after, he was by the side of Dick Davis, with his cocked revolver at his head. Davis had just replaced the cylinder containing the cartridges, in his carbine. The muzzle was pointing towards the ground. All he had to do to be ready for battle, was to raise the muzzle, wheel and fire. Had Captain Skelton been an instant later, he would have, in all probability, been killed. But he was at the side of Davis, ready to blow his brains out if he moved his weapon a hair's breadth. The Captain demanded of Davis his surrender. The latter hesitated, and glancing at his companion, saw that he had not reloaded. The Captain again asked him if he would surrender, when Davis coolly replied: "I guess I will have to, seeing there is no help for it." Skelton said: "Then drop that carbine d---n quick." Davis saw in the flashing eye of the little man before him, that he stood in the presence of his master and dropped his carbine on the ground. An ominous movement of the Captain's revolver, quickly decided the other to follow the example of his chieftain, and "ground arms." Skelton then compelled them to march backwards until he was between them and their arms. He then stood guard over them until some of his men returned from the pursuit of the other guerrillas, and took them in charge. Davis then said to Skelton: "If you had been a moment later I would have saved your bacon." Skelton did not know at that time, that he had captured the scourge of Northern Mississippi, and Southwestern Tennessee. His distinguished captive carefully concealed his name, which was not learned until he was marched into the Irving Block at Memphis, where he was recognized by the officers, who had had him in charge once before. But he knew that he had waked up the guerrillas, who, in all probability, would rally and attempt to release their comrades. He was forty miles from camp, and having

228

several prisoners, deemed it prudent to return before they could unite against him. Before he had crossed the river, a body of guerrillas, attracted by the firing, came dashing upon his rear guard. He wheeled a portion of his command to the rear and charged the rebels and put them to flight. By the time he returned, the rest of his command had crossed the river, and were engaged on the opposite side. Hastily crossing, the Captain ordered a Sergeant to take ten men and charge the guerrillas, who were dismounted and posted behind the trees. The Sergeant and his men were driven back on the main command. Capt. Skelton then selected a trusty sergeant and ten men, and directed him to take charge of the prisoners, proceed down the river and get to camp with them if possible, but if the worst came, not to let one of them escape, while he with the rest of the command fought the enemy back. Placing himself at the head of his men, Skelton led them in the charge upon the guerrillas, and put them to flight, and pursued them in a wild chase through the woods for over a mile. The Sergeant in charge of the prisoners, seeing the rebels routed, concluded his best course would be to follow up Skelton, and did so.

Capt. Skelton had proceeded but a mile further, when he discovered in his front a body of rebels, greatly out-numbering his entire command, drawn up to oppose his further advance. He was expecting, every moment, the guerrillas he had driven on the opposite side of the river, to rally and come upon the rear. Not a moment was to be lost. He deployed as skirmishers, while on the run, twenty of his men, and led them in a charge on the rebels. The latter stood long enough to fire one volley, when they broke and fled in all directions. The Captain then proceeded without further interruption, to camp, arriving there before dark. Although under fire a part of the time, not a man of Skelton's command was hurt. In this little expedition Capt. Skelton displayed great tact and undaunted courage. The service he had rendered humanity and the Federal army was almost incalculable.

Captain Skelton was peculiarly fitted for such enterprises just described. He was ingenious, quick to form his plans, and possessed courage that shrank from no danger. At times his courage partook of the character of rashness. In every fight or battle, he was always in advance of his men. He did the most of the fighting himself. It was invariably his practice on coming in sight of

229

an enemy, to charge. The enemy invariably ran, and separating into small squads, scatter in the woods. Skelton singling out the largest squad, would pursue it until he had captured one or more prisoners. He participated with the regiment in all its raids, expeditions, marches and battles, except those of the Missouri campaign. On the consolidation of the regiment, he was assigned to company C, but was soon promoted Major, and served as such till the muster out of the regiment.

Lieutenant Elijah S. Blackford.

Elijah S. Blackford resides one and a half miles from Warsaw, in Kosciusko county, Indiana. He is a farmer by occupation. He was born in Butler county, Ohio, on the 7th of March, 1825. In 1848, he came with his father to Fayette county, Indiana, and in 1852, he went to Kosciusko county, his present home. In 1863, he enlisted as a private in company I, of the Seventh Indiana Cavalry, under James H. Carpenter, of Warsaw, Indiana, but was mustered with the company September 3d, 1863, as First Sergeant. He served in that capacity with the regiment, until November, 1864, when he was promoted to 2d Lieutenant. On the 1st of March, 1865, he was promoted to 1st Lieutenant, *vice* Lieut. Charles H. Hare, dismissed. He was frequently sent on scouting expeditions, in which he displayed good judgment and pluck. Especially was this the case, when with twenty-five men, on the 14th of May, 1865, he was sent from Lagrange, Tennessee, toward Corinth, to protect workmen employed in repairing the telegraph on the Memphis and Charleston railroad. At Middletown, on the 22d of May, 1865, while on that duty, a "Night Hawk," so called in that country, because they were Union men, compelled to hide themselves in the daytime, but who roamed about at night, and killed guerrillas, came to his camp, with the information, that Bent Rogers, a notorious guerrilla, was at his house, three miles distant, and offered his assistance in capturing him. The next morning, the Lieutenant, with four trusty men, with the "night hawk" for a guide, proceeded to the residence of Rogers, where they found him in bed. His wife appeared at the door in answer to the Lieutenant's rap, and declared that her husband was not at home. The Lieutenant pushed the door open, went into the bedroom, and found Rogers hastily dressing himself. He arrested him and took him to his camp, and from there to

Lagrange. On the way there, at a house, he saw hitched to the fence, a splendid white horse, with an officer's saddle, with a pair of navy revolvers in the holsters. He asked Rogers what that meant. The latter said that it was a horse belonging to "one of our men." At that moment, a tall, fine-looking man, came out of the house, walked leisurely to the horse, mounted it, and rode out into the highway, just as the Lieutenant and his party came up. Rogers introduced the stranger as "Capt. Higgs." The Captain rode by the side of Lieutenant Blackford for quite a distance and chatted pleasantly. In a hollow by the side of the road, were three men dismounted and holding their horses. When opposite, one of them said: "Well, Bent, they have got you at last." Rogers replied: "Yes, they have got me." Captain Higgs turned out of the road to the men in the hollow, politely excusing himself as he did so, while Lieutenant Blackford proceeded toward La-grange. Both sides being equal in strength, neither dared to make an attack. Rogers made no effort to escape. He heard the order given to the men, before starting, to shoot him dead if he made such an attempt. He undoubtedly deemed it prudent to go quietly along. He informed Lieut. Blackford that Higgs was a notorious guerrilla chief in that country, and that the men in the hollow were members of his band.

Rogers was safely delivered to the military authorities at La-grange, sent to Memphis, tried by a military commission, con-victed of robbery, and sentenced to ten years imprisonment in the penitentiary at Alton, Illinois.

On the 7th of June, 1865, Lieutenant Blackford was detailed to serve on a military commission at Memphis, Tennessee, of which Colonel George W. McKeaig was president. Before that commis-sion, Mat Luxton, a notorious guerrilla, and a half brother of the rebel General N. B. Forrest, was brought for trial for his crimes. Owing to the difficulty the Government had in getting witnesses, the trial dragged along for eighty days. But at last he was con-victed of murder and of being a guerrilla, and sentenced to suffer death. He, however, managed to escape, probably by bribing the jailor.

His friends offered thousands of dollars for his release. His mother, and Col. Forrest, his half brother, attended his trial almost daily. He was ably defended by Captain Henry Lee, a Union officer.

While waiting for witnesses in Luxton's case, the Lieutenant went to Sanatobia, Mississippi, with another commission to collect the evidence relating to the ownership of certain cotton, in the possession of W. T. Avant, of Fayette county, Mississippi. On the 5th of July, 1865, he was detailed on another military commission, and served on it, at Memphis, until the close of the war. He was therefore prevented from going with the regiment to Texas.

Capt. Bales being dismissed from the service, the Lieutenant was commissioned Captain of company I, but as the war was over, and being anxious to return to his family, he declined to muster. He soon resigned and returned to his home in Kosciusko county, Indiana.

CAPTAIN ROBERT G. SMITHER.

Robert G. Smither was born in Marion county, Indiana, September 27th, 1846. On the 28th of July, 1861. At the early age of fourteen, he entered the military service, during the rebellion, as a private of company I, of the 26th Regiment of Indiana Volunteer Infantry. He served in that regiment until the 4th of November, 1862, when he was discharged from the service on surgeon's certificate of disability. He reenlisted in company H, of the Seventh Indiana Cavalry, of which company he was soon after appointed First Sergeant. On the 30th of September, 1864, he was mustered as 2d Lieutenant of the company. On the 1st of June, 1865, he was commissioned Captain, and after the consolidation of the regiment, assigned to company A, and mustered as its Captain on the promotion of Captain Moore to Major. He was with the regiment in all its raids, expeditions, campaigns and battles. He was severely wounded in the neck, in the sabre charge, at the battle of Okolona, February 22d, 1864. In a charge of the regiment, at the battle of Egypt Station, Mississippi, on General Grierson's raid, on the 28th of December, 1864, he was severely wounded in the right thigh. For the last three months he was connected with the Seventh Indiana Cavalry, he served on the staff of General George A. Custer, as commander of his escort, consisting of two companies.

After his muster out of the volunteer service, he was appointed First Lieutenant in the Tenth Regiment of United States regular cavalry, which position he still holds.

Since the close of the rebellion, he has been stationed on the frontiers among the hostile Indians. His appointment to a Lieutenantcy in the regular army is sufficient proof of his ability as a soldier and officer.

LIEUTENANT FRANCIS M. WAY.

Lieutenant Way enlisted with General Thomas M. Browne, in company B, of the Seventh Indiana Cavalry. He was mustered into the United States service, on the 28th of August, 1863, as First Sergeant of company B. On the 1st of October, 1863, he was promoted First Lieutenant of the company. He took part with the regiment in its early operations in Kentucky and West Tennessee. On the return of the regiment to Union City, from Jackson, Tennessee, he got a leave of absence, to visit one of his children that was dangerously ill. Before his return, the regiment started on its march to Colliersville. On returning, he proceeded directly to Memphis, and rejoined his command at the former place. He then took command of his company, and gallantly led it through the dangers and trials of the expedition to West Point. At Ivy Farm, on the evening of the 22d of February, pursuant to orders, he dismounted his company, and formed it for the support of the battery of the 4th Missouri Cavalry, but was soon ordered to horse, and joined in the sabre charge. Company B was the last company, and Lieutenant Way the last man to leave the field. After the army had retreated some distance, he was sent back with a force to reconnoiter, and ascertain the purposes of the enemy. On reaching the field, he discovered that they were making no preparations to pursue, thus showing that they had received considerable punishment. On returning to the regiment, it being dark, the Lieutenant was in considerable danger of being shot by his own men. He was riding a white horse, and in the darkness, was thought to be a rebel scout. The words: "shoot that man on the white horse," was passed from man to man, but the darkness that caused that trouble, proved to be his shield of protection, and he escaped unhurt.

He commanded company L, on the expedition to Port Gibson, and Grand Gulf, in the summer of 1864.

When Forrest dashed into Memphis, Lieut. Way was at White Station, with a detachment of the regiment, that did not accompany Gen. Smith to Oxford, Mississippi. The troops at that post occupied a precarious position, and expected every hour to be captured. While there had been considerable picket firing, yet no direct attack had been made on the camp. It was not known there, which side held Memphis, whether Forrest or the Federals. The commanding officer dispatched Lieut. Way, with ten men, to ascertain. He proceeded cautiously toward Memphis. On coming in sight of the picket line, he saw the officer in charge, posting his men behind trees, and making preparations for defense. The Lieutenant posted his men in a good position, and then rode forward alone, to ascertain whether the pickets were friends or foes. When within hailing distance, he called for the officer to step out and hold a parley. He did so, and proved to be a Union officer. From him the Lieut. learned that Memphis was still in the hands of the Federal army. He returned to camp with the joyful intelligence.

He was with the detachment of the regiment in the last invasion of Missouri, by the rebel General Price.

When Price was at Independence, communication with Gen. Rosecrans, at Lexington, thirty miles distant, was kept up by means of a courier line, with posts at intervals of three miles. Lieutenant Way was placed in command of that line. The country swarmed with "bushwhackers," who killed many of the couriers.

After the fight at Independence, Lieut. Way was taken sick and sent to Lexington. He did not recover sufficient health to be again able for active duty, and on the 11th of February, 1865, was discharged on surgeon's certificate of disability. Before his discharge, however, he was commissioned Captain of company B, but declined to muster as such.

He was a strictly temperate man, and did not, during his entire service, taste a drop of any kind of liquor.

He returned to his home, at Winchester, Indiana. He still is, and for a number of years has been, postmaster at that place.

LIEUTENANT CHARLES H. GLEASON.

Lieut. Gleason was born July 5th, 1845, in Utica, New York. He enlisted in company A, of the Seventh Indiana Cavalry, in LaPorte, in the month of July, 1863. He passed through all the gradations of rank from Corporal to 1st Lieutenant, and Adjutant of the regiment. For about three months he was acting quartermaster of the regiment. He was with the regiment in nearly all its expeditions, raids and battles. He acted as Adjutant on the expedition in Missouri after Gen. Price, in his last invasion of that State. He was a young man of irreproachable character, a brave soldier, and a reliable officer.

At the battle of Brice's cross-roads, in Mississippi, June 10th, 1864, the Author saw him under the severest fire during the day, and was impressed with his coolness and courage.

He served with the regiment until its final muster out. Since the close of the war, he has resided at Sardis, Mississippi, and was for six years Clerk of the Circuit Court. He is now manager of a hotel in Sardis. He married in Memphis, Tennessee, and has one child, a daughter, three years old.

LIEUTENANT WILLIAM H. CRANE.

William H. Crane was born February 28th, 1840, in LaPorte county, Indiana. He is a farmer by occupation. He enlisted as a private of company C, Twenty-ninth Regiment of Indiana Infantry Volunteers, on the 7th of September, 1861. He served with the regiment in the siege of Corinth, in the spring of 1862, and on the march to Bridgeport, after the evacuation of the former place, and in the pursuit of Bragg to Louisville. On the 30th of December, 1862, he was discharged from the regiment, by reason of sickness, caused by the exposures incident to the severe campaigns through which the regiment passed.

He reenlisted in the Seventh Indiana Cavalry, and was mustered September 3d, 1863, at Indianapolis, as a Sergeant of company F, of that regiment. He performed active duty with it up to the 21st of February, 1864, at West Point, Mississippi. On the morning of the 21st, his face was severely burned with powder, from broken cartridges, that he was assorting. While so engaged, a spark from the campfire flew into the powder, which exploded in his face. He was unable to take part in the battle the next day.

He came very near being captured on the evening of the 22d. The driver set him out of the ambulance, to get Lieut. Donch, and Capt. Parmelee, but found the portion of the field, where they fell, occupied by the rebels. On returning, he forgot Crane, and had passed him a considerable distance before he remembered him. He started back on the run, and by the time he got the Lieutenant into the ambulance, and started up, the rebels were but a few rods from them. He did not recover from the powder burn so as to be able to participate in the Guntown expedition in the following month of June.

He was with Capt. Skelton, in his night attack on the rebels, at Lamar Station, Mississippi, and fought bravely. He took command of the portion of the company that got separated from Capt. Skelton, marched it to Lagrange, Tennessee, and from there in safety to the regiment at Holly Springs. He was with the expedition to Port Gibson, Mississippi, and in the Missouri campaign in the fall of 1864.

In the latter campaign, when Gen. Pleasanton was approaching Independence, Missouri, he had command of the extreme advance guard, and in coming in sight of the rebels, charged them, captured a few prisoners, and put the rest to flight.

Soon after his return to Memphis, from this expedition, he was commissioned 2d Lieutenant of company F.

He was with the detachment of the Seventh Indiana Cavalry, that accompanied Gen. Grierson on his famous raid through Mississippi, in the winter of 1864-5, and proved himself a reliable officer. He was with the regiment in all its operations and marches afterwards.

On the consolidation of the regiment, he was transferred to company A, of the new organization, and was soon afterwards promoted 1st Lieutenant of the company.

On the 18th of January, 1866, he was mustered out with the regiment. He returned to his home in LaPorte county, where he still resides.

Captain John Donch.

John Donch was born on the 28th day of July, 1824, at Mecklar, Hessia Castle, Germany, in which country he lived till 1851. He served five years, as a private soldier, in the standing army of that country. In August, 1851, he came to America, landing at New York City, since which time he has been a citizen of this country.

In 1852, he went to California, and engaged in mining until the fall of 1853, when he went to Lake county, Indiana, where he has ever since resided.

He entered the United States service, during the rebellion, on the 25th of September, 1861, as a private in the Thirteenth Illinois Cavalry, and was in active service with that regiment, in Missouri and Arkansas. He was promoted to 2d Lieutenant of the regiment, and served as such until the 10th of January, 1863.

On the 10th of August, 1863, he enlisted at Indianapolis, as a private, in company A, of the Seventh Indiana Cavalry. On the 24th of August, of the same year, he was mustered with the company as Sergeant, and on the 1st of September following, he was promoted to First or orderly Sergeant of the company.

On the first of November, 1863, he was commissioned 2d Lieutenant, and on the 26th of the same month, and before he had mustered on his first commission, he was promoted 1st Lieutenant of his company. These promotions followed in rapid succession, and were conferred on a worthy soldier.

He was with the regiment in all its operations in Kentucky, Tennessee and Mississippi up to the battle of Okolona, February 22d, 1864. In the gallant sabre charge, made by the regiment at Ivy Farm, on the evening of that day, he was shot through the right arm, and also in his body. He became unconscious and fell from his horse, and was supposed to be dead, and when the regiment retired, he was left on the field. On regaining consciousness, he went to a log cabin a short distance from where he fell, and was received by the rebel soldiers there in a brutal manner. They cursed and swore at him, and threatened to kill him. True to the principles of the chivalry, they deprived him of his watch and pocket-book. A rebel surgeon dressed his wounds. A chivalric bystander asked the doctor, with a knowing wink, if the Lieutenant's hand needed amputating. The doctor replied: "This man will fight no more while this war lasts," and thus his hand was saved. He lay for that night on the ground, beside a large number of other wounded.

On the next day he was taken, with others, in a wagon to Okolona, and placed in a temporary hospital, where he remained nine weeks. During most of that time, he was in a critical condition. But receiving from the surgeon and nurses proper attention, he was so far recovered at the expiration of nine weeks, as to be able to be moved to Cahawba, Alabama. From that place, at the expiration of four weeks, he was taken to Macon, Georgia, and imprisoned with sixteen hundred other federal officers.

When General Stoneman was making his raid on Macon in 1864, with the intention of releasing the prisoners at that place, the rebel authorities sent six hundred of the prisoners to Charleston, South Carolina, and six hundred to Savannah, Georgia. Lieut. Donch was of the number sent to the latter place. From there, with other federal afficers, he was sent to Charleston. At that place the rebels exhibited the highest type of chivalry, by compelling the prisoners to stand under the fire from the federal batteries, that were bombarding the city. For eighteen days the Lieutenant was kept in the yard of the State prison, without any shelter whatever. His clothing was nearly worn out. His bedding consisted of an old, nearly worn out horse blanket. At night he slept on the bare ground, with his old boots for a pillow. His food was principally worm-eaten rice. While in that place he took the scurvy, and was sent to a hospital out of the city. While there, the yellow fever broke out among the prisoners, of which many of them died. But the Lieutenant escaped that plague.

On the 13th day of December, 1864, he was paroled. He reported at Washington city, where he received a leave of absence, with orders to report at Camp Chase, Ohio, at its expiration.

His appearance at his home in Lowell, Lake county, Indiana, astonished his friends, who believed him dead. He was himself astonished to learn that he had been treated as a dead man, and that his estate had been administered on, and his affairs settled up. He instituted proceedings to set aside the administration. He established his identity, and the court, thinking him a rather lively dead man, annulled the letters of administration, and the proceedings under them.

He then went to Camp Chase, where he remained till the 31st of March, 1865. At that time he was exchanged, and ordered to rejoin his regiment, at Memphis, Tennessee, which he did on the 19th of April, 1865.

He went with the regiment to Alexandria, Louisiana, and from there on the long, dreary march to Hempstead, Texas.

On the consolidation of the regiment, he was transferred to company C, and was soon promoted Captain of the company. He was with the regiment in all its marches in Texas, and was mustered out of the service with it on the 18th of February, 1866. He was a brave soldier, and a capable officer. He fought desperately and suffered much for his adopted country.

Since his return from the war, he has been twice elected

238

Sheriff of Lake county, which office he still holds in this centennial year.

CAPTAIN SYLVESTER L. LEWIS.

Captain Lewis entered the military service during the rebellion, at the early age of seventeen. He enlisted under General Browne, in company B, of the 7th Indiana cavalry. On the 28th of August, 1863, he was mustered as 2d Lieutenant of that company. He was promoted successively, 1st Lieutenant and Captain of company B. He was mustered as Captain, April 9th, 1865. He was at that time but eighteen years of age, and was probably the youngest Captain in any of the Indiana regiments.

As an officer he was brave and capable. He did as much, if not more, hard, active duty, as any other officer of the regiment. He was in the battles of Okolona, Brice's Cross Roads, Port Gibson, and Grand Gulf, Mississippi, in brief, in every raid, expedition, and battle in which the regiment took part.

He performed more scouting duty about Memphis than any other officer of the regiment. That kind of service, during the year 1864 and the Spring of 1865, was extremely hazardous. He was mustered out of the service Sept. 19th, 1865, on the consolidation of the regiment.

A GUERRILLA ATTACK UPON OFFICERS AT DINNER. DEATH OF
A BROTHER OF DICK DAVIS.

The following is furnished by General Browne.

Many circumstances, at the time of their occurrence really thrilling, are constantly transpiring in the field that will never find a place in the history of this war. They are not, taken alone, little things, but they spring up in the over-awing shadows of those that are so hugely great that they pass unnoticed by the historic eye. A great victory—the sanguinary field with its thousands mangled and slain—the fearful charge of infantry against intrenchments, or the sudden and impetuous dash of cavalry upon the enemy's line of glittering bayonets, must ever occupy the foreground of the picture—must ever stand in the way of individual instances of courage and the lesser incidents of peril. The fame of how many personal acts of heroism is tied up in the laurel wreaths that crown the stately brows of Grant, Sherman and Sheridan? He who would attempt to make these small events of war interesting, may fail, but as I have no literary reputation at stake, I take the hazard of the effort.

Our cavalry camp at White's Station was situated in a beautiful grove, on undulating ground; the stately trees threw out their long leafy branches, shutting out the scorching sun, giving us a cool shade for horses and men. It was in that most delightful of Southern months, May, we pitched our tents and went into camp, after a winter and spring of long marches and rapid raids through Western Tennessee and Northern Mississippi, to give a season of rest to our weary men, and to recuperate our jaded and broken-down horses. One day, while at this camp, as I was seated in front of my tent, under the thick boughs of a thrifty dogwood, enjoying my morning paper and my pipe, a young man in the unchanging garb of butternut, so common in this country, presented an order from headquarters, giving him permission to look through the camp for a pair of mules which he professed to have lost. He scrutinized the quadrupeds at the picket ropes, failing to discover his missing property—visited our sutler's tent, drank a few glasses of lager, and then quietly walked out of camp.

A day subsequent to this event, Capt. Elliott, Lieut. Ryan and Lieut. Woods, having grown tired of their unvarying meals of "hard tack and greasy bacon," thought to enjoy a more refreshing repast at a farm-house, which stood but a short distance beyond the pickets. Having previously ordered it, they repaired to the place a short time before noon, enjoying the keen appetite of hungry soldiers, which they expected to appease with the coming dinner. Supposing that they would meet a no more formidable foe than a venerable chicken or tough beef steak, they went unarmed.

Now that the reader may fully understand what is to come, it is necessary that we should take a short survey of the farm-house and its surroundings. It was a two-story structure, with a verandah on the north, a long kitchen at the rear, and several Negro cabins on the right or west side. To the front and north was an open lawn of about one hundred yards in extent, at the edge of which, adjoining the woods, was stationed a picket reserve of some twenty-five men. To the south-east was a wood reaching to the yard fence, and some half mile beyond, the crooked Nonconnah creek coiled through the thickets of trees and bushes.

As it happened Col. W—— had, on that morning, sent into

240

the country a foraging party of some twenty men, of the 4th Missouri cavalry, to procure some little delicacies for his mess table. This party of foragers had been beyond the creek and were returning by a road that led them to camp, and which passed near by the farm-house where our half famished officers were "snuffing from afar" the odors of the dinner pot. When passing carelessly through the woods that line the margin of the creek, and within a half mile of camp, a little cloud of white smoke puffed curling up from the bushes—the sharp crack of a half dozen revolvers fell upon the ear, and three of them—one killed and two wounded—were in an instant put *hors du combat;* the others surprised and frightened by the suddenness of the ambuscade, scampered away "pell-mell, helter-skelter," without stopping to give fight or to ascertain the numbers of the foe. The guerrillas, for such they were, made instant and vigorous pursuit, and an exciting race of half a mile ensued. The Missourians made the best time, and made camp a short distance in advance of their pursuers. The bushwhackers, seeing they had lost the race when at our very lines, suddenly changed their direction, and dashed up to the rear of the farm-house, keeping it between themselves and the picket reserves.

Our officers were, at this time, quietly seated in the kitchen, smacking their lips in anticipation of the good things that would soon be in readiness for them, all unconscious of what was transpiring without. In a moment afterwards, however, they were brought to a sudden sense of their forlorn and defenseless condition, by having a fellow of warlike appearance thrust the muzzle of a revolver into their faces, and demanding "an immediate and unconditional surrender." Their astonishment at this apparition may be imagined. In beating a hasty retreat lay their only hope. To fight without arms, against revolvers, was an odds too fearful to be contemplated with coolness. The guerrilla was between them and the door, and escape in that direction was cut off. They couldn't jump through the roof, and being in the rear of the house, they could neither be seen or heard by the reserves. Fortunately the kitchen windows were up, and in a twinkling, Elliott and Ryan went through them, but not without being greeted with a bullet that whistled harmlessly by their heads. They ran into the main building, thence up stairs and out on the upper verandah, and called vigorously to the reserves, who, without losing a moment's time, responded to their frantic appeal for help by moving on "a double quick" to the house.

While this was going on, the women, children and Negroes, were screaming and running wildly in almost every conceivable direction, making the scene peculiarly grotesque and exciting. Woods and the guerrilla, were, in the mean time, having a single-handed bout in the kitchen. Woods was too late in his attempt to escape, and was compelled to rely upon strategy. Adopting measures adequate to the emergency, he closed with his antagonist and kept him so busy, that he was unable to use his revolver. A rough-and-tumble-combat was progressing with about equal chances of success, when the footsteps of the approaching soldiers admonished the bushwhacker that events were thickening about him, and that it was high time for him to call off his forces and retreat. He suddenly faced about and ran from the kitchen door in the direction of the Negro quarters, but before he could reach his destination, four bullets rattled through his carcass and he fell instantly, *dead*. The four others of his gang, who accompanied him, but did not dismount, fled early in the fray without having fired a shot.

The flight of the frightened foragers, and the firing of the pickets, created quite a commotion in camp. Happening to be on horse-back at the time, and half a dozen officers and twice as many men similarly situated, we gave pursuit to the fleeing guerrillas, but before we could reach them, they had scattered in the creek bottoms, and our effort to capture them was unavailing. Our dead and wounded were found and cared for, and we returned to camp. As we returned, the dead marauder lay under the shade of a forrest tree, surrounded by a knot of soldiers. He was immediately recognized as the man who had visited camp the day before, seeking his *lost mules*. He was a member of the band of guerrillas of which Dick Davis was the leader, and was a half brother to that noted robber chieftain. The boys made his grave at the edge of the woods near the farm house, where his remains now lie; and two large gate posts, constituting his head and foot boards, are the only monuments reared to his memory.

Lieutenant Thomas S. Cogley.

I was born on the 24th of November, 1840, at Liberty, the

county seat of Union county, Indiana. My father, Robert Cogley, was a physician of that place. The most of my life has been spent in my native state. In 1859, I went to LaPorte county, Indiana, from the state of Iowa, where my father at that time resided, and since that time LaPorte county has been my residence. I was living and attending school in the city of LaPorte, in the county of that name, at the outbreak of the rebellion. On going to dinner from school, I read for the first time, the proclamation of the President, calling for seventy thousand volunteers, to suppress the rebellion. On returning to school after dinner, I stepped into a recruiting office that had just been opened, and wrote my name as a volunteer. On arriving at Indianapolis, it was ascertained that the company had more names on its roll than could be mustered with it. The officers selected the number they were authorized to muster, and there were left fifteen or twenty others, among them myself. We felt as if we were disgraced for life, and some of us got together and resolved never to return to LaPorte county to be laughed at. The 8th Indiana regiment of three months troops was not full, and I enlisted in company C of that regiment, and served with it until it was mustered out on the expiration of its term of enlistment. I was with it in the battle of Rich Mountain in West Virginia. After being discharged, I returned to LaPorte, thinking I could do so with honor. In the Fall of 1861, I enlisted under Capt. Silas F. Allen, in company C, of the 29th Indiana infantry volunteers, and on the 30th of August, 1861, was mustered as 1st or orderly Sergeant of the company. I served with that regiment, without losing a day, up to the second day of the battle of Shilo, April 7th, 1862. On that day I was wounded in the right knee with a minnié ball, while the brigade to which the regiment was attached, was advancing on the double-quick, to relieve the brigade of Gen. Ruseau which had exhausted its ammunition. With a large number of other wounded, I was sent home to Indiana till my wound healed. I rejoined the regiment at Stephenson, Alabama, after the siege of Corinth. I marched with the regiment and Buel's corps to which it was attached, from Stephenson to Bridgeport on the Tennessee river. And with it from the latter place to Louisville, Kentucky, in the chase after Bragg. From Louisville, with the Second Division under Gen. Sill, to Frankfort, and from there by forced marches to Perryville, not arriving there, however, until after the battle. From Perryville we returned to Louisville, and from there marched back to Nashville, Tenn. The hardships and exposures of that severe campaign so impaired my health, that I was discharged by reason thereof, on the 14th of January, 1863. I then returned to LaPorte, and began the study of law. Finding it difficult to apply myself to books, when there was so much being said and written about battles, in August, 1863, I enlisted with Capt. John Shoemaker in company F, 7th Indiana cavalry, and was appointed Orderly Sergeant of that company. Being at home on leave of absence when the regiment left Indianapolis, it had reached Colliersville, when I rejoined it, and therefore I was not with it in its operations in Kentucky and West Tennessee. I was with it in the expedition to West Point, and in the sabre charge on the evening of February 22d, 1864; on the expedition to Guntown and in the battle of Brice's Cross Roads, June 10th, 1864; on the expedition to Port Gibson and Grand Gulf, Mississippi, in July of the same year.

I was with Gen. A. J. Smith's army on his expedition to Oxford, Mississippi, up to August 14th, 1864. On the night of the 14th of August, I was captured in the fight Capt. Skelton had with the rebels at Lamar, Mississippi, an account of which is given in his sketch. Almost at the very onset I was shot in my right side with a revolver, the ball striking the lower right rib, and following around in front and lodging over the pit of the stomach, but I was still able to keep the saddle. South of the town was a ravine from twenty to thirty feet in width and from six to ten feet in depth. The rebels, on reaching it, tumbled over each other into it, and managed to get on the other side where their officers succeeded in rallying them. Capt. Skelton managed to withdraw his men at the ravine, but I did not hear the order to retreat, and at the rapid rate at which my horse was going did not have time to observe correctly what the rest of the company were doing, and on reaching the ravine, made no effort to stop my horse, in fact, the first knowledge I had that a ravine was there, was when I was nearly thrown over my horse's head, when he struck the opposite bank, and with great difficulty, kept from falling backward into the ravine. By the time my horse had fully recovered an upright position, the rebels had partially formed and were advancing towards the ravine. I knew my horse could not recross it without momentum to carry it over. Besides, I had no idea that my own men were retreating, but thought that having discovered the ravine in time to avoid it, had gone around and would be with me in a moment. I saw between myself and the rebel line an officer, whose uniform in the night looked like those of Union officers. Thinking it was either Capt. Skelton, or, Capt. Wright, who possibly had arrived with reinforcements, I rode towards him. I thought it prudent however, before getting too close to him, to ascertain whether he was friend or foe. For that purpose I called out to him: "What command do you belong to?" Receiving no answer after a pause of a moment, I again said: "Are you a federal officer?" Our horses had been approaching each other on a slow walk, and by the time I asked the second question, I was close enough to see that the person in front of me was a rebel. I saw his right arm raising, and I supposed it was for the purpose of bringing his revolver to bear on me. Intending to get the first shot if possible, I hastily fired at but missed him. He instantly spurred his horse toward me, which struck mine so violently as to nearly knock it off its feet, at the same time thrusting his revolver at my body with the evident intention of shooting me through. But the muzzle struck my right arm just below the elbow, as I was raising it to fire at him again, and on firing his revolver the ball passed through my arm. Seeing that I was wounded he rode away without saying a word or paying any further attention to me. An instant later I was in the rebel lines, and had it not been for my sabre, would have escaped notice, and probably got away. The rebels did not have sabres, and seeing one on me, attracted the attention of a rebel, who, leaning forward in his saddle to look at me, exclaimed: "By G---d that it is a Yank, surrender!" I said: "Certainly, sir," and handed over my revolver which I still held in my hand. Two of them led my horse a few rods to the rear, and made me dismount. The first thing they demanded was my pocketbook. I produced it, and was amused to see with what eagerness they looked through it expecting to get money. Finding none, they wanted to know "why in h---l" I had none. At that time there were but two Confederates with me, the rest were at the front. One of the two, magnanimously offered to let me escape. The other objected, saying it was known that a prisoner was taken, and if they allowed me to escape, they would get into trouble. The other rebel then grew wonderfully strict, and cocked his musket and aimed it at me, and threatened to kill me if I made an effort to run. I told him he need not be alarmed, for I was too badly wounded to run if I had a chance. He affected not to believe that I was wounded, saying that it was a Yankee ruse to get a chance to run. In their haste to get my pocketbook, they forgot to deprive me of my sabre. One of them seeing it pretended to be alarmed, and presenting the muzzle of his musket at my head, demanded it. I had just handed it over and lain down on the ground, when an aid came up with an order for me to be taken before the commanding officer. Accordingly, I was taken on to the field in the midst of a group of officers, one of whom commenced interrogating me in a very harsh manner. He would not believe that his command had been put to flight by only thirty men, and intimated rather plainly that it was his opinion that I was lying about the number of men who had attacked him. I laid down on the ground in front of his horse, and found it impossible, from the intense pain from the wound in my side, to avoid an occasional groan. The officer wanted to know if I was wounded. I told him I was. His manner immediately changed to kindness, and in the rest of our conversation, I thought from his tone of voice that he really sympathized with me. While we were talking, a rebel officer came dashing up, and said he believed the "Yanks" were about to open fire on them from a battery on an opposite hill. The commander ordered a Captain with a company forward to reconnoiter. The officer proceeded a short distance, and mistaking the members of our company, who were riding about trying to get together, for artillery, returned and gave it as his opinion that the "Yanks" had artillery and were preparing to open fire. In the meantime I informed the commandant that there was quite a force of Federal cavalry at Holly Springs. That information made him exceedingly nervous. And well it might. It was but a few miles across from Holly Springs to the road on which he had to retreat, and if the troops at that place got information of his position, they could easily cut him off. When the officer reported artillery on the opposite hill, the commander instantly ordered a retreat. It was begun and continued in haste.

I was placed under guard in the centre of the column and was compelled to keep up on foot. That, I was not able to do very long. The wound in my side involved a portion of the right lung. The increasing inflammation, and the rapid walking, causing my

246

breathing to be more rapid, rendered my sufferings almost intolerable.

Unable to go further, I stopped. That caused the troops in the rear to halt. The guard threatened to shoot me if I did not go on. At that time I believed I was in the hands of guerrillas, and that my death was only a question of time. That belief nerved me to bid the guard defiance. He was about to carry his threat into execution, when the adjutant of the regiment came dashing up from the rear, to ascertain the cause of the interruption of the march. Seeing the guard with his musket leveled at me, he knocked the muzzle upward with his hand, and demanded of him his reason for treating a prisoner in that way. The guard explained that he was obeying orders. The adjutant then ordered him to move on with me slowly, while he went to the rear to get an animal for me to ride. He then spoke to me kindly, and told me to walk on a short distance, when he would have something for me to ride. In a few moments he returned with a mule, off of which one of their men had been shot, and assisted me in mounting it. He then got me a canteen of water, the contents of which I immediately drank, when he ordered one of the men to refill it for me. My condition was then splendid in comparison with what it had been, but still I suffered greatly. The mule, I was riding, was a small short-legged animal, and could not keep up with the column by walking. It was constantly lagging behind, and the guard every few minutes had to whip it and make it trot to catch up. At such times, the pain caused by the jolting was intense. Every few minutes during that night, and until 4 o'clock in the afternoon of the next day, that was my experience. The next day, at the request of some of the officers, I related the manner in which I was captured, which, they told to Col. Kelley, the commander of the expedition. My account agreed so nearly with his own, that there was no doubt but that he was the man I encountered in front of his lines, and that he was the one who shot me. After my story had been told him, he appeared opposite, and rode for quite a distance a rod or so from me, scrutinizing me carefully, but did not speak a word. He looked upon me with anything but a friendly eye. From the subdued conversation of the officers, that I overheard, I learned that Col. Kelley was dreading the anger of Gen. Forrest, for allowing himself to be beaten by inferior numbers. I could not but notice that I was regarded with more than ordinary interest, as I underwent an inspection from every officer in the command. Some of them sought interviews with me, and expressed their unbounded admiration of the feat of one company in making them run.

With one or two exceptions, I was treated well, so far as the circumstances would permit. No attention had been paid to my wounds, because the columns did not halt but once from the time of commencing the retreat, until it crossed the Tallahatchie river in the afternoon of the next day. After crossing the river at New Albany, the command halted for a brief rest. While there, the surgeon dressed my wounds. I laid down on my back on the ground, and sitting astride of my body, the surgeon cut into the flesh in the pit of my stomach, and extracted the ball.

During the march, the soldiers manifested their kindness by giving me water. One insisted on me taking his last cracker. Not being hungry, I at first refused, but he urged me to take it so persistently and with such kindness, that to please him, I did so. At New Albany, with some of their own wounded, I was placed in a lumber wagon, and after a march of five or six miles further, camped for the night. With the other wounded, I was taken to a house, the lady of which, spared no pains to make us comfortable. She gave greater attention to myself than to the others. She placed a featherbed on the floor for me to sleep on, and gave me first something to eat. The rebel wounded complained of that. She then explained that her motive for so doing was, in the hope that some Northern mother would bestow the same kindness on her own son, who was a prisoner of war in the distant North.

The next day we were taken in the same jolting, uncomfortable vehicle to Pontotoc, where I again slept on a comfortable bed. The next day, we were taken to Okolona, on the Mobile and Ohio railroad, and from there by railroad to Lauderdale, Mississippi. At that place, I was placed in the hospital, established for the reception of the badly wounded from the battlefields in the north and interior parts of the State. The garrison consisted of convalescents.

While there, I received the same care and attention given to the rebel soldiers. The food was poor and scanty, but it was the best the Confederate government could furnish. It was plainly evident to those familiar with the internal affairs of the rebel government, that it could not last much longer. There was an undisguised discontent among the rebel soldiers. What disgusted them more than anything else was, the utter worthlessness of Confederate money. The soldiers would frequently say to me, that if their money was as good as our greenbacks, they could whip the North. What the rebel government got from the planters, they had to take almost by force.

While at Lauderdale, the soldiers were paid off, in Confederate script. Some of them drew several months pay, and gave it all for a watermelon and a few half-ripened peaches.

I knew that as soon as my wounds were sufficiently healed, I would be sent to some prison pen. I resolved to attempt an escape, rather than run the risk of ending my life in such a place. I soon learned that the guards were placed on their posts around the hospital enclosure, at four o'clock in the morning, and relieved at eleven o'clock at night. That between the hours of eleven p.m. and four a.m., there was no one to prevent a person from leaving the premises. My plan evidently was, to leave the hospital some time after the guards were relieved for the night. To do so, without attracting suspicion, I had for several days, previous to starting, invented several excuses for going out of the hospital, between eleven and twelve o'clock at night. This occurred so frequently that nothing was thought of it. I resolved to make the attempt to escape on the night of the 10th of October, 1864. On the evening of that day, some of the rebel soldiers bought some sweet potatoes. One of them baked two very large ones and gave them to me. I took them to my bed and wrapped them in my blouse, intending to save them for the next day while on my journey. The head of my bed was at a window. I availed myself of a moment when no one was looking, to toss my blouse, hat, and boots out of it; for, I was afraid if I put them on when I left, that it might cause a suspicion that I did not intend to return. At eleven o'clock, I heard the guard relieved. All in the apartment where I was, except myself and the steward, were asleep. The latter was deeply interested in a novel, he was reading. About half an hour after the guards were relieved, I got up, put on my pants, and went to the door. The steward looked up but immediately resumed his reading. I passed out, got my hat, blouse, and boots, went to the east end of the enclosure, and put them on, and after pausing long enough to know that I was not being watched, got over the fence, went to the Mobile and Ohio railroad, a few hundred yards distant, and started north on it as rapidly as I could walk. That was the hardest night's travel I ever had in my life. I was constantly imagining that I was pursued, and consequently taxed my strength to the utmost.

The transition from sickbed, to the violent exercise of walking on a railroad track in the dark, was radical in the extreme, and no one in my enfeebled condition, unless nerved with the energy of despair, could have endured the fatigue.

The ties were laid unequal distances apart, which necessitated taking long and short steps, thereby rendering travel more laborious. It being very dark, I frequently missed the ties, which caused me to stumble and fall. About four o'clock in the morning, I reached Gainsville Junction, twenty miles from Lauderdale. There was a locomotive on the track, and men were moving about with lanterns. I stepped off to the right side of the railroad, intending to go around the station. I soon found myself ascending a very steep hill, covered with a heavy growth of cedar. On gaining the summit, I paused to rest. The station was just below me, and I could hear the men talking. From the fragments of their conversation, I learned that a construction train was about to depart. Not knowing which way it was going, I thought it prudent to wait and see, as I would be in some danger if it was going in the same direction I was.

The exercise of my morning's walk, gave me a good appetite, and while waiting for the train to start, and daylight to come, I ate one of my sweet potatoes. It was my plan to travel at night and conceal myself in the daytime. I chose the railroad, instead of the wagon road, to avoid the necessity of inquiring the way, which I would have been compelled to do, had I taken the latter, and would have been constantly running the risk of detection. I knew the Mobile and Ohio railroad ran north, and that no trains were run at night, and by taking the railroad I would be comparatively safe. I had been in the habit of carrying with me on our expeditions, a war map. From it I knew there was a branch road from the Mobile and Ohio road to Columbus, on the Tombigbee river. But it had escaped either my attention or recollection, that there was a branch road to Gainsville, on the same river. My ignorance or forgetfulness of that fact came near costing me my life, as will be seen further on. I felt that I was in a good hiding place for the day, and that I ought to rest. But I thought that when I was missed in the morning at the hospital, that efforts would be made to recapture me, by means of blood hounds.

The rebel officers had taken particular pains to impress on my mind, that that was the way they pursued and captured their runaway prisoners. Nearly every day I read in the papers they brought me, accounts of Union prisoners being hunted down with those ferocious animals. I therefore resolved to travel that day and put as many miles as possible between me and Lauderdale. At daybreak I resumed my journey. I made a circuit to the right, to avoid the station. After traveling a mile, I came to the road to Gainsville. Thinking it was the Mobile and Ohio road, I took a direction through the woods, parallel with it. After walking an hour or two in that way, I went on to the track to see if the coast was clear, intending if it was, to travel on the railroad track, as it would be easier than dodging through the brush in the woods. About half a mile ahead, I saw a party of men at work repairing the road. I then went into the woods on the left of the railroad, intending to get far enough from it, to pass the working party without being seen. I went quite a distance into the woods, out of sight of the railroad, and started north, which direction was indicated by the moss on the trees, supposing I was going parallel with the railroad, but in fact I was getting farther from both roads. I traveled two hours in the woods, thinking it safer to do so than to venture on the track. I sat down on a log to rest. While resting, I mechanically broke off some twigs in reach of me, and with the end of one, gouged holes in the decayed surface of the log. I then started, as I supposed, in the direction of the railroad. Not finding it after going quite a distance, I quickened my pace to a very rapid walk. Hour after hour went by, and I was no nearer the railroad than when I started. A suspicion that I was lost flashed across my mind, and with it a natural feeling of alarm, and the abandonment of my common sense. Distrusting my compass, the moss on the trees I followed the direction of the sun, as rapidly as I could walk, and part of the time on the run. Toward evening, when the sun was well down toward the horizon, I came to the identical log on which I sat in the morning the rest. There were the twigs I left sticking in it, the bits of rotten bark I had chipped off, and the pieces of broken twigs. I knew to a certainty that I was lost. I fully comprehended my

251

situation. I was in a pine wilderness, without anything to eat, and with no means of procuring food, the knowledge of which increased my appetite. I sat down on the log to think. I thought of everything I had heard recommended for a person in my situation. I thought of "Davy Crockett's" remedy: to go in the direction I was sure was the wrong one. I found no hope in that, for I had been in every possible direction, and had only reached my starting point. Suddenly it flashed across my mind, that the construction trains on the railroad would soon be going into quarters for the night, and that the whistle of the locomotive could be heard, in that flat pine forest, for many miles. I therefore sat intently listening for the locomotive. I had but half an hour to wait, when my heart bounded with joy at hearing a whistle much nearer than I expected. I was waiting to hear it again, so as to be sure of the direction, when I was confused by hearing in an opposite direction, the faint sound of a locomotive's whistle. A moment later, I heard again the first whistle, and concluded that the distant sound was an echo. I did not know it, but the fact was, I was between two railroads, and the distant whistle was from the Mobile and Ohio road, my proper route.

I started in the direction of the Gainesville road as rapidly as I could go. I soon struck an old abandoned wagon road, which, going in the direction of the sound of the locomotive, I followed till dark. Being fearful of again getting lost by traveling in the night, and not knowing certainly that the wagon road would lead me to the railroad, and knowing that I had but to wait for the whistle of the locomotive in the morning to get the right direction, I concluded to *bivouac* for the night, expecting to be refreshed in the morning by a good sleep. I leaned some sticks against a large pine tree, and covered them with pine brush, to shelter me from the dew. I crawled under the covering and tried to sleep. For several hours, the thoughts of my peculiar situation prevented sleep, and as the night wore on, it grew so very cold, that slumber was out of the question. Late in the night I was roused to my feet by hearing the baying of hounds following my trail. I thought the rebels had followed me with bloodhounds, and that I would soon be retaken. I was fearful of being worried to death by the dogs, before their masters could come up. I got a club, and placing my back to the tree, waited for them to come on. The baying followed the course I had come precisely, and was getting nearer and nearer. Occasionally it would cease, as if the scent was lost, and then break out again nearer and with greater vigor, as if it had been found. The dogs came so close, I could hear them snuffing. The barking ceased, and a moment later I heard a Negro calling the dogs away. I concluded that it was a party of Negroes hunting coon and opossum, a nightly custom of theirs, not so much for the amusement of the chase, as for the meat of those animals. That incident has often caused me to wonder why the hair of our heads will persist in standing on end, when the owner of it is frightened!

With the appearance of daylight, I started on my way, following the road which still went in the direction in which I heard the locomotive the evening previous.

It was evident that my strength had been overtaxed. The cravings of hunger were terrible. I was obliged to lay down and rest every few rods. It took me several hours to go one mile. I found in the road a rotten ear of corn. That greatly encouraged me, for I reasoned that I must be near some habitation. I ate a few of the grains, but they were so far decayed and poisonous, that they caused me to vomit violently for quite a while afterwards. About 8 o'clock a.m., I heard the whistle of the locomotive. I judged from the sound that the railroad was about a mile distant. On going half a mile further I came in sight of a plantation, nearly a mile off. I started for it for the purpose of getting food from some of the Negro shanties that were between me and the plantation residence. I had to cross a large field of hemp. I was so weak I could not lift my feet above the hemp, which was bent over on the ground, and was therefore being constantly tripped and thrown to the ground. I had to abandon walking, and make the rest of the distance through the hemp by crawling on my hands and knees. I entered an enclosure in the rear of the Negro quarters, used for a hog pasture, and covered with heavy growth of white oak shrubs higher than my head, in which I could effectually conceal myself. I cautiously approached the shanties. I saw a Negro woman at the edge of the enclosure, giving swill to a sow and pigs in a pen. I attracted her attention and asked her to bring me something to eat. She said she would send her husband to me in a moment. I requested her not to tell anyone else. She said: "You needn't be afraid, I knows whose you ahr," and started towards the shanties. To guard against treachery, I changed my position, where I could observe but be myself concealed. In a moment I saw a powerful Negro approaching the pigpen with a pail. He pretended to throw swill to the sow, then setting the pail down, looked in the direction where I was when the wench left me. Not seeing me, he got on a log, and drawing himself up to his full height, looked slowly over the enclosure, and gave a subdued whistle. Knowing that he could be trusted, I went a short distance towards him and attracted his attention by whistling. In a moment he was with me. I told him I was a Union prisoner, escaping from the rebels, and was starving, and requested him to get me something to eat. He went to his shanty and in a short time returned with a large loaf of corn bread, baked in the ashes without salt, a piece of boiled hog's jaw, and a bottle of sour milk. I made a vigorous attack on the grub, the Negro watching me eat with great satisfaction. I noticed him observing my uniform wistfully, and he mentioned what I was about to propose myself—the exchange of my army blue for a suit of citizen's clothes. A bargain was struck, but in the negotiation I observed that he had a keen eye to getting the best end of it. I was not particular, however, and would have given a fortune if I had had one, for the food he brought me. After a brief absence, he brought what was left of an old worn out broadcloth coat, without a button on it, a pair of gray pants tolerably good, an old white hat, that completely enveloped my head, and a nearly worn out horse blanket. I dressed myself in my new uniform, and was ready to assume the *role* of rebel. To make the trade perfectly satisfactory to me, my sable friend threw in an old potmetal pocket knife, and two matches. He also told me that he was to butcher some hogs that afternoon, and that he would get some of the meat, and if I would wait, he would cook some of it and bring it to me. I agreed to wait. I learned from him for the first time, that I was on the railroad to Gainesville, and had been traveling all the time out of my true route. He told me that there were no rebel troops at Gainesville, and that my best way would be to go to that place, cross the river, and take the wagon road to the Mobile and Ohio road. I concluded to take his advice. I hid myself in the bushes, and listened to the progress of slaughtering the swine. I waited patiently hour after hour for my deliverer to make his appearance with a generous slice of smoking fresh pork, but he came not. Night came but still I saw nothing of him. About nine

254

or ten o'clock, it grew quiet about the shanties, and I concluded to reconnoiter, and get some fresh meat if possible. I found my friend in the first shanty I looked into. I asked him why he had not brought the meat as he promised. He said they did not get through slaughtering till late, and that he had not yet received his rations of meat, and possibly might not get any. It was so dark outdoors, it would have been impossible for me to have traveled. The bright fire, blazing in an old fashioned clay fireplace, was inviting. I got permission to lay on the floor in front of the fire, until the moon rose. The knowledge that I might at any moment be discovered, if the overseer should happen to look in, kept me from sleeping. About three o'clock in the morning my host got up and told me he would be obliged to go to work in an hour, and that the overseer would be likely to be around at any moment, and that he had barely time to conduct me to the railroad, and get back for rollcall. Taking a loaf of bread he handed me, we started, and after a walk of half an hour reached the railroad, where my Colored friend left me, his parting words being: "God bless you, Massa!" I proceeded a few miles that day, but when night came, I traveled towards Gainesville as rapidly as I could walk. About ten or eleven o'clock, I stepped into a Negro shanty on a large plantation, and learned that I was two miles from Gainesville, that the town was occupied with rebel troops, that the ferry at the river was in their possession, and that anyone attempting to cross without a pass from the commander of the post, would be arrested as a deserter. My only safe course was to retrace my steps to Gainesville Junction and get on the Mobile and Ohio Railroad. I walked the balance of the night with my utmost speed towards the junction. I rested some during the day, and watched my opportunity when trains were not passing, to make as many miles as possible. An hour's walk after dark that night brought me to the junction. I started north on the Mobile and Ohio railroad. After four days and nights of travel, I found myself only twenty miles from my starting point. I followed the railroad without any particular adventure, to Okolona, traveling all the time during the night, and part of the time during daylight. I got my food from the Negroes, by going to their quarters in the night. At Okolona I took the wagon road to Holly Springs. I passed through Okolona at night. On the evening of the next day, about fifteen miles from Pontotoc, I saw a Negro by a splendid blazing campfire. I stopped to have a chat with him. He was going to Okolona to get a load of salt. He told me that about one hundred of the State militia occupied the town of Pontotoc, and that their business was to arrest deserters and hunt down conscripts. He told me that no one could pass through the town without written permission from the commander. I knew my only safety was to get beyond Pontotoc before daylight. I intended on getting in sight of the town, to go around it. I started for Pontotoc as rapidly as I could go. To facilitate my travel I pulled off my boots and carried them in my hands. Pontotoc was at an abrupt turn in the road. I traveled much faster than I was aware of, and reached the town sooner than I expected. I was astonished to find myself at a picket post at the turn of the road. I did not dare to retreat, for fear of being pursued if seen. It was late at night, or rather early in the morning, and the picket was sleepy. He sat on a pile of rails, on the opposite side of the road, with his back to me. Having my boots off I walked by him without making any noise, and without being observed. I passed through the town, keeping in the shadow of the buildings. At the other end of the town was another post, which I passed without being seen. I was once more out of immediate danger.

Half a mile from the town the roads forked. Not knowing which was the right one for me to take, I very naturally took the wrong one. But intending not to run the risk of getting far out of the way, I rested in a cedar clump till daylight, when I started on, and about a half a mile further, came to a log house by the roadside on a hill. I stepped in, and learned that I was on the wrong road. A free Negro and his wife lived there. Their breakfast being nearly ready, the man invited me to partake. I was sitting down to the table when someone at the gate called. I noticed the man and woman cast looks of apprehension toward me, and the former left the house hastily, and entered into conversation with some one outside. I suspected the individual was a rebel. I asked the woman if he was, and she said she believed he was. I improved the time, however, in eating. A moment or two later, the Negro came in, and told me that the person outside was a rebel soldier, in search of his horse that got away in the night. That with difficulty he kept him from coming into the house, by making him believe that his horse was in a hollow a short distance from the house, that he had gone there to look for it, but that he would soon be back for breakfast. That he, the Negro, guessed that I did not care to meet the rebel, and that I had better eat as rapidly as possible, and get away before he returned. He said he would direct me to the Holly Springs road. I drank my coffee, grabbed a piece of fried ham and a piece of bread, and under the guidance of the Negro left the house. He took me into a hollow, away from the road, and pointing out a path, told me to follow it until I came to a log house, on a plantation, a mile distant. He told me to inquire there for a certain Negro, and tell him who sent me there, and that he would understand what was wanted. My guide told me, that the Negro I was to inquire for, knew every road and by-path between there and Memphis, and that he would give me full instructions. He also told me that he thought I was a rebel deserter. That such persons came to his house nearly every day for directions and food; and that he cheerfully rendered them all the aid in his power, but that he had to be very cautious about it, for if the rebels knew what he was doing, they would probably kill him. I followed the path as directed, and soon came to a cornfield in which were some Negroes husking corn. I knew from the description given of him, the Negro I was to see. He was a tall powerful man, and the overseer of the plantation. I addressed him by name. He answered me gruffly, by asking what I wanted there. I told him I was sent to him to learn the way to Memphis. He looked very knowing and made a signal for me be silent. After husking a few minutes, he ordered the others to keep on at work, while he husked a shock of corn a few rods distant. He started toward it, and made a motion for me to follow him. When we were alone, he told me he knew who I was, and that I would have to be very cautious, or I would fall into the hands of the rebels, who scouted through the woods every day in search of deserters and conscripts. He pointed across the field to a road, that would lead me to another road, that would lead to the Holly Springs road. He advised me not to attempt to go to it in daylight, as I would be running the risk of being captured.

I hid in the field till night, when I started. I found the first road without difficulty. The night was extremely dark, and the road very rough. I stumbled and fell so often, that by the time I reached a plantation two miles distant, I was almost exhausted. I concluded to stop at a Negro shanty till the moon rose. I stepped

257

into one, and found I was within a few hundred yards of the other road I was looking for. I lay down on the floor in front of the fire to rest. About ten or eleven o'clock, some Negroes came in, and from their conversation, I learned that they had been to church. One of them wanted to know who I was, when I came, where I was going, and what I wanted. The wench told him, he knew as much about it as she did. After a few moments, he repeated his questions. He wanted to know if I was a white man. On being told that I was, he remarked that that was no place for me. That a certain rebel captain, with twenty men, was but a short distance from there, and that he would surely stop and search their quarters, as he usually did, and if he found me there, they would get into trouble. He requested the wench to wake me. She told him to wake me himself. Thinking it was time to be going, I got up, told the Negro that I had heard his conversation, and requested him to conduct me to the road that would lead to the Holly Springs road. He readily offered his services, and in a moment I was walking toward Pontotoc. In a few moments I heard the tramp of horses behind me. I got over the fence into a field of hemp, and laid flat on the ground, until a body of rebel cavalry passed, when I went into the road again, and followed them up, keeping several rods in their rear. On coming to the main road, they went toward Pontotoc, and I started rapidly in the opposite direction toward the Tallahatchie river. About 4 o'clock in the morning, I arrived in New Albany on the river. To the left, I saw some tents and a few smouldering fires, indicating that there were some troops at that point, but I saw no pickets. I crossed the river on a log, the bridge having been burned, and hurried on toward Holly Springs. I did not stop to rest that day, but kept steadily on. At noon, I stepped into a farmhouse to get dinner. The proprietor was a physician, but was not at home. The lady of the house had company. I sat down to the table with quite a number of other persons, who, to my great satisfaction, paid no attention to me, so I escaped being drawn into conversation. I learned from their remarks, that there was a rumor afloat that the Federal troops had surprised and captured Holly Springs, that morning, but that they discredited it. After dinner, observing one or two persons paying for their meals, I knew pay would be expected of me. The landlady came near me, as if to receive it. I thanked her kindly for my dinner, not having any legal tender, and, departed. She looked disgusted, and said: "yes, I understand." I had gone but about half a mile, when I saw a man coming toward me, in a great hurry, motioning with his hand for me to go back. When he got close enough for me to hear, he said the "Yanks" had taken Holly Springs, and were preparing to march further South, and if I did not want to be captured, for me to turn back. I affected alarm at the information, but instead of turning back, I walked faster toward Holly Springs.

Soon after, I met a woman in a buggy, who said she had been to Holly Springs, and that it was in the possession of the Union army. When within two or three miles of the city, I met a man coming out of the brush, with the same startling news, that the "Yanks" were in town. I could not avoid stopping to talk with that fellow, and from him I learned, that he had a store in town, and that in the morning, hearing that the Federals were coming, fled, and had been hiding all day in the bushes. He remarked that he did not think that I was all right, or I would not persist in going into town, when the Yanks were there. Seeing I was about to have trouble with him, I left him. I had hardly got out of sight of him, when I found myself face to face with two rebel officers, mounted. They were riding slowly, one in advance of the other, but were in a deep study. The first one barely glanced at me, and rode on. The second was about to pass without seeing me. However, he happened to look toward me, and made a motion with his hand, as if reining in his horse, but observing that his companion was keeping on, he went off into his reverie again, and I escaped unmolested. I thought they did not act like they would if the Yanks were in town. At the crossing of the railroad, half a mile from the city, I learned from some little boys at play there, that the report of the Yankees having possession of the place, was a canard, gotten up by a wag, for sport. I made a wide circuit around the city to the Memphis road.

Nothing of particular interest occurred until near Colliersville. It was toward evening. The uppers of my boots had broken loose from the soles, and it was difficult for me to walk in them. There was an old deserted log house a few rods from the road, nearly concealed from view from the road, by timber and bushes. I thought I would go to the house and repair my boots. I cut strips off the tops of my boots, and fastened the soles to the uppers, by boring holes through them with my knife and tying

259

them together with the strips. I had just finished the repairs, when I heard behind me, the click of a revolver. I knew full well that I was in the power of an enemy, and that my only hope of escape was to pass myself off as citizen.

Waiting a moment to recover my self possession, I rose from the floor on which I had been sitting, and turned around, as if by accident, and was face to face with a young rebel officer, mounted, at the window, with a revolver in his hand resting on the window sill. I said: "how are you?" He asked me, with a tremor in his voice: "where is your horse?" I told him I had none. He refused to believe it. I said to him: "I see you are a soldier, and from your remarks, I infer, you take me to be one. He said: "certainly, I do; everybody in this country is a soldier, on one side or the other." I told him I knew that was the case generally, but that I had failed to get into the army, because the examining surgeon rejected me as unfit for service on account of the loss of sight in one of my eyes. He remarked that they must have been more particular when they examined me, than they were at that time, when the Confederates were glad to get any kind of men. I told him I was returning from a visit to an uncle near Holly Springs, to my home near Raleigh, a small town twelve miles northeast of Memphis. He wanted to know the name of my uncle at Holly Springs, and of my folks at Raleigh. I gave him fictitious names, and could see that he was revolving in his mind whether he had ever heard of such persons in those localities. Fortunately, as I learned from him afterwards, he lived in the interior of Mississippi, and had but a slight acquaintance in the part of the State where we were. He, in company with several other rebel officers, was that afternoon netting quails. He carried the nets. While we were talking, another officer emerged from the bush, who, seeing me, wanted to know who I was. The one I was with, replied: "Oh, just a man I am talking with." Just at that time, some one of their party found a flock of birds, and was calling impatiently for the nets. My companion grew excited at the prospect of getting birds, but was undecided what to do with me. While seeming to be reflecting on the subject, someone of the party yelled out: "Why in h---l don't you bring those nets?" He answered: "Yes, I am coming," and started to go. I availed myself of the excitement, to travel. I jumped out of the window, bade my new acquaintance "good evening," and started.

When out of sight, I dodged into the brush, and hid till dark, when I resumed my journey with all the speed I could command. The darkness enabled me to pass through Colliersville without being seen. About a mile west of Germantown, at a farmhouse, standing quite a distance from the road, some guerrillas were having a dance. I watched them a few moments through the windows, and started on.

At White Station, nine miles from Memphis, I came very near running into a bivouac of guerrillas. I thought I would look at the ground on the south side of the road, where my regiment at one time camped. I was approaching it, when I heard a voice. I listened and heard a person waking his companions, and telling them it was time to be going. I passed rapidly to the opposite side of the road into the timber, and got by without being discovered. I was expecting that that party would come upon me, on their way to make an attack on the Federal picket posts, and, therefore, kept a constant look out to the rear. I was traveling on a hard-smooth pike. The moon had risen, and I had no difficulty in finding my way. I had such a dread of at last being captured by the enemy I had left in the rear, when so near my destination, that most of the time I traveled on the run. When four or five miles from Memphis, I heard the ringing of the bells on the steamboats at the wharf, and knew that I was rapidly approaching the Federal lines. I knew the guerrillas were in the habit of lurking about the lines to capture and kill our pickets. It was, therefore, with mingled feelings of terror and joy, when about three o'clock in the morning, when I was going at the top of my speed, I heard the command: "Halt!" ring out on the still air. I obeyed the order according to its very spirit. A ball through my heart would not have brought me to a more sudden standstill. My alarm, lest I had run into a guerrilla ambuscade, was increased by not seeing any one. After a pause of a moment or two, I heard the words: "who comes there?" I replied: "a friend." The same voice said: "What kind of a friend, we have strange friends here; my opinion is you are a damned rebel. Don't move, or I will shoot you." I heard the click of his musket, as he cocked it. The words: "damned rebel," made me feel happy. I knew I must be at the Union lines. I told the picket that I belonged to the Seventh Indiana Cavalry, had been taken prisoner, and escaped. He called the corporal of the guard, and stepping from a deep

261

Courtesy: Mick Hissick

Left to Right: LT. COL. THOMAS BROWN[E],
MAJ. CHRISTIAN BECK,
MAJ. SAMUEL E. SIMONSON,
MAJ. JOHN C. FEBLES.

shadow, cast by a high bank by the side of the road ordered me to "advance."

One has a strange feeling, on being compelled to march up to the point of a bayonet, in the hands of a guard, who will thrust it through you, if he suspects anything wrong. I advanced to the picket, and stood with the point of the bayonet against my breast, while the corporal satisfied himself that I was unarmed, when I was taken to the reserve to give an account of myself. They all remembered Captain Skelton's fight at Lamar, and that he lost one prisoner. They were satisfied I was what I represented myself to be, and while waiting for daylight, got me some breakfast.

It being supposed that I was dead, my appearance at the regiment created some surprise. I found a commission as Second Lieutenant waiting for me. A vacancy in the office of First Lieutenant, had occurred by the resignation of Lieut. Dunkerly. Maj. Carpenter, who was in command, immediately forwarded my name to Governor Morton, for promotion, and in a short time I received a commission as First Lieutenant of company F.

I went with the expedition under Col. Osborn, to Bastrop, Louisiana, in the spring of 1865.

During the time the regiment remained in Tennessee, I was employed most of the time on scouting duty.

I went with the regiment to Hempstead, Texas, where, on the consolidation of the regiment, I was mustered out of the service.

I returned to LaPorte, Indiana, and during the winter of 1865-66, attended a course of law lectures, in the law department of the University of Michigan, at Ann Arbor, Michigan. After the close of the term, I returned to LaPorte, and entered the law office of the Hon. Mulford K. Farrand, as a student. On the 9th of November, 1866, I was admitted to practice law, in the Circuit Court of LaPorte county, the Hon. Andrew L. Osborn being Judge of the court. At the May term, 1874, I was admitted, on motion of Gen. Thomas M. Browne, to the Bar of the Supreme Court of Indiana, and of the United States Circuit Court. I have been in the practice of the law in LaPorte county, since my admission in 1866. In December, 1869, I was united in marriage to Miss Mary L. Farrand. With her my home has been the scene of contentment and happiness, in adversity as well as prosperity. Our union has been blessed with two beautiful and intelligent children—a girl and a boy.

This is my first attempt in the field of literature. I formed the resolution to write a history of my regiment, after learning that General Browne had abandoned the intention he formed, while in the service, of writing it. It is to be regretted that that gentleman had not the leisure to perform the task I have attempted. His happy style of writing, would have thrown around the subjects treated, a charm, and given them an interest not be achieved by any other writer.

CONCLUSION.

The Seventh Indiana Cavalry took the field when the black clouds of civil war were breaking, and when patriots saw a glimmering of hope for the successful termination of the bloody strife. Its field of operations was the great Mississippi valley; and the part taken by the army, with which it was connected, had an important bearing on the great military events, that were transpiring. The army of the Mississippi, performed its duty of securing the navigation of the Mississippi river; of interrupting the routes of supply of the Confederate armies in the southwest; and of making diversions in favor of the armies under Generals Sherman and Thomas, with eminent success. It had opposed to it, one of the most watchful, successful, daring and able of Confederate Generals, N. B. Forrest. The long and important line to be guarded, and the frequent and desperate attacks of the enemy, kept the cavalry almost constantly in the saddle.

During its term of service, the Seventh Indiana Cavalry traveled by land, on regular marches, three thousand, seven hundred and twenty-five miles; by railroad, six hundred and sixty-six miles; and by water, three thousand and thirty miles; making, without including in the sinuosity of the routes of travel, and the almost daily scouting expeditions, while the regiment was in camp, a grand total of seven thousand, four hundred and twenty miles, which will average a little over eight miles for every day the regiment was in the service.

We buried our comrades by the wayside, from Hickman, Kentucky, to the end of our wearisome march in Texas. In obscure thickets, in the Lone Star State, "in unmonumented graves," slumber our heroes, who took a gallant part in the events recorded in these pages. From the bottom of the Mississippi river; from the hilltop and the low river bottoms, where they were

264

shot down by the lurking guerrillas, and by them denied the right of burial; from the thickly-populated military cemeteries, borne there from groaning hospitals, and, the fields of glory where they fell, will members of the Seventh answer to roll-call, at the sounding of the great *reveille*. They are dead, but not forgotten. A grateful people will ever cherish the recollection of their heroic deeds and patriotic sacrifices, and reserve in their hearts a green spot, consecrated to the memory of the fallen brave. As a compensation for their sacrifices, and standing as a grander monument to their memory, than any that could be erected of marble, is our Union of States preserved, and the power of Our Government felt and respected throughout the world.

From our complex system of government, grave questions of constitutional law, will arise, and convulse the people—but every true soldier who has experienced the horrors of war, and seen the innocent, as well as the guilty, swept into its bloody vortex, will enter an earnest plea for peace—and the people, applying the test of patriotism, will settle their differences without resort to arms.

THE END.

Courtesy: Mick Hissick

UNIDENTIFIED OFFICER, 7th Cavalry

266

ROSTER.

Abadie, John, Private, Co. E.
Abadie, Philamon, Private, Co. E.
Abbott, Harris J., Sergeant, Private, Co. E.
Abdon, Armen, Private, Co. D.
Able, Thomas I., Private, Co. F.
Acker, George N., Private, Co. G.
Adair, John, Private, Co. E.
Adair, William, Private, Co. E.
Adams, John G., Private, Co. L.
Adams, Stephen, Private, Co. A.
Adamson, Alkana, Private, Co. C, F.
Agin, James, Private, Co. D.
Akerman, Frank, Private, Co. M, B.
Alexander, Wesley, Private, Co. K.
Alford, Thomas, Private, Co. H.
Allen, Adoniram, Private, Co. I.
Allen, George, Private, Co. H, A.
Allen, John, Cook, Col. Cook, Co. D.
Allerton, William, Private, Co. D.
Allin, Emeline, Col. Cook, Co. D.
Allison, George W., Private, Co. B.
Altizer, Moses, Private, Co. M.
Alyea, Aaron, Private, Co. F.
Alyea, Gideon, Private, Co. H.
Alyea, Gilbert, Private, Co. F.
Ames, Sanford P., Private, Co. E.
Anderson, David, Private, Co. L.
Anderson, Edmund, Private, Co. B.
Anderson, Francis, Private, Co. D.
Anderson, Harrison, Private, Co. H, A.
Andrews, George F., Private, Chf. Bugler, Co. H, F, and L.
Andrews, George F., Private, Co. I, A.
Andrews, James, Private, Sergeant, Co. H.
Andrews, Stillman, Private, Sergeant, Co. A, C.
Angle, Amos, Private, Co. G.
Anson, John, Private, Sergeant, Co. L, B.
Anthon, Fred, Private, Co. F.
Anthony, Franklin B., Private, Co. I, A.

HARRIS J. ABBOTT, Sergeant, Private, Co. E

268

Antle, George, Private, Co. M, B.
Armstrong, George A., Private, Co. L, B.
Armstrong, Jeremiah, Bugler, Corporal, Co. B, D.
Armstrong, Robert B., Private, Co. I.
Arnold, James E., Private, Co. I, A.
Arnold, John, Private, Co. B, D.
Arnold, John H., Private, Co. I.
Arnold, John L., Private, Saddler, Co. I, A.
Arrington, William, Private, Co. H, A.
Ash, Michael, Private, Co. I.
Aurand, Joseph R., Private, Sergeant, Co. F.
Austin, Philip, Private, Co. E.
Ayers, Edward, Private, Co. D.
Ayers, William, Private, Co. A, C.
Aylea, Jacob, Corporal, Saddler, Co. H, A.
Babb, John W., Private, Co. E.
Babcock, John L., Trumpeter, Co. A.
Babcock, William, Private, Co. I, A.
Bacon, Joel, Private, Co. I.
Bagly, Orlando, Saddler, Co. A.
Baker, John P., Private, Co. H.
Baker, William H, Private, Co. K, E.
Balbabena, Henry, Private, Bugler, Co. H.
Baldwin, Amos, Private, Co. B.
Baldwin, Edward, Private, Co. E.
Bales, Benjamin F., 2d Lieutenant, Captain, Co. I.
Baley, Tinsley, Private, Co. M, B.
Ball, Frank, Private, Co. M.
Ball, William, Private, Co. D.
Ballenger, Orlando, Private, Sergeant, Co. F, C.
Barber, John, Private, Com. Sergeant, Co. D.
Barber, Orrin, Private, Co. B.
Barger, George W., Private, Corporal, Co. I, A.
Barger, John W., Corporal, Co. I.
Barkley, Samuel S., Private, Co. L.
Barnaby, William, Private, Co. F, C.
Barnes, James C., Private, 1st Sergeant, Co. F, C.
Barnett, William, Private, Co. H, A.
Barrack, William, Private, Co. I.
Barragan, James, Private, Co. H.
Barrett, Augustus, Private, Co. K.
Bascom, George M., Private, Co. K, E.
Bates, Abram L., Private, unassigned recruit.
Bates, Andrew, Private, Co. H, A.
Bates, William, Private, Co. C.
Baugher, George, Private, Co. L.
Baum, Americus, Com. Sergeant, Co. A.

Baxter, George W., Private, 2d Lieutenant, Co. M, D.
Bearden, Benjamin J., Private, Co. B.
Beck, Benjamin, Blacksmith, Private, Co. H, A.
Beck, Christian, Major, Co. F, S.
Becker, Valentine, Corporal, Private, Co. K.
Becket, David, Private, Co. H.
Beetly, Rutherford M., Sergeant, Co. F.
Benjamin, Nathaniel, Saddler, Co. L, B.
Bennett, Cyrus, Farrier, Private, Co. I, A.
Benson, Julius L., Asst. Surgeon, Co. F, S.
Berry, Hunter, Private, Co. B, D.
Best, John, Private, Co. F.
Bible, Levi B., Private, Co. A.
Bigelow, Richard R., Private, Corporal, Co. D.
Bishop, Charles, Sergeant, Private, Co. F, C.
Bishop, Cleavland, Private, Saddler, Co. A, C.
Blackburn, Joseph, Private, Co. E.
Blackford, Elijah S., 1st Sergeant, 1st Lieutenant., Co. I, E.
Blackford, Henry C, Bugler, Co. F, E.
Blackman, Alpheus T., 1st Lieutenant, Co. L.
Blasdel, Benjamin F., Sergeant, Co. C, F.
Blocksom, John B., Private, Co. L.
Blowers, William W., Private, Co. K.
Bodle, Lewis, Private, Co. H.
Bolder, Solomon, Private, Co. H, A.
Bolen, John W., Private, Co. K, E.
Booth, Clark B., Private, Corporal, Co. A, C.
Booth, Harrison, Sergeant, Co. E.
Borgman, Henry, Private, Co. C.
Bottaro, John, Private, Co. C.
Boulden, Nathan, Sergeant, 1st Sergeant, Co. K. E.
Bowen, James, Saddler, Co. E.
Bradburn, Alexander, Private, Co. C, F.
Bradford, John, Private, Co. C, F.
Bradshaw, Mason, Saddler, Co. C.
Brandon, George W., Private, Co. G.
Brandon, Perry, Private, Co. A, C.
Branham, Charles, Private, Co. B, D.
Branham, George W., 1st Lieutenant, Captain, Co. B.
Bratton, Joshua, Private, Co. C, F.
Brenner, Daniel C., Wagoner, Private, Co. G.
Brewer, John, Private, Co. A.
Bright, James, Private, Wagoner, Co. B, D.
Bright, Lewis, Private, Co. F, C.
Briley, Samuel, Farrier, Co. H.
Brittingham, Philo E., Private, Co. M.
Brock, John, Private, Co. A, C.

Bromfield, Charles, Private, Corporal, Co. E.
Brougher, Andrew D., Corporal, Sergeant, Co. D.
Brougher, Lewis F., Q.M. Sergeant, 1st Lieutenant, Co. D.
Broughton, Elias, Private, Co. K.
Brown, Albert, Private, Co. H.
Brown, Benjamin M., Sergeant, Private, Co. A, C.
Brown, Ezekiel, Sergeant, 1st Sergeant, Co. H.
Brown, Henry, Private, Co. M, B.
Brown, Isaac, Under Cook, Co. A, C.
Brown, John, Cook, Co. H.
Browne, Alber, Private, Co. H.
Brown[e], Thomas M., Captain, Lt. Colonel, Co. B, F, S.
Browning, Reason, Private, Co. H, A.
Bruce, John, Private, Co. D.
Bryant, Samuel, Private, Co. H, A.
Buchanan, James, Private, Sergeant, Co. M, B.
Budd, Isaac, Private, Co. G.
Bundy, George, Corporal, Private, Co. A.
Bunger, Henry, Bugler, Co. D.
Bunnel, Justice, Private, Co. B.
Bunussi, Anthony, Private, Sergeant, Co. E.
Burgner, Charles, Private, Co. H.
Burke, Isaac, Private, Co. L.
Burket, Lafayette, Sergeant, Co. K.
Burns, Joseph F., Private, Co. D.
Burny, Christopher C., Private, Co. G.
Burr, Horace M., Private, Co. ?.
Burr, Silas E., Private, Co. C, F.
Burton, William, Private, Co. ?.
Buzzard, Manassa, Private, Co. L, B.
Caillia, August, Private, Co. E.
Calkins, Edward, Sergeant, 1st Lieutenant, Co. B, H.
Canon, George L., Private, Co. D.
Carey, Edwin, Private, Co. K.
Carle, Leon, Private, Co. F.
Carmichael, George, Private, Co. G.
Carpenter, Almon S., Private, Co. K, E.
Carpenter, Edward, Private, Corporal, Co. H.
Carpenter, James H., Captain, Major, Co. I, F, G.
Carr, Adoniram, Private, Sergeant, Co. I.
Carr, George, Private, Co. D.
Carrell, William, Private, Corporal, Co. H, A.
Carter, Edmund D., Private, Co. B.
Carter, Henry, Private, Co. C.
Carter, Henry, Private, Co. E.
Carter, Joseph, Private, Co. G, F.
Cartwright, Cornelius E., Sergeant, Corporal, Co. I.

Case, Clark, Private, Co. C, F.
Cashman, John M., Private, Co. K.
Cavanaugh, Charles, Private, Co. H.
Cavanaugh, Michael, Private, Co. H, A.
Chaigneau, Arthur, Unassigned.
Chandlee, Elias N., Private, Blacksmith, Co. M, B.
Chandlee, Morris J., Private, Co. M.
Channan, George, Private, Co. C.
Chaplin, Erasmus M., Private, Corporal, Co. I.
Charman, George, Private, Co. C.
Cherry, Robert E., Private, Co. K, E.
Chery, James, Private, Co. I.
Chew, William A., Private, Co. K.
Chisam, James, Private, Co. H, A.
Chitwood, Joshua, Asst. Surgeon, Surgeon, Co. F, S.
Christy, Isaac, Private, Corporal, Co. C, F.
Clark, Cassius, Private, Co. A, C.
Clark, George, Private, Co. D.
Clark, John, Private, Co. A, C.
Clark, Joseph, Private, Co. L.
Clark, Lyman, Private, Co. C.
Clark, Orrin S., Corporal, Co. A.
Clark, Samuel, Private, Co. F.
Clark, William, Private, Co. A, C.
Claverie, Charles, Private, Co. E.
Clear, David H., Private, Co. B.
Clear, James, Private, Co. B, D.
Cleland, John, Bugler, Private, Co. H, A.
Clevenger, John, Private, Co. G.
Clevenger, John G. W., Private, Corporal, Co. E.
Clifford, Henry C., Corporal, Co. I.
Cloud, James G., Private, Q.M. Sergeant, Co. E.
Clutter, John, Private, Saddler, Co. M.
Coats, Daniel, Private, Wagoner, Co. B.
Coddington, Samuel, Private, Corporal, Co. B, D.
Coffin, Charles W., Bugler, Private, Co. E.
Coffin, Joseph, Corporal, Co. B.
Cogan, John, Private, Co. K.
Cogley, Thomas, 1st Sergeant, 1st Lieutenant, Co. F.
Cole, John B., Corporal, Sergeant, Co. I, A.
Cole, William N., Private, Co. G.
Collins, John J., Private, Co. K.
Colon, Enoch, Private, Co. D.
Colshear, William H., Private, Co. C.
Conn, Joshua M., Corporal, Co. C, F.
Connell, George W., Private, Co. C, F.
Conover, Charles, Private, Co. M, B.

Conover, George, Private, Co. M, B.
Conyers, Alpheus W., Private, Co. B.
Cook, John, Private, Hosp. Steward, Co. I.
Cook, John M., Private, Co. K.
Cook, John W., Private, Co. A, C.
Cook, William A., Unassigned.
Cooper, George, Private, Co. ?.
Cooper, Reuben P., Private, Co. C.
Corbin, William S., Corporal, Private, Co. G.
Corbit, Calvin P., Private, Co. K, E.
Core, John, Private, Co. L, B.
Corey, Henry, Private, Co. G.
Cosairt, Perry, Private, Co. D.
Cost, Anthony, Private, Co. B, D.
Cotton, George A., Corporal, Co. M.
Cotton, Theodore P., Private, Sergeant, Co. M, B.
Cottrell, Charles, Corporal, Com. Sergeant, Co. G, F.
Cox, Micajah, Private, Co. K.
Cox, Oscar J., Corporal, Private, Co. L, B.
Cox, Vinage R., Private, Blacksmith, Co. A, I.
Craig, George D., Private, Co. M, B.
Craig, Joseph S., Corporal, Co. L.
Craig, Robert T., Private, Co. M, B.
Crail, John V., Private, Co. K.
Crane, Lafayette, Corporal, Private, Co. F.
Crane, William, Q.M. Sergeant, 2d Lieutenant, Co. F, A.
Crause, Jacob, Private, Corporal, Co. F.
Crawford, John R., Private, Co. A, C.
Crawford, William, Private, Corporal, Co. A, C.
Crevaston, Jacob, Private, Co. I.
Crews, Andrew J., Private, Co. E.
Crist, Sanford, Private, Co. B.
Crites, Daniel, Private, Co. F.
Crocker, William B., Private, Co. F.
Crow, Abijah, Private, Co. E.
Crow, Daniel B., Private, Sergeant, Co. E.
Crow, George, Private, Co. G, F.
Crowl, Enoch, Private, Co. I, A.
Culbertson, Alfred, Private, Co. G.
Currin, Morris, Private, Co. H, A.
Curtis, William, Farrier, Private, Co. A.
Custar, Calvin, Private, Co. L.
Cuttle, Ransel, Corporal, Co. F, C.
Daggy, Franklin, Private, Co. C.
Dahuff, Eli, Private, Co. D.
Daingerfield, William H., Sergeant, Private, Co. K.
Daily, Benjamin F., 2d Lieutenant, Captain, Co. L.

Dale, James W., Private. Unassigned.
Davidson, Harmon, Private, Co. F.
Davis, Elias, Private, Co. A, C.
Davis, George W., Cook, Col. Cook, Co. I.
Davis, Humphrey, Private, Co. E.
Davis, John H., Private, Co. M, B.
Davis, John S., Private, Sergeant, Co. A, C.
Davis, Milton, Private, Co. G, F.
Day, William H., Corporal, Private, Co. D.
Day, William, Private, Bugler, Co. M.
Deal, James, Private, Co. E.
Dean, Jackson, Private, Co. D.
Deeter, Samuel, Private, Co. L, B.
Deming, Benjamin O., 2d Lieutenant, Co. M.
Demzine, Frederick, Private, Wagoner, Co. F, C.
Denny, John W., Sergeant, Private, Co. M, B.
Denton, Justice M., Corporal, Co. I.
Depa, Gilbert M., Private, Co. L.
Desheill, John W., Sergeant, Co. D.
Deshong, Henry, Private, Co. L.
Detta, Barnard, Private, Co. H, A.
Deuble, John, Private, Co. D.
DeVersy, Joseph, Private, Co. M.
Deview, Dominick, Private, Bugler, Co. F, C.
Dewitt, Alfred O., Private, Co. G.
Dickey, Joseph B., Private, Co. G, F.
Dillman, Robert M., Private, Co. G.
Dillon, John J., Private, Co. B.
Dilman, Jacob, Farrier, Private, Co. F.
Dilworth, Richard, Corporal, Private, Co. E.
Dimmic, James, Private, Co. A.
Dingman, Joseph, Private, Co. D.
Dirlam, Stillwell, Private, Co. D, B and F.
Disbro, James M., Private, Co. D.
Dixon, Harmon, Private, Corporal, Co. M, B.
Dixon, James A., Private, Co. M, B.
Dixon, John, Private, Co. I.
Dockham, Delancey A., Private, Co. I, A.
Dohoney, Samuel, Private, Q.M. Sergeant, Co. M, B.
Doner, Daniel W., Private, Co. E.
Dorsey, Charles, Private, Co. L.
Douch, John, Sergeant, Lieutenant, Co. A, C.
Dougherty, James R., Private, Co. K.
Douglas, George P. F., Private, Corporal, Co. L, B.
Downing, Daniel G., Private, Co. G.
Downing, Leander, Private, Co. G, F.
Downing, Samuel G., Private, Co. G, F.

Downing, William T., Private, Co. G, F.
Downs, Jeptha, Private, Co. M.
Drake, Benjamin F., Private, Co. K, E.
Drake, Rollin W., Corporal, Private, Co. M.
Dresser, Charles A., Sergeant, Co. B.
Dubois, John, Private, Co. L, B.
Ducate, John S., Private, Co. C, F.
Dudley, George, Private, Co. F, C.
Dugan, Dudley C., Private, Co. F.
Duighnan, Mathew, Private, Sergeant, Co. H.
Dumont, John F., Sergeant, 2d Lieutenant, Co. D.
Duncan, Thomas, Private, Co. F.
Dundon, James, Sergeant, Co. G.
Dunkerley, George W., 1st Lieutenant, Co. F.
Dunn, Samuel P., Private, Co. A.
Dunn, Sylvester, Private, Co. H, A.
Dupuy, John, Private, Co. E.
Durkee, Clark S., Private, Co. A, C.
Dynes, William A., Private, Com. Sergeant, Co. B, F, L.
Eahart, James, Private, Co. A, C.
Eberle, Joseph, Private, Co. D.
Edgerton, Lewis F., Private, Co. G, F.
Edwards, Danford, Sergeant, Co. K.
Edwards, David, Private, Blacksmith, Co. E.
Edwards, John, Wagoner, Private, Co. F.
Egbert, William, Private, Co. L.
Eldridge, William H., Corporal, Q.M. Sergeant, Co. K.
Elkins, Francis M., Private, Co. K.
Elliott, Joel H., 2d Lieutenant, Captain, Co. E, B, M.
Elliott, John H., Private, Co. E.
Elliott, Nelson H., Private, Co. B, D.
Ellis, James L., Corporal, Sergeant, Co. L, B.
Ellsworth, William H., Sergeant, Co. F, C.
Elmer, John, Private, Co. D.
Englehart, Frank, Private, Co. H.
English, James A., Private, Co. A, C.
Ennis, John, Private, Co. L.
Ernest, Joseph, Private, Co. A, C.
Ervin, Franklin, Private, Co. C, F.
Erwin, Joseph A., Corporal, Sergeant, Co. D.
Esterly, George W., Private, Co. A.
Eubanks, George S., Private, Co. C, F.
Ewbank, Robert J., Corporal, Private, Co. D.
Ewing, John P., Private, Co. C, F.
Fairbanks, Joseph, Private, Co. ?.
Fairchilds, Henry, Private, Co. A, C.
Falconer, David, Bugler, Private, Co. M, B.

Falkner, Andrew, Private, Co. G.
Farl, John, Private, Co. D.
Farrell, Michael, Private, Co. H.
Farris, David, Private, Co. E.
Farris, Lemuel, Private, Unassigned.
Febles, John C., 1st Lieutenant, Major, Co. A, F, S.
Fegley, George W., Private, Co. D.
Felton, Joseph, Private, Co. I, A.
Fennimore, Charles, Private, Co. F.
Ferguson, Franklin, Private, Corporal, Co. A, C
Ferry, Robert H., Saddler, Private, Co. M.
Filson, William F., Private, Co. L.
Fink, William H., Private, Co. F.
Fisher, David, Private, Corporal, Co. K.
Fisher, Henry, Private, Co. A, C.
Fisher, James A., 2d Lieutenant, Co. L.
Fisher, John, Private, unassigned recruit.
Fisher, Phillip, Private, Co. C, F.
Fitch, John, Private, Co. D.
Flaharty, John, Private, Co. F.
Fleming, Milton, K., Private, Co. L.
Flynn, Charles, Private, Corporal, Co. H, A.
Flynn, William A., Corporal, Private, Co. F, C.
Foley, Francis, Corporal, Private, Co. A, C.
Ford, George, Corporal, Private, Co. E.
Forrest, Franklin, Private, Co. E.
Forrester, Bennett, Private, Co. F.
Fostnaucht, Moses, Private, Co. D.
Fox, Thomas, Private, Co. A, C.
Frame, Oliver, Private, Q.M. Sergeant, Co. F.
Frank, Martin L., Private, Co. I, A.
Frasier, William, Corporal, Sergeant, Co. F.
Frazee, George M. D., Corporal, Co. E.
Frazee, George, Private, Co. A.
Frazee, Olivet, Private, Corporal, Co. C, F.
Franzier, Eli, Private, Co. B.
Frazier, James P., Private, Bugler, Co. G, F.
Fred, Charles, Private, Co. M.
Frederick, Anthony, Private, Co. D.
Frederick, George, Private, Co. D.
Freeman, David, Private, Co. G, F.
Freeman, Ruel C., Bugler, Private, Co. M, B.
Freeman, William, Surgeon, Co. F, G.
Fribis, Frederick, Private, Co. K, E.
Fugate, John, Private, Co. F, C.
Gabler, Henry, Private, Co. F.
Garber, Abraham, Private, Co. J.

Gard, John W., Private, Co. K.
Gardner, Frederick, Private, Co. C, F.
Gardner, John J., Private, Co. H, A.
Gardner, Obediah, Private, Co. E.
Gardner, William, Private, Co. A.
Garner, Laben E., Private, Co. B.
Garrett, Nathan, Private, 1st Lieutenant, Co. B, F.
Garrett, Samuel, Private, Co. K.
Garrigus, Jacob H., Corporal, Private, Co. C, F.
Garrott, John R., Private, Co. M, B.
Gathman, John Henry, Private, Co. C, F.
Gaw, Joseph, Private, Co. F.
Gay, John, Private, Co. G.
Gay, William H., Private, Co. G, F.
Gerrard, Asbury C., Private, Co. J, A.
Gerreau, Lewis, Corporal, Private, Co. J, A.
Gibson, Thomas W., Sergeant, 1st Sergeant, Co. M, B.
Giffin Azariah, Private, Co. J.
Gilbert, Cyrus J., Private, Co. D.
Gilbert, Isaac R., Captain, Co. M.
Gilbert, John N., Q.M. Sergeant, Private, Co. M, B.
Gilbert, Noah, Private, Co. H, A.
Giles, Michael, Com. Sergeant, Private, Co. H, A.
Gillan, Alexander, Private, Co. K, E.
Gillan, William, Private, Corporal, Co. K, E.
Gillegan, Michael, Private, Co. E.
Gillespie, William, Private, Co. F.
Gilson, Edward G., Private, Sergeant, Co. H, A.
Glasscock, James, Private, Co. M.
Gleason, Charles, Sergeant, 2d Lieutenant, Co. A, C.
Gleason, John, Private, Co. H.
Glendening William, Private, Co. E.
Goad, Hiram, Private, Co. G.
Godbey, Daniel W., Private, Co. K, E.
Gogan, Charles M., Trumpeter, Sergeant, Co. A.
Gogan, William, Private, Co. A, C.
Gordon, James B., Sergeant, Co. D.
Gordon, Noah H, Private,. Co. A, C.
Gorman, Isaac A., Private, Co. E.
Goth, George, Private, Co. C, F.
Gould, Joseph, Private, Co. C, F.
Gould, Wheeler, Private, Co. K.
Graham, Slaven, Private, Co. I. A.
Grant, William, Private, Co. C.
Gray, Edward, Corporal, Private, Co. B.
Gray, George W., Corporal, Private, Co. B, D.
Gray, Isaac M., Private, Co. B, D.

Gray, James, Private, Co. K, E.
Gray, Mitchell C., Bugler, Co. J.
Gray, Morgan L., Private, Sergeant, Co. E.
Gray, Samuel J., Private, Co. E.
Graydon, James W., Bugler, Co. D.
Grebe, Daniel, Corporal, Private, Co. M, B.
Green, Charles E., Private, Co. D.
Green, Edward, Private, Co. E.
Green, Elias, Corporal, Private, Co. M, B.
Green, Henry L., Q.M. Sergeant, Co. H.
Green, James, Sergeant, Private, Co. H.
Green, William F., Private, Co. D.
Griffin, James D., Private. Unassigned.
Griffis, William C., Private, Q.M. Sergeant, Co. B, D.
Griffith, Isaac, Private, Sergeant, Co. E.
Grisham, William, Private, Co. G.
Griton, Calvin, Private, Co. L.
Grove, Jasper M., Asst. Surgeon, Co. F.
Grow, William H., Private, Co. G.
Guckert, Antony, Private, Co. D.
Gullett, Hamilton G., Private, Co. B.
Gunckle, Winfield, Private, Co. K, E.
Gurrigues, Jacob H., Corporal, Private, Co. C, F.
Guthrie, Richard, Private, Co. D.
Hager, Peter, Private, Farrier, Co. L, B.
Haley, George, Private, Co. E.
Hall, Alfred, Private, Co. B.
Hall, Cyrus, Private, Co. M.
Hall, Greenbury, Private, Co. F.
Hall, John, Private, Co. D.
Hall, Louis, Private, Sergeant, Co. C.
Hall, Rollo, Sergeant, Private, Co. H.
Hambleton, George W., Private, Sergeant, Co. E.
Hamilton, Benjamin, Private, Co. G.
Hamilton, John W., Sergeant, Co. G.
Hamlin, George, Private, Co. D.
Hammond, George, Sergeant, Private, Co. F.
Hampton, William E., Wagoner, Private, Co. I.
Hand, James, Private, Sergeant, Co. M, B.
Hanson, John C., Private, 2d Lieutenant, Co. G, A.
Hardesty, Adolphus, Private, Co. A, C.
Harding, Benjamin, Private, Co. C, F.
Harding, David, Private, Co. C, F.
Harding, Myron, Private, Corporal, Co. C.
Hare, Charles H., 1st Lieutenant, Co. I.
Harlan, Calvin, Private, Co. K.
Harrell, John R., Bugler, Private, Co. I.

Harrington, Jeffrey, Private, Co. H, A.
Harris, Mordecai, Corporal, Sergeant, Co. B.
Harsh, Edward, Private, Co. C.
Hartman, Jacob, Private, Corporal, Co. B, D.
Haskins, Nicholas, Private, Co. A, C.
Hatley, Uriah, Private, Co. K.
Hawkins, Henry, Corporal, Blacksmith, Co. E.
Hays, Richard, Private, Corporal, Co. M, B.
Hazelton, Elijah, Private, Co. B, D.
Headly, William, Private, Co. L.
Hearding, Benjamin J., Private, Co. C, F.
Hearding, David A. J., Private, Co. C, F.
Heath, Thomas, Private, Co. M.
Heaton, Seth S., Private, Corporal, Co. C, F.
Heck, John, Private, Co. G, F.
Heffernan, Hugh, Corporal, Co. H.
Heiger, Henry, Private, Co. D.
Helms, Joseph, Private, Co. I.
Helvey, Champion, Q.M. Sergeant, Private, Co. L, B.
Helvey, Robert, Trumpeter, Bugler, Co. L, B.
Henas, Christian, Private, Co. K.
Henderson, Joshua, Private, Co. C.
Henderson, Samuel B., Sergeant, Saddler Sergeant, Co. L, F, S.
Hendrickson, John M., Private, Co. I.
Hendrickson, Tunis, Private, Co. I, A.
Herrell, John, Private, Co. H, A.
Hess, Andrew H., Private, Co. D.
Hiatt, Benjamin, Private, Wagoner, Co. C, F.
Hiatt, William, Private, Co. C.
Highland, James, Private, Co. L, B.
Hight, Henry, Private, Co. I, A.
Highton, Richard, Private, Co. G, F.
Hill, Abram, 1st Lieutenant, Co. D.
Hilligoss, Burt C., Private, Co. I.
Hilligoss, Elbridge G., Private, Co. L.
Hilton, George W., Private, Co. E.
Hinds, Francis, Sergeant, Q.M. Sergeant, Co. C.
Hinds, George, Private, Co. M, B.
Hines, Solomon, Private, Co. I.
Hinshaw, John C., Private, Co. B, D.
Hinton, Theodore F. H., Private, Co. M, B.
Hire, Frederic, Private, Co. E.
Hix, Marvin, Private, Co. K, E.
Hodges, James, Private, Co. A, C.
Hoffman, Frederick, Private, Co. D.
Hoffman, Samuel, Private, Co. D.
Hogle, Sylvester, Private, Co. I.

Holliday, Wilber F., 1st Lieutenant and Regtl. Com., Co. F, S.
Holmes, John B., Private, Co. I, A.
Hoover, Richard D., Private, Co. E.
Hopkins, Charles P., Com. Sergeant, Sergeant, Co. M.
Hopkins, James A., Private, Co. K.
Horner, Berzilia, Private, Co. A, C.
Horstley, Ezekiel, Private, Co. C, F.
Hostetter, Samuel W., Private, Co. M.
House, John W., Private, Co. L.
Howard, George, Private, Sergeant, Co. M.
Howard, Thomas J., Sergeant, 1st Sergeant, Co. I.
Howell, Amasy, Private, Co. F, C.
Howser, Lawrence, Private, Co. I.
Hubbard, Martin, Private, Co. L, B.
Hubbard, William S., 2d Lieutenant, Captain, Co. K.
Huffine, Elias, Private, Co. B.
Huffman, Andrew, Private, Co. B, D.
Huffman, George D., Farrier, Co. B.
Huffman, Henderson, Private, Co. D.
Hughes, James G., Corporal, Co. A.
Hughes, John B., Private, Co. B.
Hughs, Henry H., Private, Co. D.
Hull, Joseph, Private, Co. C, F.
Hull, Samuel, Private, Co. K.
Hunaford, Daniel C., Private, Co. G.
Hunt, Edward D., Private, Co. B, D.
Hunt, James D., Private, Co. G, F.
Hunt, Jeremiah M., Wagoner, Co. E.
Hunt, Nelson H., Corporal, Sergeant, Co. I, A.
Hunt, Robert G., Private, Sergeant, Co. B, D.
Hunt, Thomas S., Private, Co. D.
Hunter, William H., Private, Co. F, C.
Huntington, George, Private, Co. A.
Hurley, John, Sergeant, Co. G.
Hurst, Frederick J., Private, Corporal, Co. C, F.
Hustis, John H., Corporal, Sergeant, Co. C.
Huston, Vinson, Private, Co. B, D.
Hyatt, Jerome, Private, Co. E.
Hyatt, William, Private, Co. K.
Inglis, Archibald F., Private, Q. M. Sergeant, Co. F.
Ingram, Lysander S., Private, Vet. Surgeon, Co. L, F, S.
Inks, James, Private, Co. E.
Isabel, George, Private, Co. C, F.
Isabel, Joseph, Private Co. G.
Iseminger, Hiram, Private, Corporal, Co. F.
Iseminger, Holbert, Private, Co. F.
Jackman, James, Corporal, Private, Co. M, B.

Jackson, Albert H., Sergeant, C. Sergeant, Co. A, C.
Jackson, James M., Private, Co. F.
Jacob, Charles, Private, Teamster, Co. K.
James, George C., Private, Sergeant, Co. D.
Jarrett, John W., Private, Corporal, Co. I, A.
Jay, James C., Private, Asst. Surgeon, Co. E, F, S.
Jean, Samuel F., Private, Co. B, D.
Jenkins, Barton B., Sergeant, 2d Lieutenant, Co. E, B.
Jennings, John, Private, Co. K.
Jessup, Henry, Private, Co. F, C.
Jillison, Josiah, Private, Co. D.
Johnson, Andrew A., Private, Co. D.
Johnson, Francis M., Private, Co. B.
Johnson, Francis M., Farrier, Private, Co. E.
Johnson, Franklin, Private, Co. C, F.
Johnson, George, Private, Co. D.
Johnson, Henry A., Private, Co. M.
Johnson, Henry C., Private, Blacksmith, Co. K, E.
Johnson, James, Private, Co. C, F.
Johnson, John, Private, Co. A.
Johnson, Nicholas, Private, 1st Sergeant, Co. D.`
Johnston, Augustus, Private, Co. H, A.
Johnston, Willard, Private, Co. H.
Jones, Aaron L., Sergeant, R. Q.M., Co. A, F, S.
Jones, Ambrose, Wagoner, Private, Co. C, F.
Jones, Avery, Corporal, Co. A.
Jones, Charles R., Private, 2d Lieutenant, Co. C, F.
Jones, George H., Private, Farrier, Co. A, C.
Jones, George S., Corporal, Co. I.
Jones, George W., Private, Co. A, C.
Jones Gustavus, Corporal, Sergeant, Co. A.
Jones, Harrison, Corporal, Private, Co. F.
Jones, James, Private, Co. K.
Jones, John, Corporal, Private, Co. G.
Jones, John H., Private, Corporal, Co. M.
Jones, John T., Private, Co. B.
Jones, Samuel H., Farrier, Private, Co. A, C.
Jones, William M., Co. ?
Jordan, Josiah, Private, Co. I, A.
Judd, Albert, Private, Co. I.
Kail, Hiram J., Private, Co. D.
Kansas, Alexander, Private, Co. F.
Karch, John E., Private, Co. E.
Keesy, John, Sergeant, Co. B.
Keith, James W., Private, Co. M, B.
Kelley, John, Sergeant, Private, Co. H, A.
Kelley, John E., Private, Co. F.

Kelley, William M., Q. M. Sergeant, Adjutant, Co. I, F, S.
Kellis, Amos A., Private, Co. L.
Kelly, John, Private, Co. K.
Kelly, Marias, Corporal, Co. C.
Kelly, Patrick, Saddler, Co. G, F.
Kelly, Timothy, Private, Co. G, F.
Kelly, Wesley B., Private, Co. A, C.
Kelly, William, Private, Co. M, B.
Kenedy, James, Sergeant, Private, Co. C.
Kennedy, George R., 1st Lieutenant, Captain, Co. C, F.
Kennedy, George, Private, Sergeant, Co. G.
Kennedy, Stephen, Sergeant, Private, Co. B.
Kennedy, William H., Private, Co. K.
Kent, Edward, Private, Corporal, Co. F, C.
Kent, William A., Private, Co. F.
Kerwan, Andrew, Private, Co. F.
Ketchall, David, Private, Co. A.
Ketcham, Jerome B., C. Sergeant, Private, Co. K.
Ketchum, Charles A., Private, Co. I.
Keys, John, Bugler, Private, Co. B.
Kile, Harman, Private, Co. F.
King, Horrace W., Sergeant, Co. I.
King, John A., Corporal, Private, Co. H.
Kisener, John B., Private, Co. F.
Kitchen, James, Private, Co. H, A.
Kitson, Daniel E., Private, Co. L, B.
Kitt, George, Private, Co. K, E.
Kitt, Randle R., Private, Co. K.
Kittsmiller, William, Private, Co. E.
Kline, William H., Corporal, Co. H.
Klum, Albert, Sergeant, Private, Co. L, B.
Knapp, George W., Private, Co. F.
Knepper, Emanuel, Private, Co. E.
Knepper, Joseph, Private, Co. E.
Knowlton, John P., Bugler, Private, Co. F. C.
Krahmer, Christian, Private, Co. K.
Kratz, Otto, Private, Co. C.
Krebs, Reuben R., Private, Corporal, Co. L.
Krinkle, George, Private, Saddler, Co. K.
Lahae, Edward, Private, Co. H.
Laird, Albert, Private, Sergeant, Co. C, F.
Laird, Joseph, Private, Corporal, Co. C.
Lake, Samuel M., 2d Lieutenant, Captain, Co. K.
Lakin, Andrew F., Private, Co. G.
Lamb, Hiram, Private, Co. B.
Lamb, Uriah, Private, Co. B, D.
Lambert, Wesley B., Private, Co. G.

Lamson, Arthur F., Private, Co. H.
Land, Samuel, Private, Co. C.
Lane, Joseph R., Private, Co. G.
Lane, Julius, Private, Co. C, F.
Lanham Samuel, Private, Co. M.
Lansing, Joseph, Bugler, Private, Co. C, F.
Lantsford, Thomas A., Private, Co. F.
Lardner, Martin, Private, Co. B, D.
Lash, John S., Private, Co. M.
Lattae Ephraim, Private, Co. H, A.
Lawson, John, Private, Wagoner, Co. L.
Leahy, William J., Private, Co. A, C.
Leason, James, Private, Co. L.
Lee, John Wesley, Q. M. Sergeant, Sergeant, Co. E.
Lee, William H., Private, Co. M.
Legg, John, Bugler, Private, Co. E.
Lehr, Eli, Private, Co. E.
Lemon, John, Private, Co. F.
Lemon, John T., Corporal, Co. D.
Lennington, John B., Farrier, Private, Co. B, D.
Leonard, Savannah, Sergeant, Co. L.
Lewis, James H., Private, Co. K, E.
Lewis, John W., Corporal, Private, Co. D.
Lewis, Sylvester, 2d Lieutenant, Captain, Co. B.
Lhammon, Thomas, Private, Co. E.
Lidge, Adam C., Private, Co. D.
Linenweber, George, Private, Co. M.
Linenweber, Joseph, Private, Co. M, B.
Link, John J., Private, Co. F.
Little, Alexander, Private, Co. B, D.
Little, Thomas, Private, Co. B, D.
Livingston, Moses, Corporal, Co. A.
Lockhart, William A., Private, Co. L.
Loftus, William, Private, Co. D.
Logan, William L., Private, Co. L, B.
Logston, Perry, Private, Corporal, Co. A, C.
Longfellow, John D., Sergeant, 2d Lieutenant, Co. K, E.
Longwell, John W., Com. Sergeant, 1st Lieutenant, Co. I.
Losch, John, Q.M. Sergeant, Co. K.
Lossing, Joseph, Private, Co. I.
Lott, John W., Private, Co. E.
Lowes, James H., 1st Sergeant, 1st Lieutenant, Co. G.
Lowry, Albert, Private, Co. L, B.
Lowry, Dennis, Private, Co. H.
Ludy, Erastus, Private, Co. B.
Lunger, Asbury, Private, Co. M.
Lutes, George W., Private, Co. E.

Luther, Henry E., Private, Co. G.
Lutz, George, Private, Sergeant, Co. M.
Lyle, James H., Private, Co. K.
Lynn, John N., Private, Co. I.
Lyons, Charles, Private, Co. L.
Lytle, Thomas, Private, Co. C, F.
Malott, Simon H., Private, Co. L, B.
Mandeville, Jared B., Sergeant, Private, Co. F.
Mandeville, Rhynear, Sergeant, 1st Sergeant, Co. F.
Mann, William H., Private, Co. K, E.
Mannewitz, Louis, Private, Co. K, E.
Maple, Ephraim, Private, Co. I.
Margeston, Isaac J., Private, Co. A.
Markle, Jordan, Farrier, Co. M.
Marquis, James, Chaplain, Co. F, L.
Marsh, John, Corporal, Sergeant, Co. A.
Marshall, James W., Sergeant, Co. C.
Martin, John W., 1st Lieutenant and Q.M., R.Q.M., Co. F, L.
Martin, Joseph, Private, Co. M, B.
Martin, Mathias, Private, Co D.
Mashone, Benjamin, Private, Co. H.
Maskell, James, Private, Co. H.
Massacre, Joseph, Private, Co. G.
Matchett, John H., Corporal, Private, Co. K, E.
Matchett, Richard E., Private, Corporal, Co. K.
Matheny, John F., Private, Co. B, D.
Matheny, John W., Private, Co. A, C.
Matherly, John H., Private, Co. F.
Mathew, John W., Private, Co. K.
Mathews, Benjamin, Private, Co. M, B.
Mathews, Jesse, Private, Co. K.
Mattox, James W., Private, Co. B.
Maulsby, Luny, Private, Co. A, C.
Mauzy, John R., Private, Co. B, D.
Maxville, James, Private, Co. H, A.
Maxville, John H., Private, Sergeant, Co. L.
Mayer, John G., 1st Lieutenant, Co. M, B.
Mayers, Jacob, Private, Co. C.
Maze, Benjamin, Private, Co. I.
McAree, John, Private, Co. K.
McAvoy, Thomas, Private, Co. K.
McBride, Edward, Bugler, Co. G.
McBride, Isaac R., Private, Co. A.
McBroom, Joel, Private, Co. B, D.
McCabe, Chester E., Corporal, Private, Co. C, F.
McCabe, Isaac, Private, Co. K, E.
McCabe, James, Private, Co. H, A.

McCann, Adam, Private, Co. M.
McCann, Charles, Wagoner, Co. H.
McCarthy, Joseph F., Co. C Sergeant, Private, Co. D.
McCarty, Abram, Private, Co. A, C.
McCarty, James, Private, Co. I, A.
McCarty, John, Private, Co. F, C.
McClary, Joseph C., Farrier.
McConahay, Robert, Private, Co. I, A.
McCorkle, John, Private, Co. I, A.
McCoy, Robert, Farrier, Sergeant, Co. G, F.
McCueon, Arthur, Private, Corporal, Co. D.
McCune, James, Private, Co. F, C.
McCune, John, Private, Corporal, Co. I, A.
McCutcheon, Alexander, Private, Co. L.
McDaniel, David, Private, Co. L.
McDaniel, Franklin, Private, Co. B.
McDermott, John, Private, Co. K, E.
McDonald, Nathan, Private, Co. M.
McDorman, Risdon, Wagoner, Co. A.
McDougal, Gilford A. Unassigned.
McFadden, James, Corporal, Private, Co. M, B.
McGettigan, Patrick, Saddler, Private, Co. B, D.
McGrain, James, Private, Co. H.
McGrath, William, Private, Co. I, A.
McKenily, John, Private, Corporal, Co. K, E.
McKennan, James, Bugler, Private, Co. G.
McKinney, Ambrose, Private, Co. H.
McKinney, David R., Private, Co. ?
McKinney, James, Private, Co. F.
McKinney, James P., Corporal, Co. H, A.
McLeod, Gamaliel, Private, Co. E.
McLeod, Lemuel, Private, Co. E.
McMahan, D., Private, Corporal, Co. B, D.
McManigal, Vance, Private, Q.M. Sergeant, Co. L.
McMellen, John H. H., Private, Co. I.
McMoyers, James, Private, Co. A.
McMurphy, Alonzo, Private, Co. A, C.
McNamara, James, Private, Co. H.
McNaughten, James, Sergeant, Private, Co. M, B.
McNeece, David H., Private, Co. F.
McQuillin, Robert, Private, Co. H.
McVey, Thomas, Private, Co. M.
McWindle, William, Private, Co. A, C.
Meacham, Jesse M., Private, Co. F.
Mead, Joseph, Private. Unassigned.
Meek, Oliver H., Private, Co. L.
Meiners, James, Private, Co. L.

Mellott, John B., Corporal, Private, Co. K.
Melville, Francis, Private, Sergeant, Co. H, A.
Mentor, John, Private, Co. G.
Meredith, Peter, Private, Co. F, C.
Merical, Jesse, Private, Co. I.
Mericle, Thomas, Private, Co. E.
Michael, Sylvester, Private, Co. I.
Middleton, Charles, Private, Co. M.
Miller, Charles, Private, Co. B.
Miller, Daniel, Private, Hospital Steward, Co. L.
Miller, Francis J., Private, Co. A.
Miller, George, Private, Corporal, Co. E.
Miller, George L., Private, Co. D.
Miller, Henry B., Private, Co. A.
Miller, Jacob, Private, Co. G.
Miller, James, Private, Co. I, A.
Miller, Nathaniel C., Corporal, Private, Co. C, F.
Miller, Robert, Private, Co. L.
Miller, Talcutt, Private, Sergeant, Co. F.
Miller, William, Private, Co. B.
Mills, John R., Private, Co. A.
Mitcham, Abraham, Private, Co. G, F.
Mitchell, Alfred, Private, Co. I.
Mitchell, Patrick, Private, Sergeant, Co. H, A.
Moist, David S., Private, Sergeant, Co. B, D.
Mondary, Michael, Private, Co. D.
Monks, George W., Private, Co. B, D.
Montieth, Thomas, Blacksmith, Co. E.
Montony, John, Private, Corporal, Co. K, E.
Moor, James, Private, Co. B, D.
Moore, Charles, Private. Unassigned.
Moore, Francis, Private, Co. E.
Moore, James, Private, Co. B, D.
Moore, John M., 2d Lieutenant, Captain, Co. H, A.
Moore, Lorain J., Private, Sergeant, Co. F.
Moore, Simon H., Private, Co. I.
Moore, Wesley, Private, Co. D.
Moore, William, Private, Co. ?.
Moore, William, Private, Co. G.
Moore, William H., Private, Co. M.
Moore, William M., Private, Co. Y.
Morden, Edward D., Private, Co. F, C.
Moreland, Rophfel, Private. Unassigned.
Morgan, Daniel B., Private, Co. C.
Morgan, William, Private, Co. I, A. [Price, Arthur T.].
Morris, Albert, Private, Co. H, A.
Morris, John F., Sergeant, Co. H.

Morrison, William F., Private, Co. I.
Mortorff, Samuel, Private, Co. D.
Mossholder, William, Private, Co. A, C.
Moyer, Elias, Private, Co. M.
Muir, Hiram, Private. Unassigned.
Mullen, John W., Private, Co. D.
Mullingate, Bernard, Private, Co. F.
Mullis, Richard, Private, Co. D.
Munjoy, Mathew, Private, Co. B, L.
Murphy, Felix J., Private, Co. A.
Murphy, John, Private, Co. B, D.
Murphy, Peter S., Private, Co. L, B.
Murray, Jeremiah, Private, Co. B.
Muthert, Henry H., Private, Co. G.
Myers, Benjamin S., Private, Co. K, E.
Myers, John, Private, Co. G, F.
Myers, John T., Private, Co. H.
Myers, Jonah, Private, Co. C, F.
Myres, Andrew, Private, Co. F.
Nash, Daniel C., Private, Co. G.
Neal, John, Private, Co. I.
Nearon, Adam, Private, Co. G.
Needham, George W., Private, Co. G.
Needham, Isaac, Private, Co. G, F.
Neff, Isaac, Private, Co. D.
Neff, William, Private, Co. D.
Nemire, James, Private, Co. C, F.
Newberger, Myer, Private, Sergeant, Co. L.
Newcomb, Oliver, Private, Co. F.
Nickey, Granberry B., Corporal, Co. B.
Nickey, Harrison C., Private, Co. B.
Nisely, Abraham, Private, Co. G.
Nixon, Thomas, Private, Co. A.
Noble, Charles F., O. Sergeant, 1st Lieutenant, Co. K.
Nocks, Scott H., Private. Unassigned.
Nolan, Richard J., Private, Co. A.
Nolan, Richard, Private, Co. M.
Norman, James, Private, Co. D.
Norton, Edward, Private, Co. D.
Norton, Rufus H., Corporal, Q.M. Sergeant, Co. A, C.
Oakey, James, Private, Co. K, E.
Obaduff, William H., Farrier, Co. G.
Oliver, Abraham, Private, Co. H.
Oliver, James, Private, Sergeant, Co. L, B.
Oliver, Levi, Private, Co. C.
O'Neil, Cornelius, Farrier, 1st Sergeant, Co. A.
Oppero, Julius, Corporal, Private, Co. K.

UNIDENTIFIED PHOTO OF MAN AND WIFE

Oppy, Henry, Private, Co. C.
Orn, Jacob, Private, Co. C, F.
Osborn, John, Private, Co. L, B.
Osborn, William H., Private, Co. C, F.
Osborn, Philip F., Private, Co. M, B.
Overman, John Q., Corporal, Private, Co. C, F.
Paff, Mathew, Private, Co. K, E.
Paine, John, Private, Co. H.
Palmer, Thomas J., Bugler, Private, Co. C, F.
Parker, James M., Private, Co. F.
Parker, William H., Saddler, Co. F, C.
Parmelee, John R., 1st Lieutenant, Captain, Co. A.
Parr, John P., Private, Co. K, E.
Parrish, Taylor, Private, Co. I.
Partie, Albert, Private, Sergeant, Co. K, E.
Patrick, George, Sergeant, Private, Co. D.
Patterson, William, Private, Co. C, F.
Patterson, William, Private, Bugler, Co. I.
Patton, Robert R., Corporal, Sergeant, Co. M.
Paxton, Benjamin, Private, Co. E.
Paxton, John Q., Private, Co. E.
Peacock, Henry S., Private, Co. B.
Peak, Bluford, Private, Co. G, F.
Pearson, Francis, Corporal, Sergeant, Co. D.
Peer, Dennis J., Private, Co. F.
Pendergrass, Samuel, Private, Co. C.
Perkins, John, Private, Corporal, Co. B, D.
Peterson, Cass M., Private, Co. B.
Peterson, Isaac S., Private, Co. L.
Peterson, Orville R., Private, Co. B.
Phillippe, John W., Private, Co. I.
Phillips, Piercy, Sergeant, Co. C.
Phipps, Joseph, Private, Co. L.
Pierce, Chester G., Private, Co. F, C.
Pierce, Horace, Private, Co. F.
Pierce, Winfield, Private, Co. A, C.
Piety, Austin H., Sergeant, Captain, Co. G.
Pinson, James A., Corporal, Private, Co. G.
Place, Maurice E., Private, Co. L.
Platt, Peter, Sergeant, 1st Lieutenant, Co. C.
Poe, John, Private, Co. K, E.
Poigus, Thomas C., Private, Corporal, Co. M.
Poindexter, Alfred, Private, Co. E.
Poinier, Jacob, Private, Co. E.
Pollett, James W., Private, Co. A.
Polly, Cyrus B., Sergeant, 2d Lieutenant, Co. B.
Pool, Henry W., Private, Co. K, E.

Porter, Coston, Private, Co. E.
Porter, Lewis H., Private, Co. A, C.
Porter, Sireneus, Private, Co. L.
Powers, James, Private, Co. G, F.
Price, Hiram F., Private, Co. L.
Price, James A., Adjutant, Co. F, S.
Pritchett, William L., Private, Co. L, B, K.
Pruet, Henry C., Private, Co. L.
Puckett, Zachariah, Wagoner, Corporal, Co. B.
Pugh, Leander, Private, Co. B.
Radabaugh, Noah F., Private, Co. A.
Ragan, James., Private, Sergeant, Co. A, C.
Rains, Allen, Private, Co. A.
Rainy, Hiram, Private, Co. A.
Rankin, John, Private, Co. G, F.
Rankin, Oscar, 2d Lieutenant, 1st Lieutenant, Co. G.
Ratts, Oliver N., Private, Corporal, Co. M.
Rausbotton, Hickason, Private, Farrier, Co. E.
Ray, Albert, Corporal, Private, Co. F, C.
Ray, Jonathan, Private, Co. E.
Rayle, Brantley, Private, Company Sergeant, Co. I.
Redding, John L., Private, Co. F.
Redenbo, Robert C., Corporal, Private, Co. H, A.
Reed, George W., Private, Co. L, B.
Reed, James M., Corporal, Com. Sergeant, Co. L, B.
Reed, Jeremiah, Private, Co. L, B.
Reed, John, Corporal, Private, Co. K.
Reed, John Q., 1st Lieutenant, Captain, Co. H, D.
Rees, John, Private, Co. C.
Reeves, Lewis, Private, Co. B.
Reinkins, John, Private, Corporal, Co. H, A.
Rex, John, Private, Co. G.
Reynolds, Edwin R., Farrier, Private, Co. M.
Rice, Stephen, Private, Co. F, C.
Richards, Henry C., Private, Co. G.
Richardson, Andrew G., Private, Co. G.
Richardson, Harvey E., Corporal, Private, Co. C.
Richardson, Harvey P., Corporal, Co. C.
Richart, Robert S., Sergeant, Q.M. Sergeant, Co. I.
Ricketts, James M., Private, Corporal, Co. K.
Ring, Richard, Corporal, Co. L, B.
Ringgold, Joseph, Private, Co. I.
Ritter, Ashbury, Private, Co. F.
Ritter, George K., Corporal, Co. A.
Ritter, John, Private, Farrier, Co. F, C.
Roberts, John, Private, Co. E.
Roberts, Samuel, Private, Corporal, Co. D.

290

Robinson, Edmund L., Sergeant, 1st Sergeant, Co. A,C.
Robinson, Francis, Private, Co. H.
Robinson, Jack, Private, Co. A.
Robinson, John W., Private, Co. ?.
Robinson, Lewis, Private, Co. I.
Robinson, Ninian, Corporal, Private, Co. B, D.
Robinson, Sumner T., Private, Corporal, Co. A.
Robinson, Thomas, Private, Co. H.
Roether, Daniel B., Private, Asst. Surgeon, Co. L, F, G.
Ross, Noble, Private, Co. I.
Roush, George W., Private, Co. C.
Rowe, David P., Private, Co. C, F.
Rowe, James, Private, Co. H, A.
Roweder, Rhymer, Private, Co. A, C.
Rowlett, John, Sergeant, Co. E.
Royce, Calvin R., Private, Co. M, B.
Ruble, Joseph, Private, Co. C.
Ruby, Joseph W., Private, Corporal, Co. B.
Rudolph, Edmund, Private. Unassigned.
Ruple, Charles, Bugler, Private, Co. F.
Russell, Benjamin, Private, Q.M. Sergeant, Co. D.
Ryan Leoklas, Private, Co. G.
Ryan, William A., 1st Lieutenant, Captain, Co. G.
Ryman, Benjamin F., Farrier, C. M. Sergeant, Co. L.
Sadler, William, Blacksmith and Farrier, Co. D.
Sahm, Seigfried, 1st Lieutenant, Co. K.
Saint, Oliver P., Private, Corporal, Co. A, C.
Salgers, John, Private, Co. D.
Salyer, George D., Sergeant, Q.M. Sergeant, Co. I, A.
Sampson, Smith, Private, Co. D.
Sampson, William, Private, Co. K, E.
Sams, Samuel P., Private, Co. H.
Sanders, Zachary T., Private, Co. M.
Santz, Ferdinand, Private, Co. C, F.
Sayler, Henry B., 2d Lieutenant, Co. ?
Schendal, William C., Corporal, Sergeant, Co. B, D.
Schmidt, Joseph, Private, Co. K.
Schneider, John, Private, Co. E.
Schnurr, Andreas, Private, Sergeant, Co. K.
Schoen, Max, Private, Ord. Sergeant, Co. H, A.
Schott, Charles, Corporal, Co. K.
Schumas, John, Private, Co. C.
Schutz, Alexander, Private, Co. F.
Schwitzer, Francis, Private, Co. ?
Scott, Sampson, Private, Co. B, D.
Scott, Walter K., Captain, Co. G.
Scott, William L., Corporal, Private, Co. L, B.

ADAM H. SHOEMAKER, Corporal, Co. F
Brother of John and Daniel Shoemaker

Scott, William W., Private, Co. K.
Scroggins, Robert, Private, Co. D.
Seibert, John, Private, Co. C, A.
Selee, Truman, Private, Co. M, B.
Semans, David H., Private, Co. B.
Senior, John W., 1st Lieutenant, Captain, Co. C.
Shae, John, Private, Co. K.
Shaffer, Daniel G., Private, Co. D.
Shaffer, Jacob, Private, Co. C.
Shaffer, John, Private, Co. C, F.
Shaffer, Joseph, Private, Blacksmith and Farrier, Co. B, D.
Shanks, John P. C., Colonel, Co. F, D.
Shannon, John C., Corporal, Private, Co. G, F.
Shanon, Thomas, Private, Co. E.
Shaw, John, Private, Co. H.
Sheets, Edwin, Sergeant, Private, Co. L, B.
Shepherd, Freeman, Corporal, Co. K, E.
Shepherd, Titman, Private. Unassigned.
Sherman, Henry, Private, Co. H.
Shirley, Jacob E., Private, Corporal, Co. G.
Shirley, John M., Private, Co. B, D.
Shoemaker, Adam H., Corporal, Co. F.
Shoemaker, John W., Actg. 2d Lieutenant, Captain, Co. F.
Shoemaker, Sanford, Private, Co. G, F.
Shoemaker, Silas M., Private, Co. G, F.
Shoemaker, William R., Private, Co. G.
Shortridge, Ireneus, Corporal, Private, Co. L, B.
Shreeve, George W., Sergeant, 1st Lieutenant, Co. B, D.
Simms, John, Private, Co. F, G.
Simonson, Samuel E. W., Major, Co. F, A.
Sisemore, Ahijah, Private, Corporal, Co. I, A.
Sisk, Reuben A., Private, Co. I, A.
Sisk, William, Private, Co. G.
Skelton, Joseph W., 1st Lieutenant, Captain, Co. F, C.
Skinner, David T., 2d Lieutenant, Captain, Co. E.
Skinner, John H., Private, Co. A.
Skinner, Judson, Private, Corporal, Co. E.
Skinner, William, Private, Co. B.
Skinner, William M., Sergeant, 1st Sergeant, Co. E.
Skirvin, Jacob C., 2d Lieutenant, 1st Lieutenant, Co. D.
Slagle, John, Private, Co. F, C.
Slater, Marcus, Private, Co. D.
Slaughter, Charles, Private, Co. G.
Sloan, James, 2nd Lieutenant, Captain, Co. E.
Smith, Ambrosia, Private, Co. I.
Smith, Charles, Private, Co. K.
Smith, Charles, Private, Co. M.

DANIEL L. SHOEMAKER, Co. C, 29th Indiana Infantry
Brother of Adam and John Shoemaker of the 7th Cavalry
(Not listed on Roster.)
294

Smith, Charles, Private, Co. I.
Smith, Charles P., Private, Co. A, C.
Smith, Chester F., Private, Co. C.
Smith, Edward, Private, Co. H, A.
Smith, George W., No. 1, Private, Co. B, D.
Smith, George W., Private, Co. B, D.
Smith, James, Private, Trumpeter, Co. A, C.
Smith, James, Private, Co. L, B.
Smith, John, Private, Co. G.
Smith, John, Private, Co. H.
Smith, Stephen L., Farrier, Private, Co. C, F.
Smith, Thomas, Unassigned.
Smith, Thomas H., Private, Co. A, C.
Smith, William, Private, Co. H.
Smith, William H., Private, Co. E.
Smithers, Robert G., 1st Sergeant, 1st Lieutenant, Co. H, A.
Smock, Jasper, Private, Co. G.
Snowberger, Robert H., Private, Corporal, Co. D.
Snyder, James C., Private, Corporal, Co. E.
Sohly, Christian, Private, Co. C, F.
Solar, Michael, Private, Co. E.
Sowers, Franklin, Private, Co. L.
Sowerwine, Isaac, Sergeant, Co. G.
Sparks, John, Private, Co. C.
Sparks, John W., Private, Co. G.
Sparks, William C., Private, Co. A, C.
Spaulding, James, Private, Co. A, C.
Spence, James W., 2d Lieutenant, Co. C.
Spicknall, George W., Sergeant, Sergeant Major, Co. D, F, S.
Spidle, Clark, Private, Co. H, A.
Squibb, Samuel, Private, Co. C, F.
Stahl, Humphrey, Farrier, Private, Co. L.
Stanetts, Abraham, Private, C.S. Sergeant, Co. I, A.
Stansbury, James C., Sergeant, Co. E.
Stark, William, Sergeant, Private, Co. C, F.
Starkey, Thomas, Private, Co. D.
Starks, John H., Private, Co. M.
Stevens, Elijah, Private, Corporal, Co. C, F.
Stevens, Eliphlet, Private, Co. C.
Stevenson, Andrew, Private, Co. D.
Stevenson, Owen, Private, Co. D.
Steward, Sanford, Private, Co. F.
Stewart, Henry, Private, Co. G.
Stine, William, Private, Co. B, D.
St. John, Albert, Private, Co. I.
St. John, Edward, Private, Corporal, Co. H.
Stoddard, Henry S., 1st Sergeant, 1st Lieutenant, Co. A.

FRANK UDES, Enlisted Soldier; Co. G
(Not listed on Roster.)

Stoner, Marcus W., Private, Co. H.
Storms, Paul, Private, Co. E.
Story, Squire A., Private, Co. M.
Story, Willard O., Corporal, Private, Co. M.
Stout, Hezekiah, Private, Co. G.
Stover, George W., Private, 1st Lieutenant, Co. L.
Straham, Clement R., Private, Co. B, D.
Straley, Joseph, Private, Co. C.
Strance, Fred, Private, Co. H, A.
Sullivan, James, Private, Co. I.
Swafford, Henry C., Private, Co. M.
Swigart, David, Corporal Private, Co. F, C.
Swihart, Milton M., Wagoner, Sergeant, Co. L.
Swindler, John W., Private, Co. D.
Swisher, Johnathan, Private, Corporal, Co. D.
Swords, Elisha, Private, Co. I.
Swords, George, Private, Co. I.
Tabb, Jackson, Private, Co. H, A.
Talley, John A., Sergeant, Private, Co. D.
Tansey, Edwin M., Private, 1st Sergeant, Co. B.
Taylor, Oren, Private, Co. F, E.
Temple, Benjamin F., Private, Corporal, Co. M, B.
Temple, Lyman, Private, Corporal, Co. A, C.
Teters, John K., Corporal, Sergeant, Co. E.
Thomas, Alpheus, Private, Co. F, C.
Thomas, Hendly, Private, Co. I, A.
Thomas, Henry C., Private, Corporal, Co. M, B.
Thompson, Andrew J., Sergeant, 1st Lieutenant, Co. G, F.
Thompson, James W., Private, Co. L.
Thompson, William F., Private, Co. M.
Thornburgh, Nathan, Private, Co. ?
Throp, Benjamin, Private, Co. B.
Thrush, Joseph, Private, Co. L.
Tidwell, John W., Private, Co. G.
Tignor, John, Private, Co. I.
Tilbery, James S., Private, Co. L.
Tingle, William D., Private, Co. K.
Titus, Francis M., Private, Corporal, Co. F.
Todd, Joseph L., Corporal, Private, Co. L, B.
Todd, Louis S., Private, Co. L, B.
Topher, Frederick, Private, Co. C, F.
Totten, Elinas, Private, Corporal, Co. L, B.
Townsend, John P., Com. Sergeant, Private, Co. F, C.
Tracy, Edward, Private, Wagoner, Co. F, C.
Traubarger, John W., Private, Co. A.
Trister, Albert, Sergeant, Private, Co. D.
Triay, John, Private, Co. H.

Sutler—VON BRUCKLIN, 7th Indiana Cavalry
(Not listed on Roster.)

Trowe, Frederick, Private, Co. C, F.
Troy, James, Private, Co. ?
Trueblood, Reason, Private, Co. G.
Truitt, Isaac H., Private, Sergeant, Co. G, F.
Trulock, John, Private, Co. C, F.
Trulock, John F., Private, Co. D.
Trulock, Varnel, Wagoner, Blacksmith and Farrier, Co. D.
Tucker, Alvah, Private, Co. B.
Turner, John, Private, Co. K.
Tuttle, Chester V., Private, Corporal, Co. D.
Tuttle, John, Private, Co. L, B.
Tuttle, Theodore F., Private, Co. D.
Tyler, Joseph N., Trumpeter, Private, Co. L.
Underwood, Philander, Private, Co. C.
Underwood, William, Corporal, Sergeant, Co. E.
Updike, Thomas J., Corporal, Sergeant, Co. E.
Van Benthuysan, Henry J., Private, Co. E.
Van Camp, Daniel, Corporal, Private, Co. E.
Vandusen, Henry H., Trumpeter, Private, Co. F.
Vandusen, Johnson C., Private, Co. F.
Vanmeter, Joseph, Private, Co. G, F.
Van Skyhawk, William, Farrier, Co. E.
Veach, James P., Private, Co. I, A.
Vest, Wiseman, Private, Co. M.
Vevasa, Peter, Private, Co. H.
Vinnedge, Francis M., Private, Co. G, F.
Vinnedge, James T., Corporal, Q. M. Sergeant, Co. G, F.
Waddle, Francis, Private, Sergeant, Co. G.
Waddle, Lemuel, Private, Co. H.
Waggoner, Adam C., Private, Co. D.
Wagner, Franklin P., Corporal, Private, Co. D.
Walker, Alexander, Corporal, Co. I, A.
Walker, Enos, Private, Co. E.
Walker, Jeremy, Private, Co. I, A.
Walker, Joseph, Private, Co. M, B.
Wallich, Jacob, Private, Co. E.
Walters, David, Private, Co. L, B.
Walton, James, Private, Co. L, B.
Wampler, William H., Sergeant, Private, Co. L.
Ward, Charles W., Private, Co. E.
Ware, John, Private, Co. E.
Ware, William, Private, Co. M, B.
Warfield, Basil M., Sergeant, Private, Co. G, F.
Warner, Israel, Saddler, Co. D.
Warnock, Jacob, Private, Sergeant, Co. F, G.
Warrick, Calvin, Private, Co. I.
Warring, Christian M., Private, Co. M.

Washam, Huey, Private, Co. M.
Wasson, James H., Private, Co. I.
Watkins, Abraham, Private, Co. K.
Watson, Allen, Saddler, Co. I.
Watson, Dewitt C., Bugler, Private, Co. G, A.
Watson, John Q., Corporal, Private, Co. H, A.
Watson, John, Private, Co. E.
Watts, John, Private, Co. E.
Watts, Joseph, Private, Co. E.
Way, Francis M., Sergeant, Lieutenant, Co. B.
Waymire, Washington, Private, Co. F.
Wayne, John, Private. Unassigned.
Ways, Benjamin, Private, Co. I.
Weeden, Harrison, Private, Co. ?
Welch, Alvin, Private, Co. A.
Welch, William, Private, Co. G.
Wells, Erastus, Private, Co. C.
Wells, Samuel H., Corporal, Private, Co. G.
West, Edward, Private, Co. M.
West, Elisha B., Sergeant, Com. Sergeant, Co. B, D.
Wheeler, Philander, Private, Co. F.
Whetsel, Aaron, Private, Corporal, Co. E.
Whetsel, William, Private, Co. E.
Whipple, John, Private, Co. D.
Whipple, William, Private, Co. F.
Whistler, David, Private, Co. I, A.
White, Benjamin B., Private, Co. L, I, B.
White, Charles. Unassigned.
White, John, Private, Co. ?
Whitham, George, Private, Co. M.
Whittaker, Robert, Sergeant, Co. F, C.
Whitten, Samuel, Private, Co. I.
Whitworth, Sandford, Private, Co. G, F.
Wiley, Alvin, Private, Co. I.
Wilkins, Nicholas, Private, Corporal, Co. I.
Wilkison, Milo, Private, Co. K, E.
Willard, Henry C., Private, Co. I, A.
Willett, Ellory P., Private, Co. K.
Williams, Christian M., Private, Co. G, F.
Williams, Clark S., Private, Co. A.
Williams, Daniel B., Private, Co. M.
Williams, Frank, Private, Co. K, E.
Williams, Harvey, Private, Co. D.
Williams, James M., Private, Corporal, Co. A.
Williams, Landon, Farrier, Private, Co. F.
Williamson, John, Private, Co. B, D.
Williamson, Luther, Private, Co. B.

Willis, Sylvester V., Private, Co. A.
Wills, Henry C., Private, Com. Sergeant, Co. K, E.
Wilson, Abraham, Sergeant, Co. M.
Wilson, Charles, Farrier, Co. C, F.
Wilson, Charles, Corporal, Private, Co. G.
Wilson, George, Private, Co. F, C.
Wilson, John, Private, Co. C.
Wilson, William, Private, Co. L.
Wince, Charles, Private, Sergeant, Co. C, F.
Windsor, Enoch M., Private, Co. G.
Winfield, William, Private, Co. H, A.
Wing, Gideon, Private, Co. I.
Winger, Christian, Saddler, Private, Co. G, A.
Winter, Lewis G., Private. Unassigned.
Wintzen, Joseph, Private, Co. K.
Wise, James T., Private, Co. M.
Wise, William A., Q. M. Sergeant, Co. A.
Withrow, Loudon F., Corporal, Private, Co. C, F.
Woerner, Leopold, Private, Co. K.
Wood, Elijah F., Private, Co. B.
Wood, Elisha B., Private, Corporal, Co. B, D.
Wood, George W., Private, Co. M.
Wood, Morris P., Private, Co. E.
Woodard, James, Sergeant, Private, Co. M.
Woodard, William, Private, Co. K, E.
Woodbury, Daniel, Private, Co. B, D.
Woodbury, John M., Private, Co. B.
Woods, Lee Roy, 1st Sergeant, 1st Lieutenant, Co. E.
Woodward, George, Private, Farrier, Co. C.
Woodworth, Barzilia, Private, Co. D.
Woolf, Andrew J., Private, Sergeant, Co. F, C.
Worgum, Henry, Private, Co. B, D.
Wrick, William, Corporal, Private, Co. G, A.
Wright, Christian H., Corporal, Sergeant, Co. B.
Wright, Henry F., 2d Lieutenant, Captain, Co. D.
Yarbrough, William, Private, Co. H.
Yost, William, Private. Unassigned.
Younce, Charles A., Private, Co. I.
Young, Joseph A., Private, Sergeant, Co. G, F.
Younglove, William, Private, Co. A, C.
Youngs, George A., Private, Co. A.
Zook, Henry K., Private, Co. L, B.
Zook, Irvin K., Private, Co. L, B.

APPENDIX A

Indiana counties of origin of Civil War regiments broken down by Companies.

Indiana Historical Society *Bulletin*
December 1961; Volume 38, Number 12, page 225.
Indiana Library and Historical Board
408 State Library and Historical Building
Indianapolis, Indiana

APPENDIX B

Report of the Adjutant General of the State of Indiana.

Volume 3, Containing Rosters of Officers of Indiana Regiments
1866, Samuel M. Douglass, State Printer
W. H. H. Terrell, Adjutant General of Indiana
Indianapolis, Indiana
Volume 7, Containing Rosters of Enlisted Men of Indiana Regiments
1867, Samuel M. Douglass, State Printer
W. H. H. Terrell, Adjutant General of Indiana
Indianapolis, Indiana

APPENDIX C

7th REGIMENT CAVALRY
(119th REGIMENT VOLUNTEERS) INDIANA

A Compendium of the War of the Rebellion
Frederick H. Dyer
Reprint by The Press of Morningside Bookshop, 1978
Dayton, Ohio

APPENDIX D

List of Exchanged Prisoners on the *Sultana* from the Seventh Indiana Cavalry

Loss of the Sultana
Rev. Chester D. Berry
Darius D. Throp, Printer and Binder, 1892
Lansing, Michigan

APPENDIX E

The War of the Rebellion: A Compilation of the Official Records of the Union and Confederate Armies
War Department, United States of America
Washington, D.C., Published between 1881 and 1901

The War of the Rebellion: A Compilation of the Official Records of the Union and Confederate Armies
Index listings for the Seventh Indiana Cavalry

SERIES 1

Volume 30-32, 39, 41, 45, 48, 49, 52.

SERIES 3

Volume 3

SERIES I

Volume 30, Part 3, Page 658.
Volume 30, Part 4, Pages 193-95.
Volume 31, Part 1, Page 817.
Volume 31, Part 3, Pages 69, 249, 285.
Volume 32, Part 1, Pages 113, 171, 193, 258, 263-65, 267-77, 281, 287, 304, 307, 582-85.
Volume 32, Part 2, Pages 302, 317, 342.
Volume 32, Part 3, Pages 518, 566.
Volume 39, Part 1, Pages 128, 130-36, 242, 374, 375, 379, 391-93, 395, 883.
Volume 39, Part 2, Pages 67, 333, 559.
Volume 39, Part 3, Page 575.
Volume 41, Part 1, Pages 332, 335, 344.
Volume 41, Part 4, Page 988.
Volume 45, Part 1, Pages 845, 847-51, 1147.
Volume 45, Part 2, Pages 61, 90, 107, 191, 294.
Volume 48, Part 1, Pages 55, 56, 57, 68, 421, 1028, 1159.
Volume 48, Part 2, Pages 814, 840, 917, 956.

Volume 49, Part 1, Pages 76, 79-81, 586, 598.
Volume 49, Part 2, Pages 539, 973, 983, 985, 997, 1101-02.
Volume 52, Part 1, Page 474.

SERIES 3

Volume 3, Page 697.

REFERENCES REVIEWED

Adams, Henry C., compiler: *Indiana at Vicksburg.* Indianapolis, 1911.

Bearss, Edwin C.: *Forrest at Brice's Cross Roads.* Dayton, 1979.

——————— *The Tupelo Campaign June 22-July 23, 1864. A Documented Narrative and Troop Movement Maps.* Washington, 1969.

Bearss, Margie Riddle: *Sherman's Forgotten Campaign: The Meridian Expedition.* Baltimore, 1987.

Boatner, Mark M: *The Civil War Dicitionary.* New York, 1959.

Brown, D. Alexander: *Grierson's Raid.* Dayton, 1981.

Burns, W. S.: "A. J. Smith's Defeat of Forrest at Tupelo (July 14, 1864)." *Battles and Leaders of the Civil War.* Edited by Robert U. Johnson and Clarence C. Buel. 4 Volumes. New York, 1884-87.

Connelly, Thomas L.: *Autumn of Glory: The Army of Tennessee, 1862-1865.* Baton Rouge, 1971.

Crute, Joseph H., Jr.: *Units of the Confederate States Army.* Midothian, Virginia, 1987.

Davenport, Edward A., ed.: *History of the 9th Regiment Illinois Cavalry Volunteers.* Chicago, 1888.

Dyer, Frederick H.: *A Compendium of the War of the Rebellion: Compiled and Arranged from Official Records of the Federal and Confederate Armies.* Dayton, 1978.

Hanson, E. Hunn: "Forrest's Defeat of Sturgis at Brice's Cross Roads (June 10, 1864)." *Battles and Leaders of the Civil War.* Edited by Robert U. Johnson and Clarence C. Buel. 4 Volumes. New York, 1884-87.

Horn, Stanley F.: *The Army of Tennessee.* Indianapolis, 1941.

Kajencki, Francis C.: *Star on Many a Battlefield.* (Joseph Karge) Cranbury, New Jersey, 1980.

Long, E. B.: *The Civil War Day by Day: An Almanac, 1861-1865.* New York, 1971.

Main, Edwin M.: *The Story of the Marches, Battles and Incidents of the Third United States Colored Cavalry.* Louisville, 1908.

Civil War Centennial Commission, Nashville, Tennessee: *Tennesseans in the Civil War: A Military History of Confederate and Union Units with Available Rosters of Personnel.* 2 Volumes. Nashville, 1964.

Terrell, W. H. H.: *Report of the Adjutant General of The State of Indiana.* Indianapolis, 1866.

The War of the Rebellion: A Compilation of the Official Records of the Union and Confederate Armies. Washington, 1881-1901.

Van Horn, Thomas B.: *Army of the Cumberland.* Cincinnati, 1875.

Waring, George E.: *Whip and Spur.* Boston, 1875.

Warner, Ezra J.: *Generals in Blue: Lives of the Union Commanders.* Baton Rouge, 1964.

——————— *Generals in Gray: Lives of the Confederate Commanders.* Baton Rouge, 1959.

Williams, John H.: *"The Eagle Regiment," 8th Wisconsin Infantry Volunteers, a Sketch of its Marches, Battle and Campaigns from 1861-1865.* Belleville, Wisconsin, 1890.